CAMILLA
FOJAS **BORDER BANDITS**

HOLLYWOOD ON THE
SOUTHERN FRONTIER

T0339383

University of Texas Press
Austin

Requests for permission to reproduce material from this
work should be sent to:
    Permissions
    University of Texas Press
    P.O. Box 7819
    Austin, TX 78713-7819
    www.utexas.edu/utpress/about/bpermission.html

⊗ The paper used in this book meets the minimum
requirements of ANSI/NISO Z39.48-1992 (R1997)
(Permanence of Paper).

LIBRARY OF CONGRESS CATALOGING-IN-PUBLICATION DATA

Fojas, Camilla, 1971–
    Border bandits : Hollywood on the southern frontier /
Camilla Fojas. — 1st ed.
        p.   cm.
    Includes bibliographical references and index.
    ISBN 0-292-71863-2
    1. Mexican-American Border Region—In motion
pictures.   2. Motion pictures—United States.   I. Title.
    PN1995.9.M48F65   2008
    791.43'658721—dc22
                                        2008001121

CONTENTS

Preface   vii

Acknowledgments   xi

INTRODUCTION: Welcome to the Alamo;
Hollywood on the Border   1

CHAPTER ONE: How the Southwest Was Won;
Border Westerns and the Southern Frontier   27

CHAPTER TWO: "The Imaginary Illegal Alien"; Hollywood Border
Crossers and Buddy Cops in the 1980s   83

CHAPTER THREE: The "Narc" in All of Us;
Border Media and the War on Drugs   109

CHAPTER FOUR: Urban Frontiers;
Border Cinema and the Global City   145

CONCLUSION: Frontier Myths on the Line;
Border Cinema Redux   183

Notes   197

Filmography   211

Bibliography   217

Index   227

n May 1, 2006, International Workers' Day, millions of workers nationwide boycotted their jobs and took to the streets to march for the rights of workers and to protest a bill that would unfairly target undocumented immigrants and allow the construction of a wall on the Mexican border. Nevertheless, to the utter disapprobation of many, President Bush signed the Secure Fence Act into law on October 26, approving the construction of a 700-mile wall on the border. In Chicago, the march commemorated its origins in the worker unrest of the Haymarket Riot in 1886, 120 years earlier. But the march in 2006 marked a new era in the predicament of workers at the bottom of the labor market. Among these workers were recent arrivals who faced post 9/11 cultural fears that associated immigrants with migrating global terror units. A recent report on border security, "A Line in the Sand: Confronting the Threat at the Southwest Border," issued by the chairman of the U.S. House Homeland Security Subcommittee on Investigations, Representative Michael T. McCaul (R), reiterates this persistent association of cross-border immigration with drug traffickers and terrorists—while adding President Hugo Chávez of Venezuela into the mix as a leader who allegedly harbors terrorists before sending them across the U.S.-Mexico border.[1] This report links control of the border and the populations who cross it with the imperatives of national security, placing every immigrant under suspicion as a potential terrorist and targeting the border as the frontline of national security rather than one aspect of a complex and multifaceted issue.

In both Los Angeles and Chicago, the marches on May 1 drew hundreds of thousands of immigrants—mostly Latino, but every immigrant group was represented—and won unprecedented publicity for an often invisible or unrecognized force in the U.S. economy. At the same time in Chicago, the largest international Latino film festival in the nation was taking place, screening a number of feature films that documented the plight of immigrants, undocumented workers, and the conditions for workers in borderland *maquiladoras*: *Al otro lado* (Natalia Almada, 2005), *Al otro lado* (Gustavo Loza, 2005), *Maquilápolis* (2006), *Preguntas sin respuestas* (2005), *Se habla español* (2005). The flood of alternative messages about immigrants, especially those of Mexican origin, and the U.S. economic, social, and cultural relationship to Mexico is now part of the daily discourse of mass media.

The May 1 marches were an incredible realization of the fictional world of the border film, *A Day without a Mexican*; this political fable set in California in 2004 became the reality faced by an entire nation in 2006. The film, an elaboration on a short feature of the same name, was a direct response to California's anti-immigrant Proposition 187 and dedicated to and inspired by ex-Governor Pete Wilson. The marches were a response to similar immigrant phobia at the national level. The filmmakers, Sergio Arau and Yareli Arizmendi, issued the following statement on this issue just prior to the marches across the nation on May 1, and their words ring with the prophetic possibilities of cinema:

In the spring of 2006, reality has imitated art. Immigration issues have exploded onto the national stage and currently there is a call for a National Boycott on May 1st—No work, no school, no buying, no selling—in support of immigration reform in the United States. All artists dream of changing the world. Our goal is to create work that is relevant to our times. If our work has encouraged social change, that is the ultimate satisfaction. In making this film, our objective was to open the dialogue on the issue of immigration by including factual information and alternative views that would change the terms of the discussion. This in the hope of having the Latino community take its rightful place as an important contributor and player in the history and future of the United States. The film was meant as a fable, a warning to be heeded.[2]

Arau and Arizmendi followed these prophetic musings with a post-march analysis in their contribution to an edited collection titled *Un día sin inmigrantes: Quince voces, una causa*. The collection explores various repercussions and permutations of these massive marches in U.S. cities and across Latin America.[3] In their essay, Arau and Arizmendi reiterate the main issues of the film, while noting that the marches initiated a momentous change in social and cultural dynamics evident in the magnitude of the visibility of immigrants and their supporters. This visibility continues to be apparent in an ensuing slate of documentary investigations and news programs focused on the border, most notably by CNN's Anderson Cooper and nativist Lou Dobbs, as well as increased coverage of border issues and discussions of immigration generally on all news stations. Though much of the English language news coverage tends towards nativism, this publicity and recognition of the vast reach of the issue has become crucial political capital for all immigrant communities. This complex interplay of media events is a hopeful sign that Hollywood film and media culture has begun to lose its ideological dominance with regard to the depiction of the border and immigrants who cross it. This landmark moment of visibility for immigrants and their struggles provided a new political and cultural context for revisiting Hollywood border cinema. Hollywood border images and storylines have added fire to the debates and cultural and political attitudes about immigrants and immigration. In the current context of "Hispanophobia,"[4] these Hollywood stories demand to be reread and understood as parables of a nation gripped by fear of difference and change.

Camilla Fojas
Chicago 2007

ACKNOWLEDGMENTS

would like to thank the many people who have supported this project in different ways. I owe a great debt to the DePaul Research Council and the DePaul Humanities Center. I would like to thank Chon Noriega and the editors at *Aztlán* for the opportunity to publish parts of chapter four. Tom Bender, Alev Cinar, and Lourdes Torres offered some extremely helpful critical comments on parts of chapter four. I would also like to thank Tom and Alev for the opportunity to contribute to their edited volume on urban imaginaries. I am grateful to Emily Park, Eric Zinner, and New York University Press for allowing me to reprint part of chapter one from a volume on mixed-race Hollywood. Mary Beltrán has been a great critic and friend and I thank her for her insights and careful readings on different parts of this work. I am indebted to María Herrera-Sobek not only for her groundbreaking scholarship on the border, which informs much of this work, but also for her invaluable and generous commentary on the manuscript. Christine Holmlund offered her support and gave me some very helpful insights on the text. To all the students of my border cinema courses throughout the years, a very special thanks. I am indebted to Jim Burr at the University of Texas Press for the opportunity to publish this work and the anonymous readers for their thoughtful readings. Elizabeth Ávila and Magdalena Fudalewicz were invaluable for their painstaking research assistance. Finally, for her patience and support, her wit and charm, this work is dedicated to Sandra Franco.

BORDER BANDITS

—Now that you're here what are you going to do? Sell us tickets to the policeman's ball?
—We're with the border patrol, ma'am, we don't have any balls.

—*FLASHPOINT* (1984)

O n January 26, 2006, the United States Border Patrol, working with agents from the Drug Enforcement Agency, discovered what many claim was the largest and most sophisticated cross-border tunnel to date. Information about this tunnel quickly hit the headlines with news flashes engineered to elicit fears about the hydra of villainy: drug traffickers, "illegal" immigrants, and terrorists. The 2,400-foot tunnel grabbed attention for its infrastructure and amenities; fortified with concrete, it boasted electric lights, a ventilation system, groundwater pumping, and was fully equipped with a pulley system for the rapid transit of "drugs and other contraband."[1] The tunnel was described by many news sources as having a south-to-north trajectory that originated in Tijuana and terminated in an industrial warehouse in San Diego. The two tons of marijuana found in the tunnel were a clue to its main function, but the discovery sparked fears: "These tunnels are known to be used for smuggling drugs and illegal aliens. They also could be used (and almost certainly are being used) to smuggle terrorists—along with weapons and explosives—into the United States."[2] The tunnel quickly became the clearinghouse for North American fears about underground traffic into the United States and about the spawning of illegal activity with roots in Mexico that pointed to conspiracies against national security. The whole scenario read like the ongoing plot of the popular television show *24* (Fox), in which terrorists find covert and illegal ways of entering the United States. No similar media ploy exists for the north-to-south traffic into major border cities like Tijuana or Ciudad Juárez where visitors from the United States go in search of illicit activities, or for unauthorized north-to-south traffic in merchandise. Instead, mainstream U.S. media depict the border as a necessary barrier to unwanted traffic while the borderlands are often represented as a repository of all things illegal. Recently, news items about such tunnels have appeared more frequently, causing some to claim that underground entry into the United States obviates the need to erect a wall against invaders from the south. These stories deny the realities of economic and political interdependence between Mexico and the United States and act as symbolic blockades to cross-border dialogue.

Since the inception of cinema, the Hollywood motion picture industry has commandeered the borderlands to tell a story about U.S. dominance in the American hemisphere. Hollywood has often exploited the trope of the southern border between the United States and Mexico to capture a range of "American" ideals and values—integrity, moral clarity, industriousness, rugged survivalism, confidence, and self-sufficiency, among others. The border is also a vital repository of threatening ideas—homosexuality, prostitution, globalization, economic liberalization, drug trafficking and abuse, sexual promiscuity, effeminacy, and terrorism—and undesirable or inassimilable people such as Mexicans, Native Americans, racially mixed characters, immigrants, war veterans, terrorists, and dominant and domineering women. Moreover, many of the lost battles of history—the Alamo and Vietnam in particular—are replayed on the border to conclusions that restore confidence in the "American way." I argue that Hollywood border films do important social work: they offer a cinematic space through which viewers can manage traumatic and undesirable histories and ultimately reaffirm core "American" values. At the same time, these border narratives shape "proper" identification with a singular and exceptional moral hero who might register anywhere from maverick to vigilante. These stories delineate opposing values and ideas—for instance, the proper from the improper and the citizen from the unwanted guest or "alien." Latino border films offer a critical vantage from which to consider these topics; they challenge the presumptions of U.S. nationalism and subsequent cultural attitudes about immigrants and immigration and often critically reconstruct their Hollywood kin.

The southern frontier is one of the most emotionally charged zones of the United States, second only to its historical predecessor and partner, the western frontier. The border has become the symbol of a strong and fortified nation that is protected on all sides from invasion and infiltration of harmful or unwanted people, ideas, and things. Though spanning many different genres, border films share a preoccupation with mobility, border patrol, immigration restrictions, and the control of various kinds of traffic into the country; they trace policy mood swings and shape cultural agenda. Many of the films that take place on or near the borderlands express "American" anxieties, messianic prophecies, and fears about porous boundaries and the integration of the hemisphere through political intervention, economic globalization, and transnational migration.

Hollywood and major independent films are not alone in the fascination and fixation on the border region, but the U.S. film industry is the most pervasive image machine of the border region for a global audience. The Mexican film industry has as long a history of depicting the border region to similarly nationalist ends, yet Hollywood rarely has taken notice. In her analysis of the rich genealogy of Mexican border cinema, Norma Iglesias notes that the border did not appear as an actual place in Mexican cinema until the 1960s, prior to which it was merely a verbal construction—something characters talked about as a point of reference in the development of the plot. By the 1960s, during the boom of the Mexican Western, the border emerged as a geographic location and space of action. Some notable films of this era are *El terror de la frontera* (1963) and *Pistoleros de la frontera* (1967), both of which are set in small border towns that harbor thieves in hiding. As in U.S. Westerns, the border is depicted as a place of escape at the far reaches of the nation that is often beyond the limits of the law.[3]

Alex Saragoza has argued that the border in Mexican film tends to represent "self-absorption, introspection, and distrust of the outside" in a manner not unexpected from an embattled nation after suffering years of colonialism and U.S. interventions.[4] By the 1980s, Mexican border films deal with the various sociocultural and familial effects of northern migration: for example, the migration and subsequent estrangement of members of families, the figuring of the United States or *el norte*, the north, as a source of economic and political freedom, or the fantasy about success in the U.S. entertainment industries. For example, *Mamá solita* (1980) and *Mojado de nacimiento* (1981) depict sons longing to reunite with their exiled fathers in the United States.

María Herrera-Sobek describes a subgenre of the Mexican border film that derives from the Spanish picaresque tradition; these films are comedies of misadventure that feature a protagonist who emanates "from the working class, possesses wit, ingenuity, humor, and an uncanny skill for survival" and who often outwits and escapes his or her captors and antagonists.[5] The titles of these films foreground their parodic and co-medic premises: *El milusos llegó de mojado* (n.d.), *El remojado* (1984), *Ni de aquí ni de allá* (1988), and *Mojado Power* (1979).[6] There is also a slate of Mexican films that offer cautionary tales about the dangers of the trans-border journey and often end in tragedy, such as the film *El vagón de la muerte* (1987). Herrera-Sobek notes that many Mexican films about undocumented immigration use *corridos*, Mexican ballads, as source material.[7] The corrido acts as "hypertext" or as an intertextual source of information that introduces themes and historical events and frames narrative meaning.[8]

Iglesias describes another border formation that emerged during the 1980s where the border is not just a film set but establishes a whole set of industrial conditions as the site of production of a flourishing film in-dustry. Mirroring the generic efficiency of the Hollywood studio system, filmmakers often used border sets multiple times for similar narratives. Many famous producers used their own properties for filming various types of border narratives, from immigration genre dramas to action and border *narcotraficante* films. The latter border subgenre became an industry commonplace, leading to the well-known "crossover" film, *El Mariachi* (1992), the production of which followed the industrial pat-terns of Mexican border filmmaking, including using sets belonging to friends and family members.[9]

There are a number of border films that fall outside of the established generic patterns of the border film industry, but that use the border as a sign of future promise. For example, *Mujeres insumisas* (1995) narrates the story of a group of Mexican women who escape to Los Angeles in search of liberation from gender oppression. Similarly, *Sin dejar huella* (2000) is about two women who meet on the road and become friends as they unite trying to evade the law en route to Cancún. The documen-tary *Al otro lado* (2005) deals with immigrants' dreams of success in the U.S.-based entertainment industry into which many Mexican perform-ers have migrated.

There is a major difference in perspective and narrative topoi between Mexican and Hollywood films about northern migration. Though both fall into the category David Maciel and María Rosa García-Acevedo de-scribe as "immigration genre films," Mexican border films are strongly nationalist, discouraging northerly migration and debunking the myth of the "American Dream."[10] They thematize the entanglements of cultural contact and the experience of displacement and economic exile, whereas Hollywood border films tend to focus on the heroic mission of the Texas Rangers, border guards, DEA agents, or other police personnel. This difference leads the more critical Mexican border stories away from their border provenance and into U.S. cities where conflicts of dislocation take place. Norma Iglesias notes that this displacement from the border had become more prevalent by the 1980s, so that the genre engaged the "problems of being Mexican in the United States," and "the problems of confrontation between Mexican and American culture," rather than life on the border or the difficulties of crossing over.[11] Some Mexican border films are part of what Herrera-Sobek calls "border aesthetics," the activist aesthetics devoted to politically transformative depictions of the border region, representations that depart from and critically reconstruct the normative and phobic images of the borderlands and border crossers in the northern imaginary.[12]

BANDITS AND BAD MEN

Hollywood has perpetrated the image of banditry along the border through misuse of history, misrepresentation of socioeconomic conditions, neutralization of political tensions, and other such sleights of hand that create and perpetuate a false mythology of the borderlands and its inhabitants. The bandit is not only one of the most abiding stereotypes of Mexicans in Hollywood history, but also the symbolic center and cardinal icon of the borderland narrative.

The bandit has roots in nineteenth-century dime novels and early silent greaser films or films with plots structured around Mexican villains such as *Tony the Greaser* (1914), *Broncho Billy and the Greaser* (1914), *The Greaser's Revenge* (1914), and the very last film to contain the term "greaser" in its title, *Guns and Greasers* (1918). The greaser film played on the association of Latinos and criminality, often portraying a roving Mexican outlaw whose main occupations consisted of every vice imaginable: lust, greed, thievery, treachery, rapaciousness, deceit, gambling, and murder.[13] After the end of World War I, the term "greaser" was eliminated in films, partly due to the demand for Hollywood films in the Latin American market where commercial viability foreclosed on overtly derogatory depictions of Latinos and partly due to a shift in villainy to "the Kaiser and the Hun."[14] The bandit, however, would not be so graciously put to rest.

The denigrating term "greaser" was popular just after the U.S. war with Mexico (1846–1848), when international and interracial tensions ran high and the borders of national identity were in flux.[15] It originates from Anglo perceptions that the Mexicans' skin color was either the result of applying grease to the skin or was deemed similar to the color of grease.[16] The former meaning derived from a practice whereby Mexican laborers in the Southwest applied grease to their backs to facilitate the transport of hides and cargo.[17] In both instances, greaser indicates a dark-skinned outlaw or bandit who is unhygienic, filthy, and unsavory, with a marked proclivity for violence and criminality. These attitudes were reflected in anti-Hispano legislation; for instance, California's 1855 anti-vagrancy act was also called the "Greaser Act" and was designed to target "all persons who are commonly known as 'Greasers' or the issue of Spanish and Indian blood . . . and who go armed and are not peaceable and quiet persons."[18] These laws were open to loose interpretations to facilitate the detainment and incarceration of anyone with dark skin or who spoke Spanish, characteristics which were associated with criminality.

Charles Ramírez Berg describes the Hollywood bandit as the outgrowth of the earlier silent-era greaser character. Like the greaser, the bandit represents the darker urges repressed in civilized society and is perceived as a psychopath who lacks a moral compass or an empathic connection to others. His bad behavior is evident in his physical composition—the aesthetic counterpart to his irrational violence, dishonesty, and illegal dealings is an unkempt appearance marked by greasy hair and missing teeth. The bandit demands moral retribution from the Anglo characters; he is a "demented, despicable creature who must be punished for his brutal behavior."[19] The bandit's female equivalent is a sexually promiscuous and loose woman, typically a prostitute.[20] According to Rosa Linda Fregoso, the border was inscribed across these women's bodies; that is, native Mexicanas, Tejanas, and Californias were coded as foreign and degenerate against depictions of civilized Anglo-American women.[21] The natives of the Southwest were depicted as inferior and as harlots and bandits, often to justify colonial expansion and the expropriation of their land and property through war and theft.[22]

The greaser and the bandit emerged after the tremendous loss of land and rights for natives of the Southwest following the Mexican-American War. Indeed, there was a rise in banditry among the displaced who took up arms against Anglo aggressors. This scenario recalls Eric

Hobsbawm's distinction between the bandit and the social bandit; the latter emerges from the underclass or peasantry and engages the tactics of banditry as social rebellion.[23]

In hegemonic U.S. histories and popular culture, the Mexican bandit is invariably an outlaw. However, Mike Davis exposes a different angle to the official story about the Mexican bandit along the California-Mexico border. He draws a lineage of violence along the border into California from the wars of conquest of 1846–1847 and Anglo gangs of the 1850s to contemporary U.S. border vigilantism. He refers specifically to *Blood Meridian*, Cormac McCarthy's unrelentingly macabre account of the violence of Glanton and his gang, an account that offers a realist depiction of racially motivated violence in the Anglo conquest of California. The violence perpetrated by Native Americans and Mexican "bandits" was often misrepresented as unprovoked, malicious, and excessive, rather than what Davis describes as acts of defense of land and property, self-protection, and sometimes retaliation. Infamous bandits like Tiburcio Vásquez, Pio Lunares, Juan Flores, and Joaquin Murieta were relegated to history as "desperados" rather than as "social bandits" or "guerilla chieftains" engaged in ongoing conflict with Anglo vigilantes and conquistadores. After the turn of the nineteenth century, perhaps the most infamous Mexican bandit and screen legend is Francisco "Pancho" Villa, a historical character framed either as a villain or a hero of the Mexican revolution.

The diverse uses of the title "Border Bandits" reveal the tensions and contradictions along the border region regarding the meaning and attribution of banditry.[24] For example, *Border Bandits* is the title of a B-grade Western from 1946 about a group of outlaws who escape to the "other" side of the border and the marshal who must bring them back into the domain of law and order in the North. *Border Bandits* is also the title of an acclaimed documentary by writer-producer Kirby Warnock about a group of Texas Rangers who committed mass murder of Tejanos based on their own lawless sense of justice. As mentioned earlier, Mexican natives of Texas were often mislabeled "bandits" by Anglo civilians and Texas Rangers to justify stealing the Mexicans' land. Without the use of the racially stigmatizing bandit label, it would have been much harder for Anglos to obtain Texas land titles and wrest control of the state. More recently, Joseph Nevins used the term "border bandit" to refer to those who attack and rob undocumented immigrants as they make the journey across the border; Nevins notes that these bandits are part of the violent repercussions of the Clinton administration's attempt to crack down on the border with Operation Gatekeeper.[25] In an atmosphere of increased policing, migrants become more vulnerable targets of crime since they are viewed as having no legal recourse against their perpetrators.

The Mexican bandit continues to live on in Hollywood through various incarnations and across multiple genres, many of which intersect with the border film, including Westerns, drug trafficking films, urban gang films, and immigrant genre films. The bandit rarely remains unpunished or unchallenged by his antagonist, the character who represents the law—most typically the Texas Ranger, border patrol agent, or DEA (Drug Enforcement Agency) agent.

INDIAN WARRIOR, MEXICAN VAQUERO, AND TEXAS RANGER

The 1920 play by Porter Emerson Browne, *The Bad Man*, transferred to the screen in 1923, told the story of a Mexican bandit; the film was remade in 1930, but this time the bandit was brought to justice by his antithesis, the Texas Ranger.[26] The Texas Rangers are considered the moral saviors of Texas when in reality they were often driven by racially and ethnically phobic motivations and the desire to secure more land for Anglo Texans. In his infamous history of the Texas Rangers, Walter Prescott Webb lionizes the Rangers as a natural response to the "conflict of civilizations," referring to the Rangers' position against the renegade Anglo, Indian, and Mexican bandit. [27] The foreword to the 1965 edition of the *Texas Rangers* (originally published in 1935), written during the escalation of the Vietnam War by then president and fellow Texan Lyndon B. Johnson, is a testament to the nationalist purpose of the tome. Later, Hollywood would unify the three types of villains described by Webb—renegade Anglos, Indians, and Mexican bandits—into the arms- and contraband-peddling "comancheros" in the Western, *The Comancheros* (1961), set in the 1860s Texas borderlands.[28] John Wayne sets things straight as the morally crusading Texas Ranger battling against this tripartite threat in a manner that justifies the role and purpose of the Rangers for contemporary audiences. For Webb, the Ranger's moral position is clear: he is "a man standing alone between society and its enemies" and "it has been his duty to meet the outlaw breed of three races, the Indian warrior, Mexican bandit, and American desperado, on the enemy's ground and deliver each safely within the jail door or the cemetery gate."[29] However, there are varying accounts of the manner in which the Rangers interpreted and enacted their "duty." For historians like Webb, Eugene C. Barker, Rupert Richardson, and others, Anglo violence in Texas and along the border was justified as part of the process of nation-building.[30]

Américo Paredes is perhaps the most renowned critic of the Webb-inspired mythology of the Texas Rangers. He examines border ballads or *corridos* as oral histories that unearth the repressed history of the experience of the Anglo invasion of the Southwest. In his book he offers the "official history" of the Rangers as a counterpoint to the subjugated histories of the natives on the frontier:

The Rangers have been pictured as a fearless, almost superhuman breed of men, capable of incredible feats. It may take a company of militia to quell a riot, but one Ranger was said to be enough for one mob. Evildoers, especially the Mexican ones, were said to quail at the mere mention of the name. To the Ranger is given the credit for ending lawlessness and disorder along the Rio Grande.[31]

Paredes contradicts this characterization and attributes the intensification of border violence and unrest to the lawlessness propagated by the Rangers, which deepened the racial divide in the borderlands. The Rangers inspired Mexican distrust of the United States while enabling the consolidation of border communities and the creation of more spirited social bandits.

The Ranger was called a *rinche* in Spanish, which quickly became an umbrella term for all "Americans armed and mounted and looking for Mexicans to kill."[32] Paredes compiled a list of Mexican "sayings and anecdotes" about the Rangers, a list that may or may not accrue to historical veracity, but that certainly provides the basis for an alternate mythology. He claims, contrary to purported Ranger heroism, that the Ranger always carries an extra gun so that when he kills an unarmed Mexican he can deposit it with the body, that the Ranger prefers to kill armed Mexicans when they are sleeping or have their backs to him, that the Ranger prefers to hide behind U.S. soldiers, and that he engages in retaliatory killings and murder by proxy—a practice described by an ex-Ranger in the documentary cited earlier, *Border Bandits*. Paredes gives credence to only one part of the Ranger mythos, the Ranger dictum to "shoot first, ask questions later," which confirms the existence of the rampant injustice of indiscriminate murder through racial profiling.

Like Paredes, John Weaver charges Ranger historian Webb with confusing fact with myth in his account of the Texas Rangers. Julian Samora, Joe Bernal, and Albert Peña further note that this mingling of fact and myth is partly a consequence of the self-promotional work of the Texas Rangers as evident in the many memoirs and autobiographies of these men.[33] These official histories often remain uncontested as the only extant records of the period since many Tejano and Native American records were destroyed or delegitimated.

GREATER MEXICO

María Herrera-Sobek invokes a hidden history of Mexican involvement in the making of the culture of the Southwest and of the United States. She cites an example that has become the major foundation of the Western and of national identity: the origin of the cowboy.[34] Herrera-Sobek notes the irony that the cowboy, "that archetypal embodiment of what has been imprinted in the popular mind as quintessentially American," is actually an outgrowth of the Mexican *vaquero* who brought the skills of generations of ranch and cow work to the southwestern United States.[35]

However, Charles Zurhorst, in his work *The First Cowboys and Those Who Followed*, notes that the cowboy has been described in opposition to Mexicans, citing Mirabeau Buonaparte Lamar, second president of the Texas Republic in the late 1830s, as defining cowboys, in Zurhorst's words, as "rustlers of longhorns who hate all things Mexican."[36] Zurhorst cites many different texts that claim to have located the origin of the cowboy, including one that describes the cowboy as an outgrowth of the contact between Anglos and Mexicans in Texas. But in the end, he denies this history, finding the roots of the "American" cowboy in bands of men who struggled for the rights of tenants in the anti-rent rebellion of 1766 in New York: "And so, in 1766, the American cowboy, or cow-boy, was born. It is interesting to note that the first cowboy was (like his present day image) a rugged outdoorsman, dedicated to justice, and a rebel at heart."[37] These men were called "cow-boys" because they would raid farms of livestock, including cows, to fund their mission; men like these brought this practice to Texas, where they took possession of wild cattle and stole cattle that belonged to Mexicans, an account that coincides with Américo Paredes' description of the violent origins of the Texas ranch empire. Zurhorst goes on to assert that "contrary to the belief of some, the first Texas cowboy was not an offshoot of the Mexican vaquero," using as slim evidence Lamar's claims, cited above, that cowboys hated Mexicans.[38] However, Arnold Rojas notes some undeniable similarities between the Anglo cattle-handling buckaroo and its precursor, the Mexican vaquero.[39] The vaquero, a staple of the Mexican hacienda in central and northern Mexico, migrated north of the Rio Grande to disseminate vaquero culture, skills, and tradition to accommodating Anglos.[40] Zurhorst's outright denial of the vaquero in the diverse genealogy of the cowboy is part of the official history of the United States, which is itself premised on the erasure of the Mexican history of the Southwest.

Thanks to crimes from the outright theft of Mexican livestock, property, and land to the systematic extermination of native populations of the Southwest, the history of the contributions of native peoples— Californios, Mexicanos, Tejanos, and various Native American tribes— to the formation of the nation has been rendered invisible to dominant popular narratives. Like Paredes, Herrera-Sobek explores this hidden history through the oral tradition of the *corrido*, which documents the events surrounding the introduction of vaquero culture in what is now the Southwest of the United States.

The obliteration of the Mexican genesis of southwestern culture persisted late into the twentieth century in cinematic constructions not just of the cowboy but also more generally of the borderlands. Recent work by critical filmmakers in the border genre has brought to light much that has hitherto been repressed, rendered invisible, or marginalized; for instance, the "other" history of the Alamo in *Lone Star* (1996), the depiction of the Mexican vaquero in *The Three Burials of Melquiades Estrada* (2005), or the experience of crossing the border in *Babel* (2006).

HOLLYWOOD BORDER CINEMA

Much of border cinema derives from its precursors, the silent greaser film and its offshoot the Western, particularly the latter for its persistence into the present. Although Westerns take place in the Southwest, a smaller subcategory of these take place on or near the border or explicitly traverse the border as part of the story. Many more Westerns are set in small isolated frontier towns or depict expansive vistas traversed by gunslinging outlaws and marauding Indians. Hollywood border cinema offers a vision of the United States at its defining limits, and its popularity roughly corresponds to the crises and mood swings of national immigration and border policies. The border acts as a political symbol of national order and control, namely, the control of the national labor market and immigration from the south. Though each border film is unique in the specificities of narrative, a discussion of genre is useful for charting the changing currents of its social and cultural significance. The assertion of genre is ambitious; it implies cohesion among individual texts whose meanings often extend beyond a single genre. And border cinema designates texts linked more by a common geographical or symbolic referent than a shared ideology or textual meaning.

In an attempt to excavate the history of genre, Rick Altman distills two millennia of literary theory, reading for its usefulness to film theory in terms of its major theoretical pitfalls. Most notably, he finds that the assessment of genre as an independent entity bespeaks a lack of attention to the role of the reader and critic. The migration of genre theory to film analysis immediately heightened the institutional and industrial horizons of aesthetic production.[41] Thomas Schatz describes the genre film of the classical era of the big studio factories, from the 1930s to the 1960s, as one that "involves familiar, essentially one-dimensional characters acting out a predictable story pattern within a familiar setting."[42] This pattern was not accidental; it followed industrial capital efficiency by recycling sets and marketing stories and stars who had already garnered success, thus making the films surefire hits.

Film critics often describe the genre film as a commodity designed to maximize studio profits.[43] However, Altman contests this shorthand of genre criticism. He argues that there is at least one case of studio executives attempting to create and define a genre to no avail.[44] The genre film, in his estimation, is not so entirely determined by market forces. Genres are both "static" and "dynamic"; they refer to similar narrative systems, but change according to historical circumstance and subsequent transformations in cultural attitudes and the individual disposition of the reader-critic.[45] Altman likens genre-theorists to city-planners who plan but cannot control the use of the city: "Just as city-planners once thought that people would automatically inhabit their city as designed, so genre-theorists once believed that readers and viewers would automatically follow the lead of textual producers."[46] The individual social and cultural conditions of the spectator or the group dynamics of the audience as well as the actual conditions of viewing—whether in the cinema or on DVD or VHS, alone or with a group—in short, all material circumstances, personal philosophies and psychologies, and contextual factors contribute to the experience of the film and the production of its meaning.[47] Regardless of the shifting and alterable conditions of viewing, film genres are very resilient conductors of meaning. A genre persists because the major cultural conflicts to which it refers remain unresolved.[48]

Gloria Anzaldúa describes the border as a wound caused by the violent encounter of First to Third World; indeed, it is a space that resonates with trauma, a wound that refuses to heal, and so it becomes the object of tremendous cultural work.[49] The border genre, like the Western, emanates from a long literary history that preceded its cinematic incarnation. From dime novels to silent greaser films, popular Westerns, and action films, the border signifies a North American complex and neurosis about self-identity. U.S. popular culture defines national identity against the borderlands and their mythologized inhabitants: an inchoate mass of criminals, sexual deviants, and racialized outsiders. The more independent review of the genre by Chicano, Latino and Native American filmmakers recycles border imagery to a different end, though one that equally impacts the conception of national identity and cultural belonging.

Border films anticipate the critical work of Latin/o American cultural studies by moving beyond the nation and foregrounding contact across the hemisphere, particularly between the United States and Mexico. Border films, though often ideologically retrograde, make this contact a point of departure of the narrative. They are tacitly hemispheric in focus for the many forays from and into Mexico and the international efforts at border patrol and control, as well as the truly distinct globalism of border cultures. Studies of the border inevitably traverse the boundaries separating geographies and fields of interest. Borderland criticism, as Héctor Calderón and José David Saldívar have noted, is thus deeply dialogic and relational.[50]

Pablo Vila challenges the idea that the borderlands are a utopian space of multiculturalism and a globalized ideal of internationalism, multiplicities, and *mestizaje*.[51] He argues that binational relations produce divisions and intensify identification within difference. He explores how binaries are generated in this region; he finds that it is more a place of conflict and contention than cohesion and confluence.[52] Through extensive interviews taken from 1991 to 1997, Vila documents the various social categories that organize borderlands discourse and contribute to ongoing tensions among ethnic, racial, and regional groups. Unique among his findings is the idea that Mexican-Americans view Mexicans as alien "others," which is contrary to the critical view of a historical Anglo-Mexican dichotomy. This nationalist disidentification has roots in the denigration of all things Mexican perpetrated in social and cultural discourses and mass media. Mexican-Americans profess a particularly intense disidentification with Mexican migrants and recent arrivals as a way of consolidating a tenuous sense of place and belonging. On the other hand, Vila finds that Mexicans also view Mexican-Americans as "other," specifically as *pochos*, "rotten or discolored ones," a denigrating term for those of Mexican origin raised in the United States without a sense of cultural heritage or fully developed Spanish language skills.[53] Recently, some Mexican-Americans have reclaimed the term "*pocho*," emptying it of its negative connotations, to describe different permutations of language, such as Spanglish, and hybrid Mexican and U.S. cultural identity.[54] This latter resignification puts its meaning closer to that of "Chicano," a politically inflected term of Mexican-American racial and ethnic solidarity and pride.

Many critical Latino border films depict these scenarios, particularly *El Norte* (1983), *Lone Star* (1996), and *The Gatekeeper* (2002). In *El Norte*, a Mexican-American character calls the Immigration and Naturalization Service on an undocumented worker in order to eliminate competition for a job—this lack of political solidarity is a part of competition for scarce resources in which Chicanos and Mexicans alike are at the bottom of the labor market. A Mexican character describes this same Mexican-American as a *pocho*. Likewise, in *Lone Star*, a woman who had herself crossed the border without the proper documents becomes a successful restaurateur who is unsympathetic to the troubles of undocumented immigrants. Finally, in *The Gatekeeper*, a mixed-race Mexican-American border patrolman identifies with border vigilantes in his internalized phobia of all things Mexican. These films expose these attitudes as unfortunate consequences of internalized Hispanophobia and a lack of a politically inflected sense of solidarity for Latinos facing exclusionary nativism. Many Chicano and Latino activists have worked to create a sense of political community among the various factions and generations of Latinos of the borderlands and beyond. For instance, one of the oldest border organizations, the League of United Latin American Citizens (LULAC), originated in Corpus Christi, Texas, in 1929 to fight for the rights of Mexicans, Chicanos, and all Latinos facing discrimination, segregation, and injustice.[55]

In many Hollywood border feature films, the depiction of peaceful interracial and international relations is part of U.S. free trade ideology that denies the political and sociocultural realities of tension across the borderlands. Claire F. Fox examines the culture of the border region during the last three decades of the twentieth century, documenting misrepresentations by U.S. mass media of the border as a place of peaceful relations. She initiated work on border cultures out of her outrage at the 1989 Hollywood movie *Old Gringo*, which depicts the border as a place of serene and depoliticized transit suggesting a history of tranquil U.S.-Mexico relations. Fox dug deeper into the industrial relations in the production of the film itself and found that the Mexican film studio, Estudios Churubusco, had been commandeered by U.S. producers to maximize profits *maquila*-style. The film became a model of free trade production in the voracious search for the lowest possible production and labor costs.[56]

Old Gringo is a perfect instantiation of the pervasiveness of a North American Free Trade Agreement (NAFTA) ideological gloss, evident not just in the manner and relations of production but in the context and production of narrative meaning. Fox explores border imagery across various media to trace the persistence of the national in this post-NAFTA and thus post-national era. Her work dovetails with the works of scholars and critics who have examined the role of the border as a major symbol in bi-national politics. For many scholars, the borderlands are both a geographical location and a paradox of the social status and identity of Chicanos and Latinos.

FRONTIER NARRATIVES

In *Border Bandits: Hollywood on the Southern Frontier*, I begin the genealogy of Hollywood border films with classical post–World War II Westerns from the late 1940s to the 1970s, followed by the return of the Western hero as the border patrolman in the 1980s, the drug trafficking Hollywood film and television border stories, and finally the critical Latino border films of "Hispanic Hollywood" from the 1980s and onward that shift the border genre to major urban centers. In the final installment of this genealogy, I examine recent revisionist Westerns, including *Brokeback Mountain* (2005) and *The Three Burials of Melquiades Estrada* (2005).

Border films have stock characters—the sultry Latina, the pious female Mexican immigrant, the righteous cowboy/border guard, the job-taking male immigrant, the crooked drug runner—and stock sets and scenery—the open desert, abandoned border towns, the canteen, the whorehouse. Many of these border films belong to other genres or types—the Western, the action film, the drug trafficking film, and Latino film—but they are all Hollywood productions on, near, or about the border region, the roughly 2000-mile line separating and joining the United States to and from Mexico. Hollywood border films are not about the immigrant experience or cultural conflict; rather, they are concerned with fortifying U.S. national identity during times of cultural transition. Border films provide a vital history of the United States through key cinematic moments, from the "birth of the nation" after the U.S. Civil War, the post–World War II era, the civil rights era, the Reaganite 1980s, and the liberal "multicultural" 1990s to the current state of border anxieties relating to fears of drug trafficking and terrorism after September 11, 2001. The heritage of most of these films can be traced back to the original border genre, the Western, some more obliquely than others.

Many Westerns take place on the border region between the United States and Mexico, which accounts for the prevalence of titles like *Rio Grande* (1950), and *Rio Bravo* (1959), all referring to the river as a natural demarcation between nations, rather than one that is the result of war. The Western, the most enduring Hollywood genre, has always been associated with U.S.-style masculinity, the battle between civilization and barbarism, and the dramatization of the founding values of the early nation. But Westerns might also be examined for shared provenance, the preoccupation with Native American nation formation and immigration, the relationship to Mexico, and the presence of Mexicans and Mexican-Americans.

Though the "frontier" typically connotes its western incarnation and the uncivilized "Indian" territory beyond it, the southern frontier, Mexico, and the Mexican past of the United States are of equal relevance in the construction of the moral universe of the Western. Mexico carries various meanings: it represents a victorious sign of territorial expansion —since the United States expropriated almost half of its land mass in 1848—but it also represents the possibility of loss, of the need to continually defend the national frontier from hostile invasion or re-annexation. Mexico is the racialized and primitive wilderness where western male heroes go to reinvigorate their masculinity—often with the help of Mexican women—and where mixed race characters and relationships are common, and it often represents the uncivilized past of the United States, the idyllic land that, in post–civil war era stories, replaces the terrain just beyond the western frontier. Border films, and Westerns in particular, dramatize the nation as a lived experience in a local setting; the United States is a nation born after the U.S. Civil War and out of the illusion of the complete resolution of civil disunion, and many border narratives displace the internal conflict between the North and South of the United States onto the north-south continental divide.

In chapter one, I analyze the role of the Western as the foundation of many of the fundamental ideas and tropes of the border genre in a contemporary context. I begin with post–World War II Westerns for several reasons. These films comprise the most popular Westerns, the epitome of the genre, and audiences still watch them with deep nostalgia. They are also the most accessible films of the genre, constantly replayed on commercial and cable television, and they make up a large part of the archive of Westerns available for video and DVD rental and purchase. This era is also known for the dominance of big-budget Westerns with high production values, coinciding with the height of the genre. The nostalgia for the postwar Western also has to do with the affective engagement demanded from the viewer. These films are more complex and psychologically compelling than their predecessors, reflecting the more complex social and cultural conditions following the war. Thomas Schatz notes that the tone of the Western changed dramatically after the war: "As American audiences after World War II became saturated with the classic Western formula and also more hard-bitten about sociopolitical realities, the image of the Western community changed accordingly, redefining the hero's motivation and his sense of mission."[57] According to Schatz, the Western had gained a psychological dimension that stemmed from the Western hero's "growing incompatibility with civilization as well as the cumulative weight of society's unreasonable expectations."[58] Moreover, by the late 1940s and early 1950s, Westerns were the primary media vehicle for analyzing U.S. national identity in terms of its global position[59], as exemplified in Fred Zinnemann's *High Noon* (1952), which uses individual rights and community responsibilities as an allegory for the U.S. role in the cold war. Following Richard Slotkin, Stanley Corkin examines films of this era as major events of the cold war that perpetuate and animate the ideology of U.S. world dominance.[60]

Richard Slotkin notes that the beginning of the cold war inaugurated the "Golden Age of the Western," the twenty-five year period in which the genre peaked in popularity, an era that began with the Korean War and ended with the U.S. intervention in Vietnam. The Western provided a safe generic frame in which to encode and allegorize subjects that were not socially acceptable topics of verbal or visual discourse, topics that included race relations, sexuality, and cold war politics.[61] This deepening of the psychological fabric of the genre also informed the work of critics concerned with the role of the audience and the contextual factors in cultural and individual interpretation of film texts. The postwar films tended to invite spectators deeper into the world of the film with the more complex dynamics of voyeurism and identification. These Westerns tended to question the conventions of the genre, including the social role of the hero, giving these films considerably more impact for viewers in similar social predicaments.

In all of the Westerns of this study, the forays into Mexico are foundational events for the creation of U.S. national identity. The frontier stands in for the expansion of the nation in both actual and symbolic terms. Westerns hearken back to an earlier historical period typically between 1865 and 1910, one that is far enough from the era in which it was produced that it seems to have little or no connection to the present. Yet the genre, in its nostalgia for the past, is both intimately tied to the present and curiously future oriented; it offers a forecast of what is to come if the southern border is not more strictly policed. The United States bears the entire burden of enforcement since the land just north of the Rio Bravo is a relatively recent acquisition. The U.S.-based cowboys and cavalry try their best to break the bad habit of Mexican travel into land that was once part of Mexico; the history of the Mexican identity of the Southwest is one that the film industry has long repressed.

Chon Noriega has written of the "repressed history" of the classical Westerns, most of which were produced from 1930 to 1960 but take place during the border conflict era—from 1848, or the signing of the Treaty of Guadalupe Hidalgo after the Mexican-American War, to 1929, also the year of the Wall Street crash that marked the beginning of the Great Depression in the United States, the effects of which resounded throughout the hemisphere. During this era, the United States violated the Treaty of Guadalupe Hidalgo many times and consolidated its expansionist grip on the Southwest through various other nefarious means. The Western, however, depicted the hostile takeover of the Southwest by the United States as a benevolent and just endeavor by hardy pioneers. Noriega notes that the years of the consolidation of the classic

Western are consistent with the era of mass deportation of almost four million Mexican "immigrants"—many of whom were legal citizens—the internment of Japanese Americans, and the push-pull policies of the Bracero Program (1942–1964), a short-term labor program for unskilled Mexicans.[62]

Most Westerns depict Mexican-Americans in derogatory stereotype or grant them secondary status as citizens—but only if they capitulate to an assimilationist narrative. The borderlands are the symbolic topos of the impossible predicament of Mexican-Americans in what Charles Ramírez Berg has described as the cultural pluralism of assimilation, where ethnic difference represents a means of staving off too much ambition for success in the dominant culture for fear that Latino success would cause the displacement of Anglos. Instead, success for the racialized character is determined by his/her willingness to assimilate as a second-class citizen.[63] For instance, in the liberal post-1960s border Western *Rio Lobo* (1970), the mixed race Mexican protagonist/sidekick Pierre Cordona almost outshines John Wayne with his dazzling good looks and sense of justice, but Wayne silently recovers his place as the undeniable moral center of the story. In the end, Cordona succeeds in accomplishing Wayne's mission, which fixes him squarely in the ancillary position of sidekick.

By the 1980s, the Western had gained a new guise as the border film, in which the cowboy returns as the border patrolman and the sheriff as an agent of the Drug Enforcement Agency (DEA). Examples of border films include *Borderline* (1980) with Charles Bronson, *The Border* (1982) with Jack Nicholson, and *Flashpoint* (1984) with Kris Kristofferson. In chapter two I argue that the border patrolman is the new incarnation of U.S. moral values, of a serious and exemplary devotion and duty to the nation and its peoples. The border films of the 1980s share a post-1965 preoccupation with issues of immigration, particularly relating to fears of increased immigration from Mexico. Public opinion framed sojourning Mexicans as the cause of a depressed national mood and mass media followed with portrayals of the 'perils' of the immigrant invader, using tandem signals of danger and economic strain.

According to Leo Chavez, from 1965—the year that national origin quotas were dismantled—to 1999, the cover images from various popular news magazines told a compelling story about an immigrant "invasion" as an economic and political burden.[64] In a study that complements the work of Chavez, Otto Santa Ana reviews the imagistic language of metaphor in popular news stories and finds the language to be typical of warmongering rhetoric; these stories often describe incoming populations as violent forces of invasion and intrusion.[65] Likewise, Kent Ono and John Sloop study the rhetoric of the responses to California's Proposition 187 and find that images and information about this immigration policy are part of a larger social and historical matrix. Proposition 187 evokes centuries of systems of meaning regarding immigration, calling upon the long memory of history of the 1882 Chinese Exclusion Act, of the Immigration Acts of 1891, 1903, 1907, 1940, and so forth.[66] These critics agree that mass media is the place to look for public opinion, the public sentiments that shape policies and enable them to be enacted socially. Popular images and discourses about immigration were oriented toward the creation of new policies and the intensification of those already in place. Border films from the 1980s make good on the implied promise of the border patrol to guard the nation against undocumented immigrants, drug traffickers, and terrorists, while they also draw the viewer into their moral world and its political imperatives. Border cinema often has the benign appearance of a medium that hearkens back to a simpler era of gunslinging outlaws and lawmen, yet the prevalence of figures of renegade moralism or vigilantism personified by actors like John Wayne recall a history of U.S. cultural, political, and economic interventions in the rest of the hemisphere, justified as acts of U.S. beneficence. The Latin American male character is typically some permutation of the bandit that the Anglo moral hero will vanquish to audience delight or he is a sidekick figure who aids in the accomplishment of the Anglo hero's plan. The female equivalent to the bandit occupies an equally marginal position. To Rosa Linda Fregoso, the "Mexicana" faces the paradox of being hyper-visible as an object of "derision" and "desire" who embodies the "moral limits of white womanhood."[67]

LATIN/O AMERICAN DRUG LORDS

The ruthlessness of Latin/o American drug traffickers has been a favorite theme of Hollywood border films. In Orson Welles' *Touch of Evil* (1958) the Grandi brothers are depicted as part of the menace of the border as its resident drug users and pushers—though it is unclear whether this vice is associated with a larger market or a larger sphere of distribution. By the late 1980s, a wave of Hollywood border films and television shows about drug trafficking began to appear, most notably: *Extreme Prejudice* (1987), *Deep Cover* (1992), *Traffic* (2000), *A Man Apart* (2003), and *Kingpin* (NBC, 2003). Most of these films and shows feature the heroic mission of the DEA, FBI, and undercover cops in the capture of Latin/o American drug traffickers. In chapter three, I discuss how these films locate the responsibility of the "drug menace" in Latin America, either for lack of cooperation in the "war on drugs" or for enabling the production and distribution of contraband headed to a U.S. market.

The Latin/o American drug trafficker, though a major figure in Hollywood border films, did not really gain popularity until the 1980s, during the era of the collapse of many Latin American economies, the drop in oil prices for Mexico and Venezuela, the depreciation of local currencies, and the subsequent fortification of the U.S. economy, all of which was followed by massive northbound immigration. The prosperity of the 1980s, the overwhelming association of U.S. 1980s culture with rapid wealth, the strong dollar, dizzying investment returns, and all the trappings of affluence are notable across the landscape of U.S. popular culture. These conditions created a new wave of high risk Hollywood film and television border media that are dramatic, fast-paced, and full of glamour. The media fascination with drug war dramas also coincides with contemporary attitudes about border policy fueled by resentment about immigrants grabbing at U.S. affluence—i.e., taking jobs and women from Anglo men. From the 1990s into the present moment, the war on drugs has dovetailed with the low intensity war on the border and, more recently, with the war on terrorism as multiple fronts of the same offensive.

Beginning in the early 1980s, critical Latin/o American border films shift the genre's focus of criticism to major urban centers. A couple of notable exceptions to this trend are the films by director Robert M. Young: *Alambrista!* (1977) and *The Ballad of Gregorio Cortez* (1982).[68] Many Latino border films link the national boundary with the separation of neighborhoods in what many consider the largest border city in the United States, Los Angeles. These films explore the literal separation of Latino neighborhoods from the rest of the city and how immigrants face various borders and impasses within the city. Los Angeles–based films like *Real Women Have Curves* (2002), *Bread and Roses* (2000), *My Family/Mi Familia* (1995), *El Norte* (1983), *Star Maps* (1997), and *Mi vida loca* (1993) depict local communities as spaces drawn from the unhappy realities of economic hardship: daily struggles for survival that involve wage reductions, lack of health care, public assistance, gang membership, and working without documents.

In chapter four, I explore urban divisions as a consequence of economic and political disparities across the hemisphere. I examine *El Norte, Star Maps,* and *Bread and Roses* for their depictions of border crossing characters who settle in Los Angeles. The experiences of these characters lend insight into the various conditions and dynamics of globalization in the Americas. *El Norte* exposes the conditions for border crossers in the city in the 1980s and *Star Maps* examines the "boom" in Latino culture from the perspective of an aspiring actor in Los Angeles. Finally, *Bread and Roses* engages many of the issues of border films like *El Norte* and *Star Maps,* but then takes a very different narrative course. *Bread and Roses* depicts the city as a place of divisions, but emphasizes the urban political histories of labor activism. *Bread and Roses* acts as a training film of labor activism for undocumented immigrants; it offers a model of escape from the vicious cycle of poverty and invisibility for Latinos in the city. In the film, Hollywood is not some glossy meta-reality grafted onto urban space, but a real industry whose daily operations involve lawyers and financial institutions that contract out their cleaning services to exploitative firms.

LATINO BORDER FILMS AND CULTURAL BELONGING

After a number of cultural and political changes, most notably NAFTA, the Immigration Reform and Control Act of 1986, and the rise of new technologies of communication, the border imaginary in the city was presented differently by filmmakers. By the late 1990s, the anti-immigrant phobia and hysteria of the 1980s was eclipsed by an uninterrupted history of migration from Mexico and other parts of Latin America, which returned Los Angeles to its Latino and Hispanic heritage.[69] As neighborhoods changed, immigrant settlements dispersed, and communities went cybernetic, the social and economic boundaries of the 1980s manifested differently. Partly as an effect of the rise of the "Hispanic Hollywood" and the success of films like *El Norte,* Latinos had consolidated what Renato Rosaldo calls "cultural citizenship," or the social and cultural practices that establish place and belonging for marginalized populations.[70] Latino cinema is a vital foundation for new forms of membership both as cultural texts of historical value and as individual film texts that demand affective and transformative modes of engagement. By the 1990s, an era often referred to as "Hispanic Hollywood," a cultural revolution had taken place. Latinos in Hollywood cinema and other forms of media had begun to reap the benefits of their long cultural history to reassert their rightful place at the center of popular culture. Gustavo Leclerc and Michael J. Dear claim that it was not just Latino cultural production but also the sheer force of the surge in the Latino population that revolutionized and reclaimed Los Angeles; everything about the city and the state of California from place names to representatives in city and state governance has the mark of its Latino and Hispanic heritage; the culmination of this heritage is apparent in its current leadership under native Angelino and Chicano Mayor Antonio Villaraigosa. In *La Vida Latina en L.A.*, Dear and Leclerc gather various artists and writers who reconstruct the Latino heritage of Los Angeles lost to the "official history" of the city, and many turn to the city itself as a vital archive and archeological record.[71] They document changes in the cultural landscape of Los Angeles apparent in "cultural events on the street; in magazines, art, and television; and in universities, homes, and the workplace."[72]

For the Latino Cultural Studies Working Group, cultural practices, from those of everyday life to linguistic and artistic expression, in the words of William V. Flores and Rina Benmayor, "cross the political realm and contribute to the process of affirming and building an emerging Latino identity and political and social consciousness."[73] They eschew the rigid legal definition of citizenship for a flexible socio-political notion of citizenship that is more inclusive and descriptive of Latino realities; "In this way, immigrants who might not be citizens in the legal sense or who might not even be in this country legally, but who labor and contribute to the economic and cultural wealth of the country, would be recognized as legitimate political subjects claiming rights for themselves and their children, and in that sense, as citizens."[74]

Latino cultural productions constitute claims to membership that express and enact citizenship for all Latinos, from naturalized citizens to undocumented immigrants. Many films of Latino cinema locate their stories in Los Angeles because of its unique position as home to the second largest Mexican population outside of Mexico as well as a sizable population of South Americans and Central Americans. Indeed, almost every film mentioned by Flores and Benmayor as "standard stock in video stores"—*Zoot Suit, La Bamba, El Norte, Stand and Deliver, American Me,* and *Mi Familia*—is set in Los Angeles.[75] These films are part of a growing and vital tradition of re-examining global city spaces as the political centers of the nation that dramatize new configurations of North American identities. They are part of larger social processes of contestation of hegemonic political identities as cultural practices that perform and interpret political belonging. Rather than a city doomed to Hollywood film and television representations of social divisions, we might reimagine Los Angeles (and cities like it) as a powerful template for the creation of cultural membership, for civic and political agencies that impact national political sentiments about the definition of citizenship. Los Angeles is a major locus of Latino cultural citizenship, a place that benefits from the special resources of cultural and racial diversity and that profoundly affects national debates about citizenship and belonging for marginalized populations.

Post–World War II Westerns, border immigration films of the 1980s, and post-1980s narco-trafficking films all set the terms for the later production of critical Latino border films that impact the debates on citizenship and immigration in the United States. The new border Westerns are being written by those who were mostly denigrated as bandidos, outlaws, and unwanted immigrants or who were only considered worthy if properly assimilated to the American way. For instance, in King Vidor's *Duel in the Sun* (1946), part of the story involves Chinese workers laying railroad tracks across McCanles ranch lands; the Anglo Texans consider the railroad an invasion that is represented and intensified by the presence of the Chinese workers. Contemporary border Westerns are reconstructed dramas told from the marginal perspectives of secondary and often maligned characters. At the helm of a contemporary revisionist Western that reexamines its masculine culture is Chinese national Ang Lee, who locates his revolutionary and poetic meditation on gay male desire in the mythic frontier Southwest in *Brokeback Mountain*. The short story on which the screenplay is based was written by Annie Proulx, who writes the marginal into the center of typically masculinist Western plots. Chris Berry has claimed that the story integrates Western melodrama with the Chinese "family-ethics" film that was popular during Lee's childhood.[76] The story tells of Ennis and Jack, who form a deep emotional and physical intimacy while corralling sheep on Brokeback Mountain in Wyoming. We follow them through the years as they try to repress their mutual desire and live "normal" heterosexual lives. Recalling the brutal gay bashing of Matthew Shepard in Wyoming, Jack is, to Ennis' imagination, fatally gay-bashed, leaving Ennis alone and bereft. *Brokeback Mountain* questions cowboy masculinity and its exclusion of women and all that is deemed "feminine." By the end, Ennis is isolated and alone in his outcast desires, but he finds a way to reincorporate women, through his daughter, into his world.

Another example of a reconstructed border narrative is *The Three Burials of Melquiades Estrada* (2005), which has almost everything that border films have offered over the years. Directed by Tommy Lee Jones but written by screen playwright Guillermo Arriaga—best known for writing *Amores Perros* and *21 Grams*—*The Three Burials of Melquiades Estrada* is a revision of the border Western from the perspective of the South. In *The Three Burials of Melquiades Estrada*, the Mexican vaquero, described by Herrera-Sobek as the repressed precursor of the all-American cowboy, returns to the Western as a hero and protagonist and as migrant labor to the United States. The return of the vaquero is complicated; he is a humanized character, but his perspective is effaced by the overwhelming emotional excesses of the main Anglo character. Pete admires and appreciates his friend in a manner that says more about how he feels than how Melquiades reciprocates or experiences this friendship. Melquiades passively reflects the care and concern of Pete, whose care only intensifies the sympathetic portrayal of the Anglo hero, a dynamic symptomatic of hierarchical interracial and transborder relations.

Though this book is concerned with cross-genre border films, it begins and ends with Westerns, since even Latino border films cannot escape the legacy of the Western. In Westerns, the southern frontier marks the limitation of movement, the outer limit of the nation beyond which there is land that cannot be readily conquered. The border delimits freedoms typically associated with the western frontier; Western heroes "make a run for the border" and escape into Mexico, seeking profit and pleasure and escape from the law or other restrictions of North American culture. In border films, the border is variously a significant backdrop, another character in the story, a symbolic zone, a line between opposing forces and values, a line separating barbarism from civilization, the horizon of modernity, and the outer limit of a nation. Whether the border is one or all of these things in each of the border films of this study, it nonetheless is always a reminder that each film is part of a national narrative, part of the many texts and symbols of the myth of the United States as capital of the Americas.

ONE

HOW THE SOUTHWEST WAS WON

The western frontier has always been a defining symbol of the United States, signifying the wide and open range and the opportunity to settle new territories where the only hindrance to this forward expansion is the hostile and bloodthirsty Indian and the Mexican bandit. The frontier is a repository of these and other romantic legends of the Old West. James Folsom calls it the "intangible" but very real marker of difference between the new republic and its European predecessors.[1] Frederick Jackson Turner's lecture at the 1893 World's Columbian Exposition in Chicago, "The Significance of the Frontier in American History," was a turning point not just in historical studies, but also in the history of the United States. Turner shifted the point of reference of U.S. history from the original East Coast settlements with their European roots to the "all-American" western frontier.[2] Turner wrote, "The existence of an area of free land, its continuous recession, and the advance of American settlement westward, explain American development."[3] The frontier signified the North American difference from Europe as well as its independence from colonial forefathers.

There is another frontier that marks limits and boundaries beyond which there is land that cannot be so readily ceded. The southern frontier plays a large role in the Western as the symbolic opposite of the open western frontier. The border indicates the perimeter of the nation rather than the possibility for its expansion; it represents the modern nation as a fully crystallized formation. The appearance of the borderlands in Westerns immediately puts the nation on the line; the southern national boundary competes with the western frontier to delineate and define "America." Moreover, it is a boundary that must be protected and defended. Border Westerns are energized by a sense of common defense as a nationalist imperative.

The end of the nineteenth century marked yet another turn in the definition of the role and place of the United States in the world system. The emergence of the southern frontier defined the United States against Mexico and the rest of Latin America while it signified U.S. prominence as a military power. The southern frontier activates a distinctly North American sense of nationalism as limit and defense, an idea that resounds throughout the border genre; the United States is viewed in border Westerns as a place of both limits and limitations and of regulations and restrictions while Mexico is depicted as a place without limits, laws or restrictions. In many Westerns, the border replaces the western frontier and provides a different line of access to the freedoms that once typified the roaming frontiersman. Over the international line, southwesterners might escape the restrictions, laws, and limitations of U.S. culture to enjoy the same liberties associated with the western frontier before it was settled and civilized.

The prevalence of the southern frontier in Westerns presents an alternate view of U.S. history from the vantage of the Southwest and the international line that connects and separates nations in the hemisphere. By their very name, Westerns are a genre of western expansionism, of a manifest destiny west of the Mississippi River; for this reason, the genre has rarely been identified with the southern frontier, though the relationship of U.S. citizens to Mexico and Mexicans is a dominant trope of the genre. Following Pierre Vilar's notion that "the history of the world is best observed from the frontier," the cultural history of the United States' rise to empire might be best examined through popular conceptions of the southern national boundary.[4] Many Westerns, if not most, conveniently skip over Polk's war with Mexico and replace it with the post–civil war United States' assistance of and alliance with Mexico against French imperialism—a pleasing self-image molded on the post–World War II good neighbor ideology. In these Westerns, the border is a mere technicality between nations; mercenary soldiers from the United States cross without incident into Mexico to extend a dominion that poses as good neighborliness. Most Westerns make use of the border region, many cross the border, and many make the southern U.S. frontier a major character in the story. Since the borderlands are comprised of land that once belonged to another nation, the area has always been a zone of defense from which U.S. property and territory are jealously guarded. The border is often a stage upon which historical psychodramas get reenacted to U.S. ends; for instance, the battle at the

Alamo is revisited anew in several Western films with different outcomes. Moreover, the border is a place where mythic national icons are lionized, including the Texas Rangers, the cavalry, the border patrol and the hardy Anglo settlers of the Southwest.

By the turn of the nineteenth century, the frontier of U.S. westward expansion and progress was no longer a catalytic symbol; it was broken asunder and replaced by the southern frontier as the representative of U.S. modernism, evident in the new forces of industrial expansion—railroads, telephones, automobiles—that linked previously disparate geographies and opened new markets. The southern line replaced the western frontier as a major organizing symbol of popular culture because it defined the nation on different, more modern terms: the United States was now bounded, limited, and exclusive. Hollywood used the border to symbolize the expansion of the global power and influence of the United States and convey its messianic duty to international "protection" and "assistance" through intervention. To give contour to this picture, I explore a few popular border Westerns from the post–World War II period to the late 1960s: *Duel in the Sun* (1946), *Rio Grande* (1950), *Vera Cruz* (1954), *Rio Bravo* (1959), *The Comancheros* (1961), *The Wild Bunch* (1969), and *Rio Lobo* (1970).[5] These films share a common historical periodization, regardless of time of release, during or after the U.S. Civil War and the Mexican struggle against French imperialism, and a few of the films refer significantly to the Alamo. In fact, most Westerns take place during the era between 1860 and 1890, with the turn of the century signaling the demise of the frontier and the Old West.[6] This periodization loosely follows the invention of the newfangled post-1848 boundary between the United States and Mexico. The new border evoked concerns about U.S. identity, especially about the large numbers of Mexican nationals who suddenly, by the shift of a line on the ground, had become U.S. residents. The border genre emanates from this historical period in which the border gained increasing symbolic resonance at the same time that the boundaries of national identity were challenged by "outside" forces.

Though I follow the historical arc of the films' settings, Westerns often have dual or even multiple temporalities; these include historical setting, era of production, duration of film, and time period in which the film itself is viewed. The Western may refer to a historical era, but in many cases, the historical referent is necessarily vague, pointing to an allegorical past or presenting the past in broad strokes. A post–civil war setting, for instance, often has more symbolic resonance than historical accuracy; it means cultural unrest, disunion, social divisiveness, pessimism, and a jaded nationalism. Hollywood tends to gloss internal post–civil war national divisions and displace national tensions onto the area south of the Mexican border. The post–civil war era Western provides the perfect frame for the psychodrama of national reintegration and cohesion; it presents a story of messianic nationalism that transforms civil war skepticism about integration into true and redemptive faith. The border plays a special role in delineating national history; often, as in *Vera Cruz*, the messy drama of national reunification is played out in Mexico, mediated by a woman (who may also become the hero's wife), and the characters' return to the United States signifies the inauguration of a modern and reunified state. Many Westerns define U.S. identity against a defining outside which appears variously as Mexico and Mexicans, the roaming and warring Indian nations and Indians, and racial miscegenation and racially-mixed characters.

From the mid-1940s to the late 1970s, the United States experienced massive cultural, economic, and political changes, yet the Western, by all appearances, stayed aesthetically the same. Even in its contemporary context the Western is steeped in nostalgia for a fictional time when moral questions were answered swiftly. Westerns meet their audience's desire for continuity and moral stability through their unchanging landscapes: the untarnished vista onto Monument Valley or the open and unadulterated plains of the West.

After World War II, the cultural mood of the United States was one of optimism. The war catapulted the United States from the depression of the earlier decade and initiated the onward rush of industrial growth. Though the United States participated in the war, it did not have to endure the burden of rebuilding, and subsequently surged ahead of other war participants in the competition of industrial output. During this era of incredible industrial and economic growth in the United States and to a lesser extent Europe, Latin America seemed to lag behind. Part of this slowness of growth was a direct result of a lack of skilled labor.[7] Thus, in many Westerns of this era like *The Comancheros*, professional hired guns from the United States travel into Mexico to perform special skills and deliver knowledge. The message in these Westerns was consistent with President Truman's insistence in extending technical assistance to Latin America to boost industrial growth. Mexico is often represented as the beneficiary of aid from the United States, and this assistance formed the basis of an ongoing construction of U.S. interventionism as benevolent and disinterested. Moreover, these Westerns portray the United States as having been invited to participate in the national affairs of Mexico. This was in part the case after 1954 when the Mexican currency was devalued and fixed to the dollar to stem inflation.[8] The result was that Mexican exports were suddenly priced well below market for the United States consumer. Though not a free market economy during this period, Mexico was wide open for foreign investment and the United States was quick to cross the border for its economic aggrandizement, continuing a long tradition of border crossing.[9] The United States continues to be represented as free to cross the southern border for the "good" of Mexico, but the travels of Mexican migrants have increasingly become the subject of fears of invasion in Hollywood border narratives.

RACIAL BORDERS IN THE SOUTHWESTERNER

Duel in the Sun (1946) establishes one of the primary tropes of the border genre in that the international line allegorizes the boundaries between races. The depiction of interracial relationships sets the terms for the political objectives of border narratives to either subjugate the racial other through assimilation as a second-class citizen, a scenario typified by John Wayne's sidekick Mexican characters—often played by actor Pedro González-González—or to depict the racial other as an outlaw character, either a bandit or a loose woman, who must be eliminated.

Duel in the Sun, otherwise known as "Lust in the Dust" and often referred to as a Texas Ranch epic[10], is a cross between a Western and a psychosexual melodrama centered on mixed-race Indian-Mexican Creole Pearl Chavez. Thomas Schatz calls *Duel in the Sun* a "prototype New Hollywood Blockbuster" that combines top stars, a big budget, an epic storyline, and high-gloss production values.[11] Producer David O. Selznick was hoping to exploit his earlier success with *Gone with the Wind* (1939) by drawing on an all-star cast of Jennifer Jones (Selznick's future wife), who had just won an Academy Award as Best Actress for *The Song of Bernadette* (1943), Gregory Peck, Joseph Cotten, Herbert Marshall, Lillian Gish, Lionel Barrymore, and Walter Huston.[12] Perhaps this parade of Hollywood pedigree is what lured audiences to the box office to watch a rather unusual story featuring a *mestizo* character with a Spanish surname, Pearl Chavez, as the lead protagonist.[13] A review of the film in *Time* magazine contemporary with its release sums up the Hollywood moral concisely: "The audience learns (thanks to the

1.1 Jennifer Jones as mixed-race Pearl Chavez in *Duel in the Sun*.

1.2 Pearl is adopted by the McCanles family: Lillian Gish as Laura Belle McCanles, Lionel Barrymore as Senator Jackson McCanles, and Joseph Cotten as Jesse McCanles.

Johnston office) that illicit love doesn't really pay in the long run but for about 134 minutes it has appeared to be loads of fun."[14] Indeed the story follows the dictates of the anti-miscegenation laws that were in effect until 1967 as well as the interdiction of the Hays Production Code against interracial relationships.

Pearl Chavez's story is tragic from beginning to end. Her mother is a debauched Indian dancer in a border town cantina and her father, the "white half,"[15] is a gambler. Her father is derogatively referred to as a "squaw man" in a manner reminiscent of the treatment of the protagonist of the play, *The Squaw Man*, shot for the screen in 1914, 1918, and 1931. Her father murders her mother for infidelity and is executed for it. Pearl, left parentless, is sent to live with her father's second cousin and ex-betrothed, Laura Belle McCanles, and her family on a Texas ranch. Like her mixed-race predecessor, Ramona (of the eponymously titled novel and film adaptations), Pearl falls in love with one of the brothers in her adopted white family. The threat of incest or of "unnatural" intimacies across the family generations is a constant refrain in the story.

As mentioned earlier, the story begins in a Mexican border town outside the limits of the United States, but almost immediately shuttles Pearl to a Texas ranch, ignoring the legal implications of this international move. We might presume that Pearl has bi-national citizenship; but the real question is whether or not she experiences bi-national cultural belonging. She is literally invited into the micro-national formation of the barricaded Texas ranch—its secure borders a symbol of U.S. victory in the U.S.-Mexican war—but her mixed-race presence is the catalyst for havoc and unrest that disrupts the domestic tranquility of the Anglo McCanles clan. Upon her arrival to the ranch, Jesse, the older McCanles son, introduces it as "a million acres of McCanles empire," to which Pearl responds, "Empire? Isn't this still Texas?" Indeed in Western mythology, Texas is the center and symbol of the larger national empire and a vital part of the economic expansion of the United States. By the 1880s, large ranches like the McCanles ranch—a possible reference to the well-known McAllen ranch and its eponymous town—were becoming major industrial engines and, as depicted in *Giant* (1956), centers of oil wealth.

Duel in the Sun might be best described as a hybrid generic formation, with this hybridity reflected in both the form and meaning of the narrative. The melodramatic tone sets the emotional pitch high and inspires a more intense identification on the part of the viewer. The characters, especially the "bad" ones, evoke the Western outlaw even though on the surface the story seems to depart entirely from the defining features of the Western myth, especially thanks to the racialized sexuality and overwrought sentimentality that seem to dominate all other plot preoccupations. Unlike in other Westerns, marginal themes are central to *Duel in the Sun*. A mixed-race Native American woman is at the center of the plot, but her centrality serves a specific purpose: she is the focus of a cautionary tale about the fateful consequences of racial mixing.

Duel in the Sun was one of the first films to depict intimacy and irrepressible attraction between Anglo and mixed-blood Native American characters. Unlike other mixed-race melodramas in which the major drama centers on the female characters' issues of identity, this film is a drama of ambivalent attraction to the Native American character that reflects the national drama over the role and status of Native Americans.

Philip Deloria, writing about the status of Native Americans in U.S. popular culture, argues that "playing Indian"—just as actress Jennifer Jones is doing with Pearl Chavez—has long been a major trope of narratives of U.S. identity. Hollywood has always been at the center of the performance of the Indian and constitutes one of the largest archives of demeaning stereotypes that serve white mastery. In Jacquelyn Kilpatrick's analysis of Native American representation from early Hollywood to the present, she finds three basic stereotypes of Native Americans: primitive and of lesser intelligence, sexually promiscuous, and heathen or spiritually closer to the earth.[16] It is not surprising that Pearl embodies all three stereotypes at once and thus represents a social menace who must meet her demise. These stereotypes still resounded after World War II, when there was considerable public concern about the political fate of Native Americans regarding their potential for either assimilation or self-governance.

To Laura Mulvey, *Duel in the Sun* is fundamentally a Western whose generic space is transformed by the core narrative preoccupation with Pearl Chavez, "a girl caught between two conflicting desires."[17] Stanley Corkin also argues that the film transforms the Western genre, shifting its central terms to the feminine. Yet, neither critic acknowledges the racial dimension of the erotic tension among the characters and how this might affect the film's critical interpretation and cultural meaning. Pearl Chavez as a mixed-race character is seemingly modeled on the tragic mulattos of melodramas like John Stahl's *Imitation of Life* (1934)—though for mixed Native American and Latino characters of Westerns, passing for white is never an option since the role of the ethnic or racial outsider is played up for high drama. The mixing of the Western and melodramatic genres reflects the thematic concerns about the mixing of races in that both mixtures lead to a demise perpetuated by the "weaker" term; "Indian" passion overwhelms Anglo morality just as the feminine melodrama erodes the stoic masculinity of the Western. The moral imperative of the story is to reestablish boundaries between the two cardinal terms of border stories: civilization (U.S.) and barbarism (Mexico and Native America).

The prelude to *Duel in the Sun* frames the story in national terms— Orson Welles, in voice-over narration, presents the following preface to the film, which "two years in the making, is a saga of Texas in the 1880s when primitive passions rode the raw frontier of an expanding nation. Here the forces of evil were in constant conflict with the deeper morality of the hardy pioneers. Here, as in the story we tell, a grey fate lay waiting for the transgressor upon the laws of god and man." The story is full of the language of fate and fatedness, of chance and misfortune, and of the laws of nature or forces beyond human control that are posed against the force of human will. On the side of will are the Anglo "hardy pioneers" and the hardworking Texan ranchers and on the side of fate are all the racialized and foreign characters who exhibit degenerate traits and a lack of control. The former are heroes and nationalists who are to be celebrated and the latter are outlaws who must be corralled, exiled, or extinguished. This opening gambit establishes the terms that justify an exclusionary nationalism within a story set after the Chinese Exclusion Act of 1882 and when, in Texas, the era of the cattle drives and the open range were replaced with enclosed and secure ranches lined with fences. In fact, a major subplot is that of the railroads trying to lay tracks across the McCanles ranch lands; the railroad is considered a trespassing invasion and the Chinese workers a nuisance. The laying of the railroad symbolizes both a racialized immigrant invasion and the linking of lone star Texas to the rest of the United States, which in turn allegorizes the linking of the United States to the rest of the world.

Thus, behind the salacious characterization of mixed-race Pearl Chavez is a story about the status of Texas in the United States and a dazzling portrait of an unnamed border town just beyond the state limits.

The film's setting—Texas in the 1880s—is crucial to the framing of mixed-race Pearl. The state was going through growing pains in these years as Anglo settlement increased its size, so there was considerable uncertainty about the future role of its Mexican and Native cultural heritage.

The story has the curious imprint of an actual historical circumstance involving a cross-racial liaison that caused considerable disquiet at the time. One of the major ranches of the Texas Ranger period of history, the McAllen ranch, was inhabited by James McAllen and a young Mexican girl, Santos Tijerina; the intimate mixed-race relationship between McAllen and Tijerina was a scandal for the town and the girl's family in Mexico.[18] According to some sources, the girl's family sent a troop of Mexican hit men to seek revenge on James McAllen, which resulted in an Alamo-esque night of shooting that McAllen miraculously survived. McAllen called in the Texas Rangers to find the men responsible for the ambush; when these men could not be found the Rangers killed two innocent Mexican men in their place—a common practice of "revenge by proxy" among the Rangers. The McAllen ranch is haunted by this interracial relationship, which perhaps served as material for the writers of *Duel in the Sun*, a film that also features a doomed and embattled mixed-race relationship that ends in a bloody shoot-out. It is certainly possible that the McAllen ranch with its history of interracial romance and treachery returns in *Duel in the Sun* as the anagrammatic McCanles ranch. However, *Duel in the Sun* shifts the story, if in fact it is citing it, to concerns that were more prevalent in the period just following World War II: concerns about the role of the United States in the hemisphere, about the southern boundary, and about the social and political place of Native Americans in U.S. society.

After World War II, U.S. policy toward Native Americans changed from advocating "retribalization," or the restoration of Native American cultural and political sovereignty as set forth in the 1934 Indian Reorganization Act (also known as the Wheeler-Howard Act), to advocating assimilation. As a result, Hollywood, caught in the policy mood swing from autonomy to assimilation, depicted Native peoples in a deeply ambivalent manner.[19] Many postwar Westerns, including *Duel in the Sun* (1946), *Rio Grande* (1950), *The Searchers* (1956), and *The Comancheros* (1961), contributed to the cultural attitudes and policies toward Native Americans that established key terms of U.S. national identity by depicting Native Americans as either friends or enemies of the state. *Duel in the Sun* transcends this discourse of good and bad Indian to present a cautionary tale about the moral pitfalls of full Indian integration through lack of limitations on racial miscegenation. The story plays on social fears that full Native American integration into the mainstream would lead to the "Indianization" of the white man.

Though *Duel in the Sun* is set in the late 1880s when federal Indian policy tended to advocate autonomy, the film was released after World War II, at a time when the government was systematically terminating Native American political rights. Thus relevant to the story is an 1888 law regulating marriage between white men and Indian women which sought to limit the expansion of Indian communities through marriage: "Be it enacted . . . that no white man, not otherwise a member of any tribe of Indians, who may hereafter marry, an Indian woman, member of any Indian tribe in the United States, or any of its Territories except the five civilized tribes in the Indian Territory, shall by such marriage hereafter acquire any right to tribal property, privilege, or interest whatever to which any member of such a tribe is entitled."[20] These five "civilized" tribes—Cherokee, Choctaw, Chickasaw, Creek or Muscogee, and Seminole—were considered civilized because they were more assimilated to European-American ways of life, mostly as farmers and planters. They were also more likely to mix with European-Americans to produce "mixed-blood" offspring. Lawmakers feared such marriages might result in reverse-assimilation, or the "Indianization" of white men, and further consolidation of the Indian nations. This scenario is not explicitly addressed in *Duel in the Sun*, though some aspect of the fear of reverse-assimilation is coded as the deleterious influence of Pearl's character. Her love interest, Lewt, is already a bad character, but becomes worse in the presence of Pearl, whose presence initiates and secures his demise.

In the opening scene, we are introduced in a matter of minutes to the entire depraved Chavez family, who enjoy every vice available in the Mexican border town where they reside.[21] Pearl, mirroring her mother, dances on a platform outside a saloon while her mother dances inside on the bar. Also inside the saloon, Pearl's father plays a game of chance; it is through this dysfunctional family portrait that we begin to associate chance, misfortune, and fate with Pearl's character. She is fated to mime her family history, a fact which suggests that her racial makeup is a congenital weakness. She is doomed to embody the erotic life of her mother and to exhibit the murderous impulse of her father. She will replay both histories when, through her sensual weakness, she attracts a lover whom she is fated to murder. The whole scenario will play out in the high emotional tones of melodrama.

Linda Williams designates melodrama as one of the "body genres" that evoke intense bodily reactions in the viewer, in reaction to the display of intimate emotions across a body literally and rapturously "gripped" by an excess of affect.[22] Melodrama has a particular temporality structured by its central fantasy of loss, which Williams describes as "too late!" The title *Duel in the Sun* refers to a fated scene of double loss, in which a duel leads to the tragic death of the protagonists. This tragic scene affects us with a sense of being "too late": of knowing the fate of the lovers, as foreshadowed by the history of Pearl, and yet not being able to do anything to forestall it. We arrive late to the scene; we failed to heed the warning clearly forecast by the original scene of miscegenation at the border.

Duel in the Sun is the film that inspired Laura Mulvey to build upon her schema regarding the "masculinization" of the spectator in Hollywood film. Mulvey writes, "As the spectator identifies with the main male protagonist, he projects his look onto that of his like, his screen surrogate, so that the power of the male protagonist as he controls events coincides with the active power of the erotic look, both giving a satisfying sense of omnipotence."[23] Thus in her original formulation, the woman on screen is objectified for a male voyeuristic pleasure, which assumes a male-identified spectator. Female and male spectators alike are shuttled into this masculine spectatorial position. Yet Mulvey rethinks the position of the female spectator based on the sexual crises of Pearl as the central character in the Texas ranch melodrama.[24] She takes as a point of departure the instability of the sexual identity of the female character as a symptom of the tensions of sexual difference. According to psychoanalytic theory, women arrive at sexual difference through repression of sexual instincts. Mulvey finds liberation of the sexual instinct for women in genre films: "Hollywood genre films structured around masculine pleasure, offering an identification with the *active* point of view, allow a woman spectator to rediscover that lost aspect of her sexual identity, the never fully repressed bed-rock of feminine neurosis."[25] A film like *Duel in the Sun* shifts the narrative terms by placing a woman at the center and making her story of internal conflict

1.3 Undeniable attraction between Pearl and Lewt (Gregory Peck).

the central drama. For Mulvey, the two brothers represent aspects of Pearl's identity and the two poles of her internal conflict and sexual ambivalence. She must choose either the ordered and civilized world of Jesse, which would entail a passive feminine identification, the proper course toward marriage, or the sexual expressivity and passion of Lewt, a relationship that Mulvey describes as "not based on maturity but on a regressive, boy/girl type of mixture of rivalry and play."[26] Both choices represent annihilation for Pearl, but the latter, with Lewt, is less repressive, thus enabling the expression of her repressed desires.

This analysis does not take into account the racial constitution of sexual identity and the sexual relations among characters. For instance, Pearl's situation reflects the status of Latinas in Westerns—Chihuahua (Linda Darnell in brownface) of *My Darling Clementine* (1946) or Helen Ramírez (Katy Jurado) of *High Noon* (1952)—as characters who intensify the rivalry between white men. Race constitutes another major point of reference in the dueling oppositions of Pearl's crises of identity. The racial position of her character shuttles between the "proper" repression of passing for white and the abject and primitive racialization represented by her mother and the post-slavery servants of the McCanles ranch. As a mixed-race character, her position is one of racial instability presented by the impossibility of being neither the one nor the other. The blind spots of the Oedipal narrative are more numerous than at first appearance; the scandal of desire is not just energized by the mysteries of sexual difference but by the obscurities and paradoxes of racial fetishism.

The sexual fetish and the racial fetish are built upon the same logic. According to Freud, fetishism corresponds to a precise moment in the formation of the little boy's psyche when he sees his mother's genitalia. At this moment, rather than embracing or acknowledging her difference, he immediately fears that the same fate might befall him. He masters this fear by disavowing his mother's lack and replacing the missing penis with something close at hand: a fetish object in the form of a foot, a shoe, or some other suitable substitute. The fetish is a useful explanatory mechanism since it uses a paradoxical logic in which something is both the same and the opposite at once. The fetish points to an attempt to control and master difference out of anxiety about loss of power and control. According to Mulvey, the masterful male gaze indicates the power to deny a frightening difference by turning the woman into a controllable object. Likewise, racial difference is associated with some anxiety-provoking occult powers; the racialized other is powerful and alluring at the same time. The Anglo subject, out of fear, neutralizes the racial other's difference to better facilitate domination by interpreting it as a sign of being simply less evolved or primitive. Thus Pearl is both feared as a woman and as a mysteriously racialized being. She is alluring to the white brothers for her difference, but ultimately is deemed too uncivilized, sensual, and unsettling. Within the logic of the plot, which reflects the cultural biases of the day, Pearl must be eliminated. For Frantz Fanon, the irrationality of these racial ideas is a direct result of its basis in ideologies of nationalism and colonialism.[27]

Pearl is a symptom of the postwar nationalist consolidation of the United States in the struggle to redefine citizenship and belonging after the war. Postwar film and media depictions of peoples of color tended to highlight the irrationality and cruelty of racism within a society sensitized by the atrocities of World War II. In keeping with this liberalism, *Duel in the Sun* is wrapped in a vague ideological veneer of anti-racism that is critical of the injustice Pearl faces from Lewt's bigoted father and the tragedy of the duel in the sun between the doomed lovelorn characters. But the larger mood of racial fetishism and the preponderance of stereotypes undermine this veil of liberalism.

Pearl symbolizes the difficulties and paradoxes of race; she enters the McCanles ranch as an exotic stranger and as a distant member of the family—like Native Americans who are both the foundation of the nation (as in Disney's *Pocahontas*) and its excluded margins. This familiarity and difference at once disrupts the domestic coherence and tranquility of the McCanles clan, who must either make Pearl assimilate to their ways or eliminate her as a threat. The problem with Pearl is her refusal to be dominated and subjugated, which reflects a similar social fear about Native Americans as inassimilable. In *Duel in the Sun* this social fear ignites anxiety about too much intimacy between the Native other and members of the Texas empire, i.e., between Pearl and the McCanles sons.

Pearl is in all instances constituted as inferior to the white women around her, although slightly superior to the African-American maid, Vashti. Mulvey describes Jesse's "perfect" fiancée, an Anglo ingénue with blonde hair and perfect poise, as "a phantasmagoria of Pearl's failed aspiration" to become a lady. Yet Mulvey does not describe the other important term in this dialectical crisis of identity. The African-American maid represents another more threatening reality for Pearl, who is caught in a racial dialectic between white dominance and black subordination. Vashti and Pearl share many of the same characteristics, yet Pearl has more agency and free choice by virtue of her proximity to Anglo culture. However, she is depicted as not far from the African-American maid in her moral standing and intellectual capacity. Pearl attempts to transcend her racialized fate by staking claims on several of the white male characters to thereby assimilate into the mainstream of Anglo Texas culture.

Pearl's mixed-race embodiment allegorizes the various sexual and racial dialectical oppositions and boundaries between characters: good/bad, white/racialized, pure/impure, and civilized/savage. In one of the film's early scenes, there is an obvious triangle of identification among Laura Belle, the African-American maid (played by Butterfly McQueen), and Pearl. The entry of the maid immediately introduces a racial continuum of identification along with gradations of melodramatic intensity. The dark women are associated with the overwrought emotions and excessive expressivity of melodrama, while the white women—Laura Belle and Jesse's fiancée—are depicted in subtle affective and aesthetic tones. In this scene, Laura Belle, the embodiment of civility and culture, is at the piano when the maid, Vashti, interrupts her tranquility with seemingly childish questions—questions that are actually a sign of her limited legal rights ("Can I get married?"). The camera follows Laura Belle to establish her dominant vantage over the maid. Pearl is in the background, watching with a wry grin that indicates her disidentification with Vashti and desire to identify with Laura Belle. As Pearl and Laura Belle reposition themselves alongside each other, Pearl articulates her desire to "be like" Laura Belle, but the visual contrast between the two in skin color and aesthetic tones and mood undermines this identification. Pearl vacillates between the two poles of Anglo assimilation and racialized other, but eventually settles into the grinding determinism of race; an example of this double significance occurs when Senator Mc-Canles first happens upon Pearl and interprets her unusual style of dress as either a sign of the high breeding of her father or the latest in "wigwam fashion."

Jennifer Jones' obvious brownface underscores the fiction of the mixed-race character and precludes any possible threat of actual racial and interracial depictions. Also, as a fictional character Pearl might be deemed non-threatening to the Anglo characters and the audience they represent, since her only desire is to "be good," even though her racial degeneracy sabotages these efforts. Pearl is also bereft of all the signifiers of Native American community and politics: she is entirely disenfranchised from her parents and ethnic heritage, and even her borderlands provenance obviates the larger questions of land rights and self-rule for Native peoples. The borderlands are many things for Pearl. They are the natural home for a mixed-race character but also the origin of her degraded moral values. She is alone without community or family and her mixed-race status isolates her further from both national belonging and ethnic communities. Her lack of political encumbrance makes Pearl a desirable plaything of Texan capitalists. She is depicted as too ignorant and foolhardy to contribute to native self-governance, a right established by the Wheeler-Howard Act of 1934 but under contest after World War II. The borderlands function as a kind of purgatory and no-man's-land from which her only salvation is isolation from Latino and Native communities and full integration into Anglo Texan society. This redemption encodes the postwar initiatives of full Native American mainstream assimilation. According to Donald Fixico, these initiatives were lead by "mixed-bloods," who were able to forge closer ties to mainstream society by virtue of their mixed heritage.[28]

Border films have always been concerned with immigration and assimilation in terms of the "costs" to U.S. citizens. In *Duel in the Sun*, the cost is represented as the most extreme expense, human life. True to the Western form, Pearl meets her death in a final showdown with Lewt. The film begins as a salacious tale of exotic beauty and eroticism but ends as a cautionary moral story. Racial mixing was likely more prevalent in the Old West than is indicated in these films, yet the *mestizo* character is most often depicted as singular and unique, with extraordinary characteristics. Mixed-race female characters like Pearl were too volatile and unproductive to aid in the consolidation of the nation and often were eliminated, while mixed-race men were even less popular during this era. However, by the late 1960s, the racially mixed male character had become a topic of public discourse as a figure representing the possibility for national reintegration after the divided cultural atmosphere of the post–civil rights era.

Rio Lobo (1970) features a male mixed-race character, Pierre Cordona, within the more liberal civil rights and post-feminist atmosphere of "melting pot America." Pierre Cordona, described as half-French and half-Mexican, is also "American" and fighting for the Southern Confederates, or at least he had been, since *Rio Lobo* is set at the tail end of the U.S. Civil War. John Wayne, as Union Colonel Cord McNally, has to track down Confederate rebels, among whom are Union traitors selling information about gold shipments. McNally is in charge of getting gold to the North to fund the war effort while bringing the traitors to his own style of justice. McNally will soon discover that the information about the gold shipments was sold to a couple of Confederates, including Pierre Cordona, by one of his own. In typical Wayne fashion, McNally will bring Cordona back to the side of justice. He does this simply by his exemplarity: he leads the way with his moral rectitude and others follow.

1.4 John Wayne as Colonel Cord McNally and French-Mexican Pierre Cordona (in background), played by Mexican actor Jorge Rivero, in *Rio Lobo*.

In Westerns, mixed-race male characters might exhibit ethnic and racial characteristics, but are often white enough to be deemed acceptable objects for an Anglo female audience—as in *The Searchers*. Of course as part of the convention of Hollywood mulatto and *mestizo* characterizations, these roles were often played by white performers. The character of Pierre Cordona, played by heartthrob Mexican actor Jorge Rivero in *Rio Lobo*, is a notable exception. Because of racial prejudices largely spread by dominant media, the races had particular types in the public imaginary, which were undermined by these mixed-race characters played by white actors. With these characters, attractive by dominant beauty standards, the "race" question could be addressed and dramatized in portraits that were pleasing to the eyes of the audience. For instance, in the press junket around the original release of *The Searchers* (1956), the actor Jeffrey Hunter, who plays the quarter-Indian character Martin Pawley (whose brown-tinted skin only emphasizes his blue eyes), is introduced as a promising young screen hero—suggesting that his Anglo good looks remain untarnished by this racialized role. Rivero's co-star billing opposite Wayne was a notable departure from the negative depictions of Latinos in

Hollywood during this era.[29] Yet, though Rivero would star in a couple of U.S.-based films, his Hollywood career never gained traction.[30]

In *Rio Lobo*, Pierre Cordona is mixed both racially and nationally. He is a key figure of the opposition who combines two problematic former pieces of other nations: the French empire as represented by Louisiana, and the Mexican past that comprises more than one-third of the United States. The French ambition of empire formation challenged U.S. desires to obtain full reign of the hemisphere. The presence of "Americans" from New Orleans during this time of French imperialism in Mexico was a defiant reminder of the victory of the Louisiana Purchase from France that consolidated the southern territory of the United States. Thus the conflict represented in Mexico was that of an empire striking back, ridiculing French arrogance and imperial chauvinism.

Rio Lobo was Howard Hawks' last film before his death in 1977, and it contains many of the thematic concerns of his earlier works, particularly that of the strong female lead. Hawks maintained a reputation for strong female protagonists whose roles often shored up the insufficiencies and paradoxes of masculine social norms. Yet for Robin Wood, the "Hawks woman," though often self-possessed, never ceased to be a "male determined" embodiment of male fantasy who was depicted without female bonds or friendships and always represented in relation to men.[31] Laura Mulvey describes the Hawks woman as a symptom of cultural "ambivalence about female sexuality."[32] Women are independent, yet they are depicted as sources of anxiety, challenges to male authority and gender norms, and often threats to male friendships. *Rio Lobo* maintains this tradition in the character of Shasta, played by Jennifer O'Neill, who is independent and self-possessed and upsets expectations about her presumed social role. Yet her challenge to masculine norms has distinctly racial and ethnic overtones. In the triadic rivalry among Cordona, McNally, and Shasta in which McNally is the defining center, Shasta gains leverage by virtue of her shared whiteness and patriotism with McNally. For instance, when inquiring about Cordona's romantic timing she asks, "Are all Mexicans as sudden as he is?" This comment amuses McNally and draws her into his intimacy as they bond over Cordona's racial and ethnic peculiarities.

Cordona's masculinity is undermined by his relation to Shasta, which in turn reinforces McNally's authority. For instance, when Shasta first meets Cordona he has just run out of his room to engage in gun battle without taking the time to put his pants on—he is literally caught with his pants down. The violence of the scene causes Shasta to faint, and upon waking she, too, finds herself in her underwear. Both characters, Cordona and Shasta, are presented as potentially denuded sexual objects while McNally maintains an authoritative (and fully clothed) vantage over them.

Cordona's mixed French and Mexican heritage makes him foreign and different and thus ripe for treason. This idea circulated widely in the eugenics-based ideology so prevalent during and after the U.S. Civil War, in which the mixing of races was viewed as the cause of war. Cordona is the incarnation of the boundary between the United States and Mexico at the same time that he represents the separation and divisiveness created by the civil war. Unlike Pearl, who cannot be trained to be a "lady" and is thus inassimilable, Cordona can be trained to assimilate and flourish as an "American." Though he shuttles between the designations of "Frenchy" and "Mexican," his difference will eventually be absorbed within a liberal discourse of melting pot multicultural nationalism.

Rio Lobo begins with Cordona and his men capturing McNally and using him to safely traverse Union territory, but McNally outwits them and leads them directly into the midst of a Union camp, reversing the situation so that McNally has in his charge the two confederate soldiers responsible for his capture: Captain Pierre Cordona and Sergeant Tuscarora Phillips. But this scenario doesn't last for long; the war, they discover through a newspaper headline, has come to an end. Pierre Cordona opines, in a sentiment that resounds across these post–civil war Westerns, "All this for nothing." Although the war is over, McNally's sense of justice has no limits; he continues to seek the men who committed treason and sold the information about gold shipments to the South. It is not long before all three men meet up again in Rio Lobo, where they find that one of the men guilty of treason is terrorizing the town by forcing its inhabitants under violent duress to sell their land at less than a third of its worth. This violent imperialist, Ketcham, will not stop until he has amassed all of the land and property of the town, where Cordona's good pal Tuscarora's family stands to lose its land and livelihood. McNally's mission is clear; he must go to Rio Lobo with Cordona in tow and liberate the town from the tyrannical imperialist—recalling the cold war era references to the "evil empire" of the Soviet Union.

Shasta, a woman they meet in a neighboring village, offers to guide Cordona and McNally to Rio Lobo. Strangely, the town seems full of single, young, attractive women who make it clear that they are interested and available; the appearance of these women seems to be a strategy of divergence from an increasingly convoluted plot. The semi-clad women of Rio Lobo are of different races and ethnicities. One is Mexican and two others are visibly Anglo, but all are wearing wildly incongruous outfits of long skirts and wrap-around bikini-style tops that seem misplaced in the Old West and better suited to an Elvis beach film. To varying degrees, the Anglo women show their attraction to Cordona with an aggressivity usually reserved for men. For instance, upon his arrival to a small town Cordona slips into a house to hide, whereupon he finds a topless woman who suggestively invites him to stay. She fixes her gaze on him and flirts provocatively to no avail; he neither looks nor flirts in return. He is a "Latin lover" whose stoicism makes him a non-threatening and desirable object for Anglo women. They can express their desires without the possibility that these desires will have to be actualized. Notably, the only Mexican woman shows no interest in Cordona. Any interest on her part would represent a threat to his full assimilation into mainstream Anglo culture.

Pierre Cordona's mixed-race heritage proves useful because he appeals equally to all women, and his "Latin-ness" is sensual and seductive enough to lure these single women into his and McNally's liberation cause. The mixed-race male presents this strategic initiative to integrate both post-feminist and civil rights era subjects: women and peoples of color. In the end, Cordona and McNally, with the help of these women, succeed in ridding the town of the imperial and tyrannical Ketcham.

The mature Wayne is no longer the asexual romantic lead, as in other films of his corpus like *Rio Grande* or *Rio Bravo*, but instead the aging and benevolent father figure. His role is to father the younger, handsomer lead, to socialize him, to make him a more honest and mature man and potential husband, and to make him someone who might carry on John Wayne's "American" legacy. The anti-hero turned hero/surrogate son is represented as foreign, of a mixed racial and national heritage that represents both histories of the Southwest: French and Mexican. He is a "stepchild" who is taught the ways of the father to better assimilate.

Most Westerns end with a final showdown, a kind of war between good and bad forces, which, in this case, is also the last stage in the cross-over assimilation story. Cordona has become one of McNally's men. Here the mixed-race character represents the noble mission of assimilation and national cohesion against the forces of empire. Whereas Pearl signifies the race-based dissolution of the United States, Pierre Cordona represents its protection.

Both *Duel in the Sun* and *Rio Lobo* present a popular discourse about the role and status of racial mixing and/or immigrant assimilation through the mixed-race character, and each proposes a different solution. Pearl represents the volatile condition of Native Americans and racialized immigrants in the 1940s, a time of heightened nationalism. If she were considered simply "Indian" she might be relegated to the separate Indian nations on reservations, but she is literally orphaned between cultures. The film suggests not just that she does not have a place in mainstream U.S. culture, but that she is a bad influence for white Americans. On the other hand, *Rio Lobo* reflects some of the gains of the civil rights era but remains a cold war narrative of intervention and assimilation. The film seems to make the case that mixed-race characters like Pierre Cordona are the best disseminators of the "American way" since they are able to cross racial and ethnic lines to gather a larger audience and garner more support. By the 1960s, racialized and foreign figures like the adopted Indian son in *The Undefeated* (1969), the French character in *The Comancheros* (1961), and of course Pierre Cordona are taught the ways of the father, John Wayne, and thus are brought into the fold of mainstream U.S. culture.

CROSS-BORDER INDIAN TRANSIT: SETTING LIMITS

Rio Grande (1950) and *The Comancheros* (1961) each represent cultural attitudes and policy toward Native Americans that established key terms of U.S. national identity after World War II and during the cold war era. These films use the border to set limits and delineate citizen from alien while they depict Native Americans as unfit for North American national terrain. *Rio Grande* is about the proper kind of family formation as a necessary allegory of a militarized and protected nation. The threat to nation formation is a racialized and primitive internal alien whose sovereignty and freedom threatens the firm establishment of core American values around family and military, synthesized and encoded in the 'Americanism' of "homeland security." *The Comancheros* depicts vice-ridden and rapacious Indians and the North American Comancheros who furnish them with all manner of contraband from their exile outpost in Mexico. The Comanche Indians travel back and forth across the U.S.-Mexico border without incident; like their Apache kin, they are without limits and enjoy liberal freedoms that threaten U.S. national security. But worse yet are the Comancheros who shirk their patriotic duties and sense of civilization to aid and abet the consolidation of outlaw Indian nations. These Westerns encode U.S. ambivalence about Native Americans during their increased political and social exposure in the period following World War II. Native Americans have had a dual position in U.S. culture and policy; they are regarded as either enemies of the state or potentially assimilated members of mainstream culture—either the warring Indians or "Indian scouts" of *Rio Grande*. *Rio Grande* and *The Comancheros* entertain this cultural ambivalence about Indians while using the border to assert the boundaries of national identity, to delimit between characters who reflect the national line and those who do not, between good and bad Indians.

John Ford's *Rio Grande* (1950), with John Wayne and Maureen O'Hara, is one of the most notable postwar Westerns to deal with the Indian question along the southern border. *Rio Grande* is a cavalry Western that puts women and family at the center of the plot entanglements while the major dilemma for the main character, John Wayne's Lt. Col. Kirby Yorke, is whether to follow federal orders not to cross the Rio Grande to pursue hostile Indians. As in other Westerns with similar titles, the river is invoked as a natural and fated boundary between Mexico and the United States; the Indian tribes do not respect or acknowledge the national border, which becomes cause for national and international conflict. The film, the third installment of Ford's cavalry trilogy, is unlike other films of the era, an era that Thomas Schatz has called the crucial period of the genre's development. Unlike the more complex reconstructions of the Western, *Rio Grande* continues a classical tradition of U.S. versus the Indians as part of the myth of the West.[33] Edward Buscombe notes the backward retreat in the depiction of Native Americans in this last installment of the Ford cavalry trilogy; whereas *Fort Apache* (1948) and *She Wore a Yellow Ribbon* (1949) portrayed Native Americans more sympathetically, *Rio Grande* depicted them as rapacious and violent in what Buscombe calls a "two steps forward, one step back process."[34]

The film's promotional material introduces *Rio Grande* with the following description: "John Wayne and Maureen O'Hara are embroiled in an epic battle with the Apaches and each other in this John Ford classic! Lt. Col. Yorke (John Wayne) heads to the Rio Grande to fight a warring tribe. But Yorke faces his toughest battle when his unorthodox plan

1.5 John Wayne and Maureen O'Hara in *Rio Grande*.

to outwit the elusive Apaches leads to possible court martial. Locked in a bloody war, he must fight to redeem his honor and save his family." While some, though not all, Westerns glorify Civil War battles that privileged men and masculinity, *Rio Grande* foregrounds the conflict between family and nation, specifically Lt. Col. Yorke's sense of family and his sense of national duty. Yorke is a man so bound by duty and honor that he has abnegated all the pleasure and comforts of domestic life; during the war, he had cast off his wife and son for the dubious rewards of his military career. In fact, his sense of duty required that he cold-heartedly execute orders to raze his own wife's plantation, an act that officially estranged him from his family. The line dividing official duty from personal responsibility is grafted onto that dividing the United States and Mexico. In fact, the key dilemma of the film into which all others collapse is whether Yorke will cross the border into Mexico to gain leverage in his position against the Apaches, a move that would endanger his family. The incursion of his son and wife into the coveted masculine space of the cavalry presents demands that challenge the division between private and public. The national border becomes the horizon of meaning, casting its shadow on all of the narrative happenings.

Gaylyn Studlar claims that *Rio Grande* bolsters a critique of Jane Tompkins' assertion in *West of Everything* that the power of the Western emanates from a phobic masculinity that abnegates everything feminine, including emphasis on language and expressiveness, interiority, and civilization and its constraints.[35] This masculinity is certainly a dominant trope that continues to fuel the fantasies of the Western, even Ang Lee's revisionist Western *Brokeback Mountain* (2005), where the absence of women and social norms enables the creation of a utopic space of homoerotic intimacy. Indeed many Westerns plot this homosocial male utopia across open spaces, saloons, and cattle runs where few or no women can be found and civilized social congress is unnecessary. However, Studlar faults Tompkins for her lack of sustained critique of Westerns by John Ford, an *auteur* considered by many to be the cornerstone director of the genre—especially by Andrew Sarris, whose fixation on Ford is itself epic.[36] A more than cursory glance at the Ford opus reveals a complicated relation to gender (and ethnicity and race); Studlar gives several examples, but her analysis of *Rio Grande* is of particular interest. In this later Ford Western, though Kirby Yorke is the central and organizing character, he and his ex-wife, Kathleen Yorke (Maureen O'Hara), both undergo major transformations in their gendered dispositions. He becomes more "thoughtful" and gains an interior emotional life, while she acclimates to the cavalry and accepts her obligations as a military wife. Together they work to reconcile the divided worlds of the domestic and the professional spheres.[37] For Richard Slotkin, gender differences were signs of larger social and ideological differences between militarists and anti-militarists. Slotkin argues that the film uses gender differences to resolve questions regarding the conflict between war and peace and authority and rebellion, principles that were relevant to the political conditions leading up to the Korean War.[38]

In terms of ethnicity and race, Charles Ramírez Berg challenges critical readings of Ford's Westerns which found them to be overly stereotypical and racist, citing Ford's devotion to his ethnic Irish heritage and his famous claim that his sympathy "was always with the Indians."[39] For instance, in *Rio Grande* a commanding officer who orders the silencing of peaceful chanting Indians earns the disdain of his charge, Kathleen, who reviles his imperiousness. This representation is revolutionary in the context of the classic Western, yet Ford is not completely free of the ideological moorings of his era; for every "good" Indian is a roving tribe of bloodthirsty "bad" Indians bent on ruthlessly attacking the cavalry. Slotkin faults Ford for representing the Indians in *Rio Grande* as primitive and lacking an intelligible language or form of expression, since they are only heard issuing war cries and chants. He finds that Indians are "identified with 'the horror,'" or all that is abject and frightening.[40] For Jacquelyn Kilpatrick, "American" self-definition in John Ford's films is "reinforced by its juxtaposition to the image of Native Americans."[41]

Ford's sympathies were unevenly expressed, though they extended to all members of the marginalized, and his representations of African-Americans, Mexicans and Mexican-Americans, and other ethnic groups often went against the Hollywood grain. Several scenes in *Rio Grande* confirm this tendency and mark what Ramírez Berg has called the unique "multicultural dynamics" of the John Ford Western, in which differences among ethnic or racialized groups and individuals are leveled in the service of an assimilationist narrative; for instance, at the end of *Rio Grande*, he notes, "ethnics and Native Americans are joined together beneath the American flag."[42] This scenario might read less optimistically within the larger dynamics of the border Western, that is, as an expression of the imperative to delineate a liberal multi-ethnic United States united in its military campaign for expansion. Ramírez Berg argues that the "ethnics" are integrated into the "American" landscape to provide a more inclusive image of the United States; yet *Rio Grande* features an assimilationist nationalism in which multiple loyalties are not permitted.

Rio Grande opens with a procession of soldiers returning from battle, while spectators of this solemn homecoming, all women and children, look on anxiously and respectfully; we notice that family members are secondary to the noble pursuits of their male patriarchs. This scene is the visual basis for a major plot point: while John Wayne and his cavalry battle the bloodthirsty Apaches along the Rio Grande—with orders not to cross the national line—the family he left behind for his military career slowly infiltrates his cavalry. First his son appears as part of a stable of incompetent recruits, and then his estranged wife—the mother of this son—arrives with the anti-militarist mission of having her son released from duty. She knows that soldiers can be "bought off" for one hundred dollars and plans to do so, but discovers that she must have both the commanding officer's signature, her husband's, and that of the soldier, her son, both of whom refuse to sign the releasing document. The tensions created by masculine pride and obstinacy energize the relationships in the family and those of the cavalry unit in which they are all embedded.

Lieutenant Colonel Kirby Yorke is the typical Western hero because he embodies the moral dilemmas of American exceptionalism, and the line between his two opposing choices is continually invoked as the national border between the United States and Mexico. The border is a major blockade for Yorke; if he crosses it, he violates orders. Likewise, heeding his family is tantamount to the abrogation of duty, so he is constrained on all sides. By contrast, the Apaches are defined by their freedom of movement and lack of social restrictions. In fact, the Apaches' freedom is a large part of their menace; they roam all over the new frontier, threatening to halt the expansion of the United States while representing an alternate national formation, one that is nebulous and unlimited with the freedom of congress and association to consolidate an Indian empire comprised of many tribes. After a particularly deadly attack, Yorke surveys the dead Indians and remarks ominously that they had "concentrated three tribes" and that "this means real trouble." He becomes resolute in the imperative to stop the Apache conglomerate before they cross the Rio Grande and pass out of his jurisdiction. The scene stops with the impending threat of the freewheeling tribes crossing into Mexico, so it remains up to the audience to imagine what exactly this fate might bring. Perhaps the Native Americans will form a larger conglomeration with those living in Mexico in order to launch an attack from beyond the jurisdiction of the U.S.-based Colonel Yorke.

Mexico, in Westerns of this era, is a chaotic nation gripped by instability. In fact, when Colonel Yorke tries to strike a deal with the Mexican colonel on the other side of the Rio Bravo/Rio Grande to work together to apprehend the Indians, the Mexican colonel refuses to abandon his duty to "protect the Rio Bravo." Resolutely nationalist and intent on abiding international law, he refuses military assistance from the United

1.6 Mrs. Kathleen Yorke (Maureen O'Hara) arrives at her estranged husband's cavalry outpost to collect her son.

1.7 The new recruits, including Lieutenant Colonel Kirby and Kathleen Yorke's son, Trooper Jefferson Yorke (Claude Jarman).

States, and to emphasize his nationalism, he defines the boundary in Mexican terms, using the Mexican name for the river that had been re-named "Grande" by the United States. This scene raises the question of whether Yorke will, like the Mexican colonel, uphold federally imposed limits on military action, or disregard his government's orders.

This standoff reflects the political situation of the borderlands during this era. By the end of the nineteenth century, Native Americans would become targets of both the U.S. and Mexican governments for unauthorized cross-border transit, particularly the Apaches and Comanches, who were notorious for raiding and pillaging on both sides of the border.[43] After Mexican President Porfirio Díaz overthrew the established government in 1876, the cross-border migrations of Native American tribes increased, and the border tensions reached crisis proportions in the late 1870s.[44] *Rio Grande* tacitly cites an actual event that occurred in 1877 when, after negotiations with the Mexican government for consent for either nation to cross the border to pursue Native American "criminals" failed, the United States illegally entered Mexico to accomplish this end. Yet in *Rio Grande,* this transgression only violates orders from the U.S. government, with no acknowledgment of any violation of Mexican laws.[45] By 1882, both governments agreed on a reciprocal border-crossing pact that allowed them to pursue Indians freely until indigenous incursions were almost completely neutralized by the late 1880s.[46]

In the end, Lt. Col. Yorke does indeed cross the border to issue a strike against some Apaches who attacked a caravan of women and children and carried them into Mexico, but Yorke is not punished for disobeying either government; rather, he achieves reunification with his family and accolades for his bravery. The story ends as it began, with a solemn procession of soldiers returning from battle. But this time, Yorke is injured and prone on a stretcher while his son and wife stand over him unharmed. Yorke admits to his wife, "Our boy did well," and they hold hands to seal this assertion of family reunion. The final scene is a ceremony commending the work of several soldiers, including Colonel Yorke. But the real victory belongs to his wife, Kathleen, who does a little dance to celebrate the reunion of the Yorke clan and the new possibility of having family and career success at once.[47] Thus, family is brought into the service of the nation. The wayward patriarch goes against federal orders in the larger service of the national plan to rid all barriers to expansion, and his momentary diversion from the family of the nation actually ensures its durability and longevity.

In his analysis of *Rio Grande*, Richard Slotkin finds Kathleen Yorke's position to be the central role and point of identification for an audience ambivalent about the military role of the United States in the rest of the world. Kirby Yorke dramatizes the ethical necessity of crossing the national line in order to intervene in another territory and stop the conglomeration of an outlaw Indian nation for national security. But this is a conversion narrative centered on the reaction and transformation of Kathleen, who was initially anti-militarist. By the end of the film, she is secure in her position as a military wife who supports and appreciates the mission of her husband. Though his victory results in the family's unification, it also supports consolidation of a national ideology built on the interdependence of family and military might, thus building a stronger force against cross-border Indian incursions and preparing the way for further Anglo settlement of Texas and the West.

The Comancheros (1961), produced more than a decade after *Rio Grande*, is also a story about the dangerous consolidation of a rogue state that poses a threat to the United States.[48] Here, John Wayne is the upright and law-abiding Captain Jake Cutter of the Texas Rangers, and Stuart Whitman is Paul Regret, an unrepentant gambler and outlaw. The film begins in New Orleans in 1843, just forty years after the United States purchased Louisiana from France, an acquisition that opened up the western frontier. The focus of the story is the southern frontier, represented by Captain Cutter of Texas, in collaboration with his counterpart, Regret from Louisiana—a setup that also represents the important trade relationship of Texas and Louisiana. The initial national and cultural differences will be resolved to present a unified U.S. national identity. These two characters, representing two major territories of the United States, will work together to dismantle a threateningly sovereign Comanchero nation comprised of U.S. expatriates who survive by trading contraband with Comanche Indians from their hideout in Mexico. *The Comancheros* draws on cold war era fear about rogue arms deals while depicting actual frontier era trade relations. The trade relations among these various groups of Texans—Americanos, Tejanos, Comanches and others—formed the basis of a vital political economy, but Texans were angered by the misperception that these relations were fundamentally comprised of arms trade. Texans were bent on eradicating contact among these groups, which meant intensifying the war with Native Americans, a war which would devolve into a long-standing racial and ethnic feud between whites and peoples of color.[49]

1.8 John Wayne as Captain Jake Cutter of the Texas Rangers teaches wayward Frenchman Paul Regret (Stuart Whitman) how to be a Texas Ranger in *The Comancheros*.

The *Comancheros* story glorifies the Texas Rangers as a law enforcing entity rather than as the proto-policing arm of the state of Texas, born out of a desire to claim land occupied by Native Americans and Mexican Tejanos. However, Samora, Bernal, and Peña argue that although the Rangers may have functioned like police, they were not strictly speaking a police force.[50] Police are hired by a community to maintain order, peace, and lawfulness. In short, they are elected by and accountable to the citizenry. The Texas Rangers are neither accountable to a community nor are they officially elected by any community. Rather, they were formed in the early 1820s as a volunteer organization designed to protect Anglos from Indian incursions, but the organization maintained an overarching ideology of ethnic cleansing.[51] The Rangers were a group known to spread terror by murder, robbery, and rape in order to clear the land of Native Americans and Mexicans or native Tejanos. Gary Clayton Anderson notes that although some Rangers respected the law, others used their terms of service to pillage and extort communities of Native Americans and Tejanos of their land and property.[52] Nonetheless, the official history of the United States lionizes all Rangers as heroic protectors of the Texas flag.

The title of the film indicates the enemy of the Texas Rangers, with an important nuance. It is not necessarily the Comanches themselves that the Rangers seek to eliminate, but the Comancheros, the Anglo and Mexican group that deals in arms and munitions with the Comanches. Yet before this renegade group can be eliminated, John Wayne's character must secure the cooperation of a French inhabitant of Louisiana, Paul Regret. This symbolic alliance affirms the need to form a national bond against outsiders.

The story begins with Regret engaged in a duel with a man who trumped up charges against him out of jealousy; there is a woman who prefers Regret and his opponent intends to "simplify her choice." Comically, Regret tries to guess who this woman might be, but cannot recall. Regret aims his pistol at his opponent's shoulder, but the man steps aside, takes the bullet in the heart, and dies. Only then does Regret discover that his dueling partner was a judge's son and that the punishment for his murder will be hanging. It would appear that Regret is innocent, and that an unfortunate series of incidents lead to this fate, but when an officer speaks to him of his impending arrest, Regret's reply inculpates him within the moral code represented by John Wayne, also known as "the Duke": "When one has proven himself upon the field of honor, one cannot turn tail and run like a common criminal, can one?" asks the officer. Regret replies, "One can," as he runs away, placing himself squarely in John Wayne's moral and legal path. He may not be guilty of the crime that occasioned the duel, but he is guilty of immorality and a lack of male honor. His decadence is deemed an attribute of his foreignness, or his transplanted French roots, and it is up to the Duke to school him in the mores of U.S. masculinity and moral values.

Regret escapes by boarding a boat headed for Galveston, Texas, where he becomes the desired object of a mysterious and independent woman, Pilar Graile, played by Ina Balin, who pursues him relentlessly. He initially rejects her advances, and when he finally assents, they are interrupted by John Wayne as Texas Ranger Captain Cutter, who takes Regret into his custody. The two are an unlikely and mismatched pair: Cutter is deeply trustworthy, stoic, and operates on a code of honor, whereas Regret is an effete and decadent dandy. When Regret tries to bribe Cutter for his release, Cutter responds, "I've got what you might consider a weakness—I'm honest." These opening events preface Regret's transformation along two related moral axes represented by Pilar Graile and

Captain Cutter: he will become a monogamist with respect for women and develop a sense of U.S.-defined honor and justice.

We might wonder what the Texas Rangers are doing meddling in Louisiana's affairs, as does Regret, and the answer is simple and yet telling. Cutter explains that Texas is "getting real obliging" with the other states since "down here in Texas, 'lotta folks wanna join the Union." This of course will be the Texan fate after 1848, after the Alamo and the battle of Texas. Louisianan Regret and Texan Cutter are fated to be friends since both represent former pieces of larger empires before they joined together to expand the boundaries of the United States. But the Texan feels the deeper patriotism. Expressing sentiments that recall Wayne's previous character in *Rio Grande,* Cutter tells Regret that he avoids marriage because "Texas needs every man and every gun," and anticipating his interlocutor's skepticism, adds " . . . but duty and patriotism doesn't make sense to you." Captain Cutter will work hard to eradicate this moral difference; he will tutor his charge until Regret is fully transformed into a citizen to whom duty and patriotism make sense. Moreover, Texas-style justice and patriotism are depicted as the only hope for the renegade state of Louisiana; that is, Louisiana must mime the efforts of Texans to wrest control of their state through the work of the Texas Rangers, particularly in the use of unsanctioned force and a dubious sense of law and order that is often executed without due process.

The two men form a tenuous bond as they make their way across Texas, stopping in various small towns along the way. At one stop, Cutter meets up with a colleague on the eve of a major Comanche attack. The Indians are viewed as bloodthirsty and ruthless and without the help of the equally ruthless Regret, the town may not have so successfully defended against the attack. Cutter feels indebted to Regret and feels compelled to find a way of saving him from his death—since it is Cutter's duty to deliver Regret to the proper authorities. He tells Regret that although he would like to set him free, he swore on oath to uphold the letter of the law. Regret responds, "That's important to you? . . . words," to which Cutter replies, "Words are what men live by, words they say and mean." Cutter represents the Old West in his unwavering moral sensibility, but paradoxically these same words in the form of laws can be bent for men who protect the state, a fact that gives a very telling portrait of the Ranger interpretation of law and order. Cutter is willing to disregard the law in order to protect one of his own "fellow fightin' men." He puts

Regret's case in the hands of a well-known and respected Texas judge who gathers the Texas Rangers together to commit perjury ("that's legal language for just a plain dumb-blasted lie") and sign a paper that says Regret has been a Texas Ranger for a couple of years, creating the perfect alibi. Perjury is tolerated as the means to an end, which in this case is to consolidate the Texas Rangers to protect Texas and the nation for which it stands. This scenario secures the bond between Cutter and Regret, and they commence with the mission to find the Comancheros, the Anglo and Mexican men who have set up a secret community that survives by trading guns, gunpowder, and whiskey to the Comanches.

The eponymous Comancheros do not appear until the latter half of the film, after the successful cohesion of the latest additions to the United States territory. The unity among Texans and the rest of the United States is sealed by a common defense against the Comanches and the equally dangerous Comancheros, the expatriate enemies who enable the fortification of Comanche forces. Moreover, the Comancheros represent the inverse of the democratic values of the United States, such as inclusion and hospitality to foreign peoples. After being caught by this secret society of Comancheros, Cutter and Regret are tried for being "uninvited guests," for which the penalty is death. Luckily, we discover that Pilar is the daughter of the leader of this outlaw society, and will buy the heroes some valuable time. The Comancheros are just as "murderous" as the Indians for whom they provide munitions and thus just as menacing. Their laws are arbitrary, and men are often punished by death without due process—a rather interesting analogue to the Texas Rangers' similar arbitrariness. The Rangers' violation of the rule of law is deemed justified, but a similar move by the Comancheros is depicted as the defining feature of their savagery.

The Comancheros played on the popular fear of the threat of a communist nation bent on the destruction of U.S. liberties, while it offered the psychodrama of complete resolution through elimination of this threatening formation. The film's subplot tackles the wayward immigrant, Regret, who must be acculturated to the moral imperatives of the state, an acculturation evident in the sense of duty and justice he shows in his concern for Cutter's well-being. Regret is finally completely aligned with the moral duties of the Texas Ranger and fully assimilated to the "American way." He becomes fully domesticated by settling down with ex-Comanchero Pilar—the woman he first met on the boat and who is responsible for saving his life from her evil tyrant father. Pilar is an obvious reference to Pocahontas, who likewise rescued a man, Captain Smith, held captive by her father. She is a reinscription of Pocahontas as a woman who goes against blood ties to enable and establish national bonds. Together, Paul Regret and Pilar replay the origin story of the United States; their relationship constitutes the cross-ethnic and racial ties that establish the mythic foundation of the nation. They do as many southwestern mixed-race couples have done and escape to Mexico.

In the end, Regret and Cutter dismantle the outlaw Comanchero nation, thus defusing the threat of the consolidation of a neighboring enemy state, something the United States was not able to do in its own hemisphere in the early 1960s. As in *Rio Grande,* moral or legal lapses are forgiven or rationalized if the final outcome is the vanquishing of forces that threaten the nation. The Hollywood border genre and Hollywood films in general set the tone and ideological basis for an "American" tradition of vigilante exceptionalism or ends-justify-means morality, a tradition evident in a historical trajectory from the Texas Rangers to the border vigilantism of the Minutemen.

WELCOME TO THE ALAMO: REVISING BORDER HISTORY

The name *Rio Grande* asserts northern dominion over the border region evident in the renaming of the river, whereas another film of the same era, *Rio Bravo* (1958)—remade in 1966 as *El Dorado* and in 1970 as *Rio Lobo*—uses the Mexican name for the same river. In *Rio Bravo,* John Wayne is John T. Chance, a sheriff whose only help in his Texas border town is Dude (Dean Martin), a *borrachón*, "drunk," and a lame-legged and dim-witted old man, Stumpy. These men will be aided by an arrogant young upstart, Colorado. The nicknames given to Dude and Stumpy by the town mark separate destinies against which each is struggling. And the sheriff, Chance, runs his town on luck, of which he might be running out. This scenario of a town full of half-wits and incompetent men is reminiscent of a scene in *Rio Grande* in which Yorke, alone with his Mexican-American Lieutenant (Puerto Rican actor Alberto Morin) after a disappointing battle, speaks in code about the shortcomings of his country and its army—these opinions are not offered openly, perhaps to forestall criticism and censorship. Yorke remarks, "This coffee isn't as good as it used to be," to which his interlocutor replies, "Maybe someday it'll get better and stronger," leading Yorke to respond solemnly, "This coffee's weak, but it's all we have." Similarly,

1.9 Ricky Nelson, John Wayne, and Dean Martin comprise the rag-tag team defending the town against the Burdette clan in *Rio Bravo*.

1.10 Lieutenant Colonel Kirby Yorke of *Rio Grande* opines, "This coffee's weak, but it's all we have" in an encoded reference to the new cavalry recruits. A similar sentiment informs *Rio Bravo*.

in *Rio Bravo*, Chance is stuck with a pair of incompetent colleagues, but they are all he has. He makes the most of this diverse cast of characters to stage a valiant resistance against a professional team of villains, the Burdette clan, who storm the town. The allusions to the Alamo are apparent everywhere, but the defeat of Burdette's many men by Chance's small garrison is a different outcome.

Westerns have long contributed to the mythos of the Alamo as the origin story of southwestern consolidation and expansion of the United States. *Rio Bravo* retells the story of the Alamo as one of triumph through the fortitude of "American" will and the power of individuals to topple large armies to protect all that is good and just. Two years after the release of *Rio Bravo*, John Wayne would return as Davy Crockett in *The Alamo* (1960) to keep the symbol of Texas revolutionary liberty alive. It was not until John Sayles' *Lone Star* (1996) that a U.S. filmmaker really challenged the official history of the Alamo through Pilar Cruz (Elizabeth Peña), a high school teacher who introduces the story of the Alamo as a critical assessment of Texan secession from Mexico. Indeed, Texans fought the battle of the Alamo in part to preserve the institution of slavery, which Mexico had outlawed. The myth of the Alamo attests to the powerful force of the U.S. nationalist desire to produce a sign of victory from the most abject of failures; this cultural resignification of failure has become the cornerstone of U.S. political hegemony.

Richard Flores describes the cultural production of the Alamo as a consequence of the forces of modernity in Texas, specifically the shift from a "largely Mexican, cattle-based society into an industrial and agricultural social complex between 1880 and 1920."[53] This social and economic transformation "sets in motion forces of nationalism, post–civil war politics, wage labor, bureaucratic rationalism, and the restructuring of racial and ethnic difference."[54] Flores claims that the Alamo is the ultimate emblem of Texan modernity, a myth and symbol that smoothes the transition into a new economic order and divides the Southwest and the rest of the United States along racial lines. On the other hand, the Mexican version of the narrative foregrounds the ongoing oppression of Tejano-Mexicanos by the Anglo mainstream. Flores describes this divided ideological interpretation along a racialized axis:

For Anglos, the Alamo serves as a sign of rebirth, the coming-of-age for a state and, eventually, a nation in the modern period. It is not quite the same for Mexicans. For them, the Alamo reverberates with ambivalence. It serves as a reminder, a memorial to a stigmatized identity. Such an identity emerges not from the events of 1836 but as a result of the place of the Alamo developed through the Texas Modern.[55]

The dominant cultural memory of the Alamo supports a deeply racialized understanding of the past that denigrates those of Mexican heritage. Of course, it is not just a public site that produces this official history, but a historical narrative around which different communities coalesce. Indeed this is the case in the scene depicting the parents and teachers' meeting in *Lone Star* (1996), in which teachers of Mexican heritage assert their right to tell the story of the Alamo that depicts the wider context of the event. On the other side of the issue are the Anglo parents who want the "real" story of Texan heroism told. The issue remains unresolved but the larger storyline affirms a full unearthing of the repressions in the official history that lead back to the mythologized Alamo.

HIGH NOON REDUX

Howard Hawks described *Rio Bravo* as a direct response to *High Noon* (1952). In an interview with Peter Bogdanovich he describes the process of the creation of the film:

It started with some scenes in a picture called *High Noon*, in which Gary Cooper ran around trying to get help and no one would give him any. And that's a rather silly thing for a man to do, especially since at the end of the picture he is able to do the job himself. So I said, we'll just do the opposite, and take a real professional viewpoint: as Wayne says when he's offered help, 'If they're real good, I'll take them. If not, I'll just have to take care of them.' We did everything that way, the exact opposite. It annoyed me in *High Noon* so I tried the opposite and it worked, and people liked it.[56]

Robin Wood describes this dialogic retort in terms of aesthetic freedom, where the freeform and organic character-based work of *Rio Bravo* is a reaction against its formulaic, plot-driven, and mythos-laden precursor. Each film conveys a different notion of the "American" sense of community, *Rio Bravo* being the more optimistic of the two. The heroic sheriff of *High Noon* tries in vain to wrangle help from everyone in town to fight the bad guys, whereas poor Sheriff John T. Chance never asks for help, though he always needs it and receives it unsolicited. However, *High Noon* was critical of communist hysteria and the fearful adherence to social norms. In fact, *High Noon*'s screenwriter, Carl Foreman, faced censure by the House Un-American Activities Committee (HUAC) in their communist witch hunts. Likewise, fiercely patriotic John Wayne derided Carl Foreman's *High Noon* as "detrimental to our way of life" and "the most un-American thing I've seen in my whole life."[57] But *High Noon* is nonetheless a symptom of its era as a deeply patriarchal film where women's roles are clearly defined as marginal.

There is a clear loosening of gender restraints from *High Noon* in 1952 to *Rio Bravo* in 1959, due in part to a cultural acclimation to reconstructed masculinity, to male authority and leaders who must accept a new model of consensus formation and relinquish an obsolete "father knows best" authoritarianism. *Rio Bravo* deconstructs many of the gender constraints of the Western. For instance, Sheriff Chance does not occupy the privileged narrative position of utmost control; in fact his authority is undermined by Angie Dickinson's character, who taunts and teases the sheriff with her sexually liberal savvy and wit. Her aggressive sexual pursuit of Chance makes him appear to be an impotent, duty-bound fool with a dubious sexuality.

The townspeople are outnumbered by the well-armed Burdette clan, but, as if at the Alamo, they put up a good fight. Just when Chance thinks he might gain leverage against the clan, the town hears the fateful song of the Alamo. Like the Mexicans did at the Alamo, Burdette orders a band to play "El Degüello," the cutthroat song, to send a sinister and definitive message to Chance. It is the song, Colorado informs us, that "the Mexicans played for those Texas boys when they had them bottled up in the Alamo." It signifies no mercy for the defeated and will play ceaselessly until victory is achieved. The Alamo is an appropriate symbol, representing the battle of few against many, of the thousands of Mexicans led by Santa Ana and the few Texans fending themselves inside the mission walls of the Alamo. It was a crushing defeat for the Texan separatists, all of whom were killed. The name of the film, *Rio Bravo*, may signify the Mexican victory by naming the national boundary in Mexico's favor, but the plot itself revises this history.

The Alamo came to be a powerful impetus for U.S. revenge against Mexico. At one point, Dude, not able to refrain from drinking, announces his resignation from the sheriff's crew. But upon hearing "El Degüello," he recalls why he got involved in the first place and rescinds his resignation. The whole scene is reminiscent of the Texan exhortation to "Remember the Alamo," a sentiment that energized a later defeat of the Mexican army. Moreover, just like at the battle at the Alamo, Chance and his crew, now including Colorado, decide to hunker down

1.11 Gary Cooper in *High Noon*, the film that served as an impetus for the story of *Rio Bravo*.

1.12 Angie Dickinson as Feathers taunts and teases asexual John Wayne in *Rio Bravo*.

in the jail to wait for the Feds, employing a strategy of defense rather than offense. And if that weren't coincidence enough, a hotel owned by Mexican-American Carlos boasts the name Hotel Alamo. When they are discussing possible strategies for outwitting the Burdette clan, Stumpy reminds them that Chance "can't get out of town on account of they got it bottled up," which is the same language Colorado used to describe the situation of the Texans being "bottled up" at the Alamo. They decide that Chance should stay in town and fight to release Dude, taken hostage by the Burdettes, because otherwise "Dude won't have a chance." Although outnumbered by the Burdette men, they find some dynamite—like the cannons the Texans had at the Alamo—that they use to gain leverage. As symbolic retribution for historical defeat, Chance and his men win as the Burdettes surrender. Rather than acting as a wholesale resurrection of the myth of the Alamo, the battle is dramatized to consolidate Anglo cultural mastery without reverting to the racialized divisions typically evoked by this history. Here the conflict is more clearly that of "bad" outlaws versus law-abiding if somewhat troubled citizenry. Mexicans are depicted as on the "right" side, with Pedro González-González and Estelita Rodriguez as the innkeeper couple of "the Alamo" who help Chance in his efforts. The aspects of the Alamo narrative that would signal the undemocratic, unequal, and racially stratified realities of Texas history are removed to frame a portrait of social betterment and multicultural liberalism. Instead *Rio Bravo* re-mythologizes the history of the Alamo into one that seems more liberal and inclusive of marginal members of society, including the infirm and differently-abled, Mexicans, and women who subvert traditional roles. But of course, by the final scene, almost all the marginal characters have moved into the mainstream, uplifted by their heroism. In keeping with the marginal status of Latinos in Hollywood, the Mexican innkeepers are the only characters who do not experience a transformation.

The victory has a rehabilitating effect on the whole town. Chance discovers his heterosexuality and begins to consider succumbing to the charms of Angie Dickinson's character, Feathers. Dude is cured of the trauma of the failed romance that lead to his alcoholism, claiming that "a man forgets, sometimes it isn't easy, something happens, he just forgets . . . I don't even want a drink." Chance, satisfied that he no longer has to care for Dude, leaves to claim his prize. He allows Feathers to pursue him in a reversal of the gendered norms of the Western. Everything has returned to normal: peace and community are restored, Chance is partnered, and Dude is reformed and has re-bonded with Stumpy. The film ends with the only reference to its title in the song lyrics, "By the memory of a song, while the rollin' Rio Bravo rolls along." The ending is punctuated by this oblique reference to the title in the short snippet of the song, a reminder that all has taken place so near to the border, the edge, and the other side represented by Mexico. The river invokes the fatedness of the national boundary, which persists and asserts itself even in the face of symbolic conflicts over the shape of the United States.

POST–CIVIL WAR REUNION IN MEXICO: EXPANDING THE BOUNDARIES OF INTERVENTION

Vera Cruz (1954) was one of the first Hollywood films set and filmed entirely in Mexico. Like *Rio Bravo*, it dramatizes the symbolic resolution of a lost conflict. The South lost the U.S. Civil War and contemporaneous with the film's release, the United States lost the war in Korea, but in *Vera Cruz* the United States leads the victorious struggle against the forces of the French occupation under Mexico's Emperor Maximilian. The retribution includes other compensation, since the protagonist of *Vera Cruz*, Ben Trane, after sustaining major losses in the civil war on the side of the Confederates, will not only win back his shirt and his integrity, but also his plantation, which represents the illusion that (U.S.) Southern order will be restored. Trane meets up with a less than scrupulous compatriot who fought for the other side in the civil war. They unite in Mexico and form a bond that will save their lives. Each has extraordinary skills as a sharp shooter and each has knowledge of military strategy that he developed and refined during the civil war. Together they travel to Mexico to sell these skills to either side in the Mexican struggle against the French.

After the civil war, economic and political leaders of the United States began to envision the aggrandizement of the United States into Mexico and Canada through the appropriation of markets and resources. The political and economic elites sought to extend their influence into Mexico using the same tactics and strategies that had been so effective in settling the North American West.[58] This involved first establishing financial and trade relationships, which led to developing the Mexican infrastructure, primarily through the construction of a pan-American railroad system that would bring raw materials into the United States and send products and U.S. capitalists into Mexico.[59] The U.S. characters are part of this emigration to Mexico after the civil war that would establish and maintain U.S. political, economic, and cultural interests in the region. Moreover, in his account of U.S. involvement in Mexico, John Mason Hart characterizes this early involvement in Mexican affairs as the template for foreign policy that led to the rise to world power of the United States in the twentieth century.[60]

In the contemporary context of *Vera Cruz* (1954), the special military skills brought south by the North American protagonists recall those taught to Latin Americans in the School of the Americas (SOA—now called The Western Hemisphere Institute for Security Cooperation or WHINSEC), a military training institute that was founded in 1946 to serve U.S. security and defense initiatives. In fact, after World War II the School of the Americas took over where Europe left off, replacing the military ties between Latin America and various nations of Europe— specifically France, Italy, and Germany—which helped consolidate U.S. power in the hemisphere and the world. The SOA is infamous for training officers of right-wing regimes in Latin America in practices that constitute egregious human rights abuses.[61] The SOA is not specifically acknowledged in the narrative of *Vera Cruz*; however, its ideology is propagated in the overall display of U.S. military skill and savvy that betters even the French army's best.

Mexico and Mexicans are important to the psychodrama of *Vera Cruz* because they constitute a screen for the projections of fantasies of unification and triumph and provide an arena for North Americans to demonstrate their unmatched skills in combat. The Mexican context acts as a transitional geography for the reunification of the U.S. population; it is neutral ground upon which soldiers from different sides of the civil war might join together against the American enemy, the French empire. After achieving victory against this competing empire, they will return to their native country with renewed nationalism. Moreover, the film delivers the message that foreign intervention is a means of consolidating nationalism and augmenting the military and political power of the United States. The border is the horizon beyond which lies the road to empire.

The flow of skilled men south from the United States in *Vera Cruz* counters the real conditions and traffic of workers from the 1940s until the 1960s with the Bracero Program: the result of a collaboration and agreement between President Roosevelt and Mexican President Manuel Ávila Camacho to send agricultural workers to the United States who would fill the gap left by men who had gone off to war.[62] But as the war

1.13 Emperor Maximilian competes in marksmanship with the highly skilled North Americans, Gary Cooper and Burt Lancaster, in *Vera Cruz*.

1.14 Gary Cooper and Burt Lancaster as mercenary ex-soldiers of the U.S. Civil War looking for work in Mexico.

progressed, these workers began to fill more than just agricultural jobs. Soon short-term labor seemed to initiate a long-term change in the cultural landscape of the United States. This program initiated a legacy of Mexican migration into the United States, where there was no shortage of jobs at the lower end of the labor market.

Vera Cruz, filmed entirely in Mexico, is set after the U.S. Civil War, from which the lead characters have fled. Gary Cooper and Burt Lancaster play mercenaries in search of their fortunes during the 1866 revolution in Mexico. The film opens with explanatory titles scrolling over the verdant Mexican hillsides along which groups of men on horseback travel:

As the American Civil War ended, another war was just beginning. The Mexican people were struggling to rid themselves of their foreign emperor—Maximilian. Into this fight rode a handful of Americans—ex-soldiers, adventurers, criminals—all bent on gain. They drifted South in small groups—And some came alone—

The last line coincides with the appearance over the horizon of a lone figure traversing the landscape on horseback, Ben Trane (Cooper). The solitary hero dismounts his horse and surveys the landscape, eyeing the ruins of a church-cum-ranch to which he draws closer. We will learn that Ben Trane is from New Orleans, speaks French, and fought for the defeated Confederates. The ruined building that Trane happens upon is an appropriate context for the meeting between two American expatriates that is about to take place; the building is reminiscent of the devastation left by the U.S. Civil War. Trane finds the place occupied by another "American," Joe Erin (Lancaster), from the opposing Union army. The two will join together to lead Erin's band of U.S. mercenaries in search of their fortunes. The team represents a unification of all social disunities in the post–civil war U.S.—there are men who fought for the North and men, like Trane, who fought for the South, and there is an African-American soldier who peacefully coexists with the white soldiers. All share a common skepticism and jaded indifference about civil wars and are bereft of political inclinations; their only compass is that of their fortunes.

Ben Trane is not just from the South; he is from New Orleans, a favorite locality of the Western and sign of triumphant land grabbing. Trane is part of the dispossessed South after the war, and as he claims that the "Civil War cost me everything but my shirt," he had no choice but to start wandering in search of his fortune—not to the western frontier as in earlier yore, but to the southern frontier. This displacement of focus from the West onto the border functions within the contemporary context of the film to bolster the benevolent paternalism of U.S. interventions beyond its borders, particularly in Latin America. The group of U.S. mercenaries ends up fighting in the civil war in Mexico, a war between the liberals—Juárez and his men—and the conservative-backed French occupation led by Emperor Maximilian. Yet the film portrays U.S. interest in the war as entirely apolitical; for instance, when asked if he came to fight in the Mexican civil war, Ben Trane responds, "If it pays."

Vera Cruz gives an account of the resistance to French imperialism from the perspective of the United States; it dramatizes the dissolution of French rule as a result of U.S. intervention, in this case with the help of a few strategic representatives. Historically, the French may have desisted in part due to the pressure applied by the United States, but it was the resistance of Juárez and his men that had undermined the French plan to rule Mexico.

Gary Cooper's character, Trane, is fundamentally just and honest, an expectation generated in part by the popularity of Cooper's role in *High Noon* (1951) just a few years earlier. But Ben Trane's sense of justice is linked to the "white man's burden," while Will Kane's position in *High Noon* is more abstract. In fact, to draw on Stanley Corkin's interpretation of similar post–World War II Westerns, the analogy to U.S. intervention in the Korean conflict is an important political and cultural backdrop. The continuity between *High Noon* and *Vera Cruz* created by Cooper's role in both as a seeker of justice is perhaps not coincidental. Yet Will's role is interpreted as a criticism of the mass psychology of and sheep-like adherence to the anti-communist purges led by Senator Joseph McCarthy, whereas Ben represents the responsibility of the United States to intervene abroad—in part to justify the U.S. role against communism in Korea or the similar role of the United States in Guatemala in 1954 to overthrow their president, Jacobo Arbenz Guzmán. In *Vera Cruz*, Ben would like to earn enough to restore his plantation and support his many charges; though this is seemingly a noble cause, the inhumane practice of plantation slavery as a main impetus for the U.S. Civil War is completely glossed.

Westerns present an image of confident and competent leadership that is applicable for all time, both in the historical era of the film narrative and in the present time of viewing; the nostalgia evoked by the Western for some other better, more accomplished time is curiously future-oriented. There is the sense that nothing has changed, and that the exemplarity of the heroes of these Westerns is a core component of contemporary political leadership. Though the characters and incidents change, the range of affects elicited by these post–civil war interventions into Mexico remains the same: outrage at the cruelty of the French imperial army, admiration at the skill of the Americans, security inspired by U.S. confidence and leadership, and vague dismay at Mexican backwardness. This continual return to the same characterizations and moods establishes the mythic terms of the U.S. hero as a static and enduring type.

The plot of *Vera Cruz* twists and turns to finally reach a conclusion that showcases U.S. heroism when Cooper's character, Trane, reveals the deep sense of justice behind his search for wealth—that he is not greedy but altruistically seeks to restore his plantation industry and raise his dependents from their miserable poverty. Thus, U.S. intervention is justified not just as benefiting foreign nations but also ultimately the citizens at home.

Ben, Joe, and his men were hired by the French army, ostensibly to escort the countess to a ship so that she may sail to Paris. Ben and Joe discover that the carriage in which she will be transported is full of a secret shipment of gold—presumably bilked from the Mexican treasury. The countess finds Ben and Joe snooping around the carriage and tells them that the gold will be shipped to Europe to fund the transport of more troops to secure Maximilian's imperial throne. If the Juaristas get hold of the gold, they will be able to fund the overthrow of Maximilian, so the success of either side is entirely dependent on the destination of the gold. The three decide to join together to divert the gold and divide it evenly—later, Joe and the countess greedily devise plans to secure the entire sum for themselves as a couple, while each separately has plans to take it all alone. But, unbeknownst to all three, the marquis has been eavesdropping on their plan and intends to recapture the gold for France. In the plot machinations that follow, the gold switches hands again and again, until Ben, cornered by the Mexican Juarista army, decides to collaborate with them to capture the gold. Joe congratulates him on an effective bluff, but Ben is sincere in his promise and his deep-seated sense of justice, and it is this determination that will save Mexico. Of course, in good Hollywood fashion, this sense of justice is evoked by a pretty lady, in this case by Juarista spy Nina (Spanish actress Sarita Montiel), who tries to convince Ben that the Juaristas need the gold to fund the battle to end French occupation. At first Ben is not convinced, but as his partners' treachery and cold-hearted greed become more apparent, Ben's resolve begins to weaken. While General Ramírez rests with the Mexican army, he finds out that Ben and Joe are in Mexico for the money and laughs at their folly. The General tells them, "A man's gotta have more than money, he's gotta have something to believe in," which we are to presume is the message of the film. Ben, of course, gets the message and when, after a prolonged gun battle over the gold, he ends up in a face-off with Joe, Ben tells him decisively, "That gold's going to the Juaristas." They draw their guns over the matter, which leaves Ben standing teary-eyed and heartbroken over the body of Joe Erin. Their intimate bond is now forever torn asunder, leaving Ben to pursue another more acceptable relationship and political agenda. We know that Ben Trane has "done the right thing," and his prize is the affection of the sexy Juarista, Nina. While these men had traversed the border and entered Mexico for the self-interested reason of lining their pockets—a familiar trope in the career of the United States—the heroic Ben Trane goes against his comrades by becoming involved with Mexican struggles for self-determination and is redeemed as a hero fighting for justice. If there were doubts and suspicions about the intrusion of the North south of the border, they may well be quelled by this final turn of events. It is not until the release of *The Wild Bunch* (1969) that a Hollywood Western will completely disabuse the audience of any such good intentions on the part of the United States, laying bare the violent dispositions and dark intentions that drove the settling of the West and the expansion of the sphere of influence of the United States.

FRONTIER MODERN

The Wild Bunch takes place during the later period of modernization after the turn of the nineteenth century, when the Old West was overcome by the automobile and other technological inventions. The frontier way of life was replaced by modern industrial formations such as the entrepreneurial drive of the professional gunslinger looking to profit from his skills and the appearance of trains and more advanced methods of communication. *The Wild Bunch* tells of an aging gang of outlaws proficient at robbing trains, but who no longer have their hold on the Old West. The film is not set during a nostalgic era like during the post–civil war reunification of the United States or the heroic U.S.-aided battle against French imperialism. Instead it takes place in 1913 during the Mexican Revolution. The "wild bunch" face increasing competition from other outlaw gangs, but they and other gangs are themselves becoming obsolete, a dying generation whose skills as hired guns are being replaced by technology like machine guns and cars. The border is constantly traversed as the action moves from a Texas border town to a small Mexican town. The characters travel back and forth with ease, and the border is apparent, with signs that indicate when they are leaving the United States. The border indicates a split between the Old West of the United States and the new modern ways found in Mexico—the Mexican primitivism of the classical Western is resignified as savage modernity, where modernity is the new evil. The men learn of their diminished status in Mexico; they are not mythic outlaws, as in *Vera Cruz*, but a necessary nuisance, a gang of "gringos" who no longer trade in superior skills or savvy, but merely run guns for the Mexican army.

The Wild Bunch is a departure from typical Western fare and a refusal of the nostalgia associated with the genre. When it was first released in 1969, critics and audiences found the film excessively bloody and violent, unlike other Westerns which depicted violence as an organic and necessary aspect of settling the chaotic and uncivilized West.[63] The film departs from the myths of the Western, opting instead for a disturbing realism where greed and profit are the cardinal qualities of the warring sides: the outlaw gang and the railroad men and bondsmen. The violence is sustained to real effect; we see shoot-outs in their entirety, and witness their aftermath, including the pillaging and looting of corpses for anything of value—boots, money, or gold teeth. But, in the end, we are sad to see the "wild bunch" meet their demise, since their end is likened to the end of the Old West. It could be argued that the film is more deeply nostalgic than others of the genre thanks to a skeptical mood that renders its affective core more appealing. Like the Confederates of the U.S. Civil War, the outlaws are atavistic holdovers from a feudal and agrarian era, dependent on the land and unaccustomed to industrial culture. Progress and mass production register as a loss of culture, causing the diminution of "American" masculinity. All things modern are displaced onto the border region and shuttled into Mexico. Mexico is the site of a dystopic and savage modernity, where we see the innovations of technology put to use in macabre and sinister ways; for instance, one of the characters, Angel, is dragged behind an automobile until he is nearly lifeless. Modernity is the new site of primitivism rather than a sign of progress; it causes the devolution of civilization. The Old West continues unabated. We still have the presence of the rapacious Indian and the Mexican bandit, women are sidelined and subordinated as nondescript wives or prostitutes, and Mexicans are variously trustworthy—siding with a U.S. gang, or devious—running crooked deals, killing indiscriminately, and hungry for power. Thomas Schatz describes the real villain of the film as "progress" in the guise of the banks and railroads of big business.[64] These U.S. railways linked to those in Mexico and became the major corridors of immigration after 1910.[65]

The Wild Bunch begins with a symbolic image meant to stand as an allegory for the whole film and establish its tone and mood. The image derives from a story told by the famed director of classical era Mexican cinema, Emilio "El Indio" Fernández, who plays General Mapache in the film. Fernández describes how it was common when he was a child to take a scorpion and drop it on an anthill, and relates this to the situation of the wild bunch when they enter the town ruled by Mapache.[66] The film opens with a group of Mexican and Anglo-American children hunkering over an anthill at the edge of the Texas border town, Starbuck, watching the ants attack a couple of scorpions as a group of soldiers pass behind them. The children revel in the scene, eventually covering the anthill with grass and igniting it to demolish all parties. The joy of the children is a shocking portrait of an organic and native cruelty, but the scene also puts children squarely into the storyline in various ways. The children are stand-ins for the viewers; we may perceive ourselves as innocent bystanders, but the very act of looking registers as cruel complicity in the violence. In the next scene, cavalry soldiers ride into town, park their horses, and help an old lady on her way down the street. The same soldiers then enter a bank, causing confusion when we realize they are not real soldiers, but a group of outlaws posing as soldiers to perform a bank heist. This is a stunning reversal of the role of the cavalry in the Western; it undermines perceptions of authority as a moral point of reference. This is a counterpoint to the role of the cavalry for Ford, for whom, according to Robin Wood, the cavalry is the "answer to mortality and transience" as the center of tradition, continuity, and conservation where the individual assimilates to this larger military body.[67] The cavalry represents all that is civilized and good: "honor, chivalry, duty, the sense of tradition." Without its status intact, the world of the Western is rendered incomprehensible.[68] The temperance union, another symbolic center of moral rectitude, shares this opening scene. The "soldiers" pass

1.15 The formidable outlaws of *The Wild Bunch* sally into tyrant General Mapache's pueblo looking for one of their crew.

1.16 The automobile, as a symbol of savage modernity, is used to drag Angel around Mapache's pueblo.

a temperance preacher delivering a sermon to his followers, who will later rise up to march through town. In the bank, the wild bunch's plans are foiled by an opposing gang and a town-wide shoot-out ensues. Shockingly, nobody is spared, including the temperance unionists who plan their march through town at the most inopportune of moments. Two frightened children, one of whom is director Sam Peckinpah's own son Matthew, huddle in the middle of the shoot-out, witnessing the excessive violence and near total destruction of the town, and their presence reminds us of the horrific scene we are witnessing.[69] Peckinpah places his son in the midst of the violence as if to remind himself that this realism penetrates the extra-textual reality around him. By the end of the film, in the final shoot-out that bookends the narrative, there are again child witnesses, but the final scene is a dystopic return of the first because the young onlooker becomes a gunslinger. The presence of children is meant to appeal to the innocence of the viewer. They represent the nostalgia American culture has for childhood, but they also recall the negative criticism of film reviewers and critics who say that Westerns are for children. The children are not the same in both scenes; in the first scene in the Texas border town, the cruel onlookers of the scorpion's demise are both Mexican and Anglo-American, but in the middle of the shoot-out, the children are blonde and fair, and in the final scene the gun-brandishing children are all Mexican.

Adding to the realism of the film, all communication in Mexico is bilingual, and communication in Spanish, though important to the story, is left untranslated. When the team enters Mexico, they become not heroic "Americans," but "gringos" who lose their linguistic competency, although not to their detriment—though none speak Spanish, except perhaps Angel, they all understand it and respond in English. The term "gringo" is bandied about as a derogatory term; in an inverse of the North American norm, members of the wild bunch are almost all gringos working for Mexicans. Also, the term "gringo" emerged at the same time as the term "bandido"—in the mid-1800s—but the former is often suppressed as a sign of Latino approbation of Anglo nativism. Pedro Malavet has described the term as emerging during the Mexican-American War to refer to the "green coats" worn by U.S. soldiers, while other accounts link the term to a transliteration of a song, "Green Grows the Grass," said to have been sung by U.S. soldiers while invading Mexico.[70]

The story that links all the events in the film is a simple and slim one: the team, looking for profit, decides to rob a train carrying guns they will sell to a general. This is a common thread during the revolution; the United States had a habit of selling guns to the revolutionaries.[71] The historical setting of the film is significant in this respect; in 1913, the leader of the revolution, President Francisco Madero, was assassinated by his own military chief of staff, General Victoriano Huerta. The north of Mexico, where the fictional General Mapache reigns in the film, was the domain of the main resister to Huerta, the famous "Pancho" Villa, who fought with arms supplied by the United States. In the southwest, Emiliano Zapata lead the landless peasants, whose aim was to regain land expropriated by the corrupt "liberal" government. In the south, Huerta's illegitimate rule was challenged by the governor of Coahuila, Venustiano Carranza, who became the leader of another faction of the resistance movement. Mexico was once again gripped by a civil war. In *The Wild Bunch*, the hapless general is a Federalist and a member of Huerta's force, but we never see him face the opposition, so we never really have a clear sense of his political disposition or reasons for setting up an encampment in the north. But our main clue is the year, 1913, just before the end of Huerta's rule, an end that was initiated by U.S. intervention.[72] In fact, the wild bunch are purveyors of this ending because they travel back and forth over the border without incident, although we are accustomed to this traversal and perhaps interpret it as a matter of course. Their mission is to run guns for Federalist General Mapache, though they, like all hired guns participating in Mexican civil unrest—such as those in *Vera Cruz*—are politically neutral, inspired only by a desire for profit and a heroic self-conception. The year 1913 is the same year that Woodrow Wilson preached the gospel of manifest destiny, the providential role of the United States in leading the rest of the world with a pure vision of justice and peace.

The wild bunch quickly become adversaries of General Mapache for personal reasons. The men, in their travels through Mexico, decide to stop in Angel's native town, where they are feted by the townsfolk. Angel is distracted by his search for an old girlfriend whom he has the intention of marrying. To his deep dismay, he is told that she has run off to be one of General Mapache's many lovers. The group's departure from the town the next day is laden with Angel's longing and disappointment, making their slow farewell procession a foreboding event. Later, by accident, Angel happens upon his ex-*novia* as she is approaching General Mapache. When he tells her he had hoped they would marry, she laughs in his face and walks away. He angrily draws his gun, fatally wounding her while calling her *puta*, "whore." This is a commonplace misogyny of the film; in another scene a prostitute is shot while similarly being denigrated verbally. This personal dispute, not some political intrigue or other misdealing, causes the adversarial relationship between the wild bunch and General Mapache. As in the border Westerns that precede it, *The Wild Bunch* avoids any reference to overt political affiliations.

The final installment of the story devolves into pure violence. The gringos finally kill General Mapache and the whole town comes to a silent halt. The wild bunch look at each other with recognition that this may signify the end of the tyranny of their boss; we think they may choose to abandon the scene, but they do not choose this ending. Instead, in what Peckinpah refers to as an existential decision, the men will fight to their bloody but glorious deaths. The machine gun turns the gunfight into modern warfare with efficient, indiscriminate, and total bloodshed. Unlike in the first scene, very few are left standing, and women and children also brandish guns. Another roving gringo gang rides in and loots the scene, which is for them "like a big 'ol picnic."

Throughout *The Wild Bunch*, the American team crosses the border without incident, which in 1913 was not unusual; nor were their reasons for crossing. Their contribution to the Mexican civil war is depicted as politically neutral. However, this is not the larger story of the civil disputes following the Mexican Revolution of 1910. In fact the United States, known for supplying guns to the revolutionaries, took a leading interventionist role to end the unrest in 1914. It is not coincidental that the story takes place prior to the real interference of the United States, but instead focuses on the small ways that this "American" band of outsiders aids in the demise of the illegitimate rule of the Federalists. However, like in *Vera Cruz*, their plight is never openly politicized. Part of the appeal of the Western is its seeming freedom from political ideals or concerns, or at least the lack of any fully articulated ideology. In some Westerns the only concern of the hero, typically John Wayne, is to do the right or proper thing according to an individual sense of justice, whereas Westerns with outlaw heroes like *The Wild Bunch* eschew moral responsibility in the search for profit. These two types of stories are linked by an "apolitical" desire to regain freedom and economic power and the only way to do so is to make a run for the border. With the demise of the mythology of the frontier, the cowboy and outlaw alike lost dominion over the West; out-maneuvered by the railroad and other technological innovations, the man of the West sought to reinstitute his potency by traveling south and fixing things according to his principles in Mexico. By traveling over the border and around Mexico, the cowboy, ex-cavalryman, or ex-soldier returned to his rightful place in the moral universe of the Western. Moreover, in the borderlands and in Mexico he could find women, unsullied by the liberties of urban life, who would support the hero in his plight. The main difference between the Western and its later border cinema kin is the overt display and discussion of nationalism or political leanings.

The prevalence of similar tropes and themes among these border Westerns was part of a larger ideological picture and framing of the relationship of the United States to Mexico in particular and to Latin America in general. The historical period of many of these Westerns, the mid-nineteenth century, was a crucial time for nation building and for rethinking the relationship across the Americas. During this era, the French represented a threat to U.S. sovereignty and empire in the hemisphere; the French were responsible for coining the term, "Latin America," where "Latin" referred to the common cultural heritage of the French and the Spanish. When the marquis in *Vera Cruz* arrogantly refers to Mexicans as "our people," this is meant to elicit the ire of the U.S. viewing public. The presence of "Americans" from New Orleans recalls the Louisiana Purchase from France that consolidated the southern territory of the United States. After the crucial shift in the focus of expansion in the mid-nineteenth century, from the western to the southern frontier, the United States would begin to enlarge its imperial campaign and political influence in the hemisphere and the Pacific. These border Westerns may have resonated for a cold war audience preoccupied with Korea, Cuba, and Vietnam, but they also distill a national origin story out of a more recent and accessible past, one that is geographically local and distinct. From the Alamo to the Civil War to the French invasion of Mexico, all the major battles of the Western occur somewhere along the shifting line between the United States and Mexico.

The Western is the perfect genre for this nostalgic reflection on the recent past, because the characters are hardy and solitary. They have little care for anything but the next gun battle, they saunter into the saloon at midday to escape a punishing sun, drink whiskey, and eat heartily while the women of the town wait in the wings to offer them companionship. No wonder the Western is the most popular genre for the American (male-identified) public. While the ostensible pleasure of the narrative emanates from the lack of limits on the expression of primal desires and urges, the storylines are rigged with contemporary fantasies about the expanding circumference of national influence and potency. Many of these stories are locally based, and the characters, even if they travel into Mexico, carry their regional markings with them. If they are southern, they are usually from a small border town in Texas or from New Orleans, yet if they are northern, they are simply Yanks, not associated with any particular place, which avoids the incursion of the dystopic tarnish of cities.

Along the border, the mythic origin of the nation has a distilled historical past that has nothing to do with the Puritan and European origins in the East, but is born of a gritty and "all-American" Southwest. Yet the southwest of the U.S. has more in common with the borderlands of Mexico, with its open vistas and lush vegetation, than with the "other" United States found in the northern cities. The Western is founded on the frontier, the familiar and open lands just west of the Mississippi; as this frontier vanishes and the Native Americans are driven out on the Trail of Tears, a new frontier emerges with a similar mythos but grounded by a different aspect of the imperial designs from the North; the border between Mexico and the United States becomes the new frontier of U.S. national identity. The cavalry and the mercenary soldiers who roam the borderlands will become border patrolmen and DEA agents by the early 1980s, but the mythos of these wandering men remains the same.

TWO

"THE IMAGINARY ILLEGAL ALIEN"
HOLLYWOOD BORDER CROSSERS
AND BUDDY COPS IN THE 1980S

ollywood films from the 1980s are so distinctive that we can identify them immediately, partly for their aesthetic but mostly for their mood, reassuring tone, and stories with clear moral lessons. These kinds of films provide familiar repetitions of similar stories and formulaic genres in the midst of cultural unrest and political uncertainty.[1] The 1980s were an era of major transformations: increased immigration and transit across the border, the consolidation of globalization, military defense build-up, the waning of the cold war, and the U.S.-backed wars in Central America. It was a time troubled by the recent past of the Vietnam War, Watergate, assassinations of public figures, and the revolution in social attitudes wrought by the civil rights era, feminism, gay and lesbian rights, and by the health care crises related to HIV/AIDS and Medicare/Medicaid. Hollywood border films are symptoms of this cultural morass; they encode and contain the tensions and contradictions of this era.

Several border films work together to form a coherent cultural response to the crises of the 1980s: *Borderline* (1980), *The Border* (1982), and *Flashpoint* (1984). These films have fast-paced buddy-cop plots full of chases and intrigue, desire for the forbidden immigrant (but no contact), plenty of double-crossing and risky business, and reminders of traumatic events of U.S. history, particularly Vietnam. In *Borderline*, Charles Bronson's character is a veteran cop who, after his partner is killed, goes on his own path of justice for an attractive young Mexican woman whose child was killed while they were crossing the border. In the process, he discovers that his partner's murderer is a Vietnam veteran who has created a big business with corporate sponsorship of running undocumented immigrants across the border, using the skills he learned in Vietnam to evade the border guards. This plot is revisited in *The Border*, where Charlie (Jack Nicholson), a border agent with a heart of gold, (whose partner, predictably, is killed) makes it his personal mission to help an attractive young Mexican woman reunite with her child who was seized by corrupt border officials. Charlie falls in with the corrupt border guards who aid coyotes, immigrant smugglers, in return for extra cash, but eventually exposes this corruption. British director Tony Richardson, perhaps because of his vantage point outside of the United States and Hollywood, offers a rather scathing critique of the emptiness of American consumerism and pop culture; nonetheless, the story relapses into the messianic nationalism inherited from the Western. *Flashpoint* unfolds in a more complicated series of events that invoke two unincorporated traumas of U.S. history: the assassination of J. F. K. and the Vietnam War. The story is about two maverick Texas border guards and best friends—Bobby Logan, a Vietnam veteran and Green Beret hero, and Ernie Wyatt, a young idealistic rookie—who find a large amount of cash along with the remains of a man buried in the desert, evidence which turns out to be related to the assassination of J. F. K.—a fact that federal agents will do anything to suppress (and one of the partners will be killed in the process). These films work and play well together because they all establish a Reagan era critique of big government while flirting with liberal sympathy for the plight of the immigrant. They traffic in nostalgia for the era prior to the consolidation of the policies of globalization that challenge national integrity, for the good old days of the early Westerns, populated by wrangling and free-wheeling cowboys, morally upright law enforcers, and virtuous women—best iconized by blonde ingénue Grace Kelly in *High Noon* (1952). The border film provides symbolically rich material for managing the contradictions and uncertainties of this transitional moment in history.

In these border stories there is usually at least one border cop who is sympathetic to the migrants' struggles. The liberal discourse of the film rests on this exceptional figure whose heroism and humanism redeem him and the U.S. policing efforts along the border. The immigration issue in the 1980s, while depicted in phobic terms in much of mass media, is trumped by another more compelling mood: that of exhaustion. No matter on what side of the polarized immigration debate these films might fall, liberal or conservative, they all conclude by eliciting our sympathies for the "real victim" of undocumented immigration, the overworked, exhausted, and embattled border patrolman who is threatened by downsizing, works in units that are understaffed, and who risks his life (or at least his partner's life) to protect the nation. These Hollywood narratives provide or suggest solutions that double as fantasmatic resolutions and templates for public policy: the need for better and stronger frontier security.

BEYOND THE BORDER PRINCIPLE

In the 1980s, just years after the dismantling of national origin quotas in the 1965 immigration act, the U.S. public experienced renewed fears about cross-border immigrant transit from Mexico and Central America in particular and the rest of Latin America in general. The fears were elicited in part by racial phobias about the perceived invasion of brown bodies crossing the border into the United States. The new immigration policies would no longer limit according to national and racialized origins—as in the Chinese Exclusion Act or the Bracero Program—but would fill labor deficits and promote family reunification, changes that supported the consolidation of strong family values and advancement of the U.S. economy. This sentiment was just gaining momentum after 1965 and had reached a crescendo in the 1980s, during a time not only of cultural crisis but also a time of affluence when "Americans" felt that they had something to lose. In his analysis of mass media depictions of immigrants, Leo Chavez notes a distinct shift in mood from uneasiness from 1965 through the end of the 1970s to the heightened phobia about immigration as a threat and invasion in the 1980s.[2]

The U.S. Immigration Act of 1965 coincided with the Mexican government's Border Industrialization Program, which was designed to develop the northern economy and provide employment in plants or *maquiladoras* for those displaced after the end of the Bracero Program, the short-term labor program instituted during World War II that drew workers from Mexico to fill U.S. labor shortages. Workers in these plants assembled goods with parts from the United States and other parts of the world, after which the finished product would migrate back into the United States. These mostly U.S.-owned *maquiladoras* were relocated to free trade zones along the Mexican side of the border for tax breaks, lower overhead costs, cheaper labor, and to take full advantage of proximity to the advanced transportation infrastructure of the United States to move finished products.[3] Another intended consequence of the *maquiladora* was to stem the tide of immigration into the United States by locating jobs on Mexican soil.

The changes in immigration policy occurred in conjunction with a larger global effort to expand U.S. economic interests and influence abroad. The border had become big business for U.S. corporations, especially by the 1980s, the period with the greatest increase in *maquiladora* production; from 1975 to 1980 the number of *maquiladoras* had doubled, taking full advantage of a debt-addled and severely weakened Mexican economy.[4] However, this reality is not part of Hollywood border imagery. In fact, it is evaded. *The Border* (1982) begins with a raid of a factory employing undocumented workers; however, that factory is located in Los Angeles, not along the border where most of the story's action will take place.[5]

Though border economies employed millions of workers, stemming a potential tide of immigration, most of these jobs went to and continue to go to women. The *maquiladora* has always harbored a perniciously gendered culture that privileges and seeks out female employment. There are several reasons for this. Women were desired for the perception that they have smaller hands to perform the laborious precision handiwork of assembling small parts. Women were also perceived as a more docile workforce, less integrated and less liable to form unions or demand their rights as workers.[6] Moreover, women were literally viewed as disposable units. Thus, the result of border industrialization was exactly inverse to the expectation of policy-makers: men were excluded from the border labor market and forced to seek employment north in the United States. This scenario, coupled with civil wars in Central America and the resulting exile of many Central Americans, led to increased migration of Latin American men into the United States. Hollywood was quick to notice. In Hollywood border films of the 1980s, the "illegal alien" was often coded as male and depicted in a massive horde of bodies bent on invading the United States and infiltrating the national body as carriers of cultural, economic, and political ills. Yet the female immigrant was depicted as a singular hapless victim of a changing world. She often represents industriousness, old-world values, and familial bonds; our sympathies are reserved for her. This split in depictions allows the viewer to maintain a sympathetic position while simultaneously holding contempt for the "illegal alien."

By the 1980s, the frontier of the early Westerns that signified hopeful optimism and open possibility was replaced by the southern frontier as a terrifying chasm representing national uncertainties. It evoked an experience of limitless and indistinction that occurred, not coincidentally, on the cusp of the consolidation of globalization during the Reagan years. Runaway globalization and rampant and relentless capitalism, what Jacques Derrida calls "plagues of the new world order," were linked to one of their consequences, open borders, or what Guillermo Gómez-Peña astutely renames the "new world border."[7] Why does the border converge with globalization so frighteningly well? Many interpret open borders as both cause and consequence of the global economy. Globalization is feared as an avenue of the disbursement of U.S. jobs south of the border and as the catchall term for a number of liberal policies about transnational transit of goods and people. Moreover, globalization is a cipher; like the border it elicits endless projections, and it is an empty term capable of becoming over-full with connotations. For some, globalization has become a sign of the apocalypse, where the strange replaces the known and the knowable, human relationships are instrumentalized and rationalized, racial invaders threaten a forced hybridity, a globalized future obscures the past, and corporations replace government and turn against the people. By the mid-1980s, open borders would be linked to the expansion of drug trade in the hemisphere and the eclipse of state laws by the workings of the market. The border would be linked to issues of national security in ways that intensified with each passing decade.

Most Anglo characters in border films are politically conservative; they fear a single effect of globalization, the relaxing of borders and boundaries for the purposes of free trade. There are similarities between a leftist critique of globalization from the global south and a U.S.-based right-wing critique of globalization. Both sides of the reaction to globalization emanate from popular and populist movements and rhetoric that are often profoundly nationalist. James O'Conner examines the divergent meanings of populism in the anti-globalization movements in terms of the different histories and deployment of nationalism. Often, for nations that have been subject to histories of colonialism and subsequent interventions—as is the case in Latin America—nationalism is a means to a self-sustaining economy and political sovereignty. For the United States, nationalism means sustaining formidable power and influence in the world; in short, nationalism "is another name for U.S. imperialism."[8] The conservative fear and rejection of globalization is part of a larger picture of nativism, an exclusionary and protectionist nationalism. It is also a fear of displacing the center of world power from the United States to international markets and globalized corporations. In these three border films from the 1980s, the latter conservative perspective is apparent as a function of class, in particular the class position of the central protagonist, the border patrol agent, who is a dispossessed member of the lower middle class. These border patrol agents are depicted as losing power both individually and in their professions; their loss of control parallels the lowered defenses of the nation.

Border films target globalization as the force behind the dissolution of the border, leaving in its wake a porous border susceptible to undocumented immigration, among other ills. A recurrent trope during this era was that of the "flood" of immigration—the inundation of the first world by the third world and the subsequent fear that the "strongest" nation in the world would devolve into an underdeveloped and overpopulated third world nation. Immigration was often depicted as a pandemic, an opportunistic infection that could ravage the national body. *Borderline* (1980) ends with this anxious fear; truckloads of hundreds of undocumented immigrants arrive in California en masse, filling an entire stadium-sized holding pen. They represent a dark, roving third world nation waiting to launch an invasion to engulf an "Anglo" first world United States. The immigrant is deeply overdetermined as a massive third world scourge, an invisible invader, a job and wife taker, and a risk to public health. Who will protect the public from these catastrophic implosions and unseen machinations at and over the border, and from what *Flashpoint* calls the "imaginary illegal alien"? The border patrolmen alight on the scene and save the day; in films from *Borderline* (1980) to *Traffic* (2000), they are cast as the new messiahs of national integrity and security.

The fear of immigration in the 1980s was a consequence of a confluence of social attitudes that linked race, migration, and public health. According to David Simcox, the 1980s were marked by a rising public impatience with all forms of migration into the United States. Simcox regards this trend from the vantage of various official positions, including director of the Center for Immigration Studies in the late 1980s and director of the Department of State Office of Mexican Affairs from 1977 to 1979 with an almost thirty-year career in the Department of State where he worked on Latin American labor and migration issues. He claims that the 1980s were a time when Americans "came to care more" about immigration because of a recognition of its impact on social life, both in terms of its social contributions and "a rising unease over its magnitude and seeming immunity to government control."[9] The public health language of "immunity" tacitly subtends a discourse of epidemic and uncontrollable and untreatable disease. Immigration was treated as an immuno-resistant strain of social illness at a time when the language

2.1 In *Borderline*, truckloads of undocumented immigrants arrive in California en masse, filling an entire stadium-sized holding pen.

of disease held sway in public discourse. In fact, Cindy Patton notes that the cultural obsession with disease, from the "cancer" of communism to AIDS, had turned disease into *"the* primary metaphor of the late twentieth century."[10] The 1980s in particular were marked by a preoccupation with well-being and health, disease and disorder, epidemics and health care crises from AIDS to chronic fatigue, and Medicare/Medicaid. Following on this linguistic strain, Republican Senator Alan Simpson, co-author with Romano Mazzoli of the bill that became the Immigration Reform and Control Act of 1986, describes the negative sentiments toward immigration as "compassion fatigue," which would become a major catchphrase in the media. Simcox attributes this diagnosis to several situations and events; weariness was a consequence of the public costs of southeast Asian refugees, the rise in undocumented immigration, the political activism of Iranian-American students in 1979, the 1982 Supreme Court decision in *Plyler v. Doe* that granted undocumented children the right to public education, complaints about the Mariel boatlift migrants, and anxiety about bilingualism.[11] The language of disease had an accusatory frame, especially with AIDS and immigration, in which those associated with insalubriousness and infectiousness were seen as willfully bringing harm to the public. "Compassion fatigue" was an ideological mask for more than just exhausted benevolence; it described the waning good will and rising phobia of a public wary of the economic impact of these aggressively proliferating bodies. The border is both the porous national skin unable to resist opportunistic infection and it is a container for the fantasmatic collision of infectious disease, waning economic health, risk, aberration, invasion, and the deleterious effects of the global economy. The nation, according to the Right, was fatigued and immuno-compromised, suffering exhaustion from the work of relentless immigrant roundups and the strain of various forms of public assistance. Paradoxically, the antidote for all this chronic fatigue was self-help. From talk shows to public policy, self-help was the language of the day. National wellness might be regained through individual enterprise, determination, and the *will* to health. According to Gil Troy, Reagan's successful entry to the White House in 1981 was a consequence of his rhetoric of convalescence and renewal in the proclamation that it was "morning again in America" during an economic slump and loss of national vigor and esteem.[12]

Susan Jeffords notes that the Reagan era was the era of bodies, particularly of hard bodies as a reaction against the degenerative soft bodies of the permissive Carter era. The vigorous and incorruptible body of the nation had its cinematic counterparts in the muscular bodies of heroes like Rambo or Dirty Harry. In border films, the fascination with the hard male body is clearly part of this continuum. This is particularly true in *The Border*, in which Jack Nicholson's fellow border patrolman, played by Harvey Keitel, first appears without his shirt, his muscles a reflection of his hardened attitude. Those protecting the nation were viewed as men first, real men, whose bodies were the site of the discourse of hard line nationalism. But it should be noted that the men to whom these hard bodies belonged were not the protagonists that shaped the plot, rather it was the manly but reconstructed male with a slightly softer body who would win out, the man who was both a lone ranger type and a family man. For instance, in *The Border*, Jack Nicholson is a cowboy patrolman with a clear moral code who shows his paternal benevolence by returning a baby to its mother. This illustrates what Jeffords has described as the "Reagan Revolution," where the hard body image was transformed so that "the hard body and the 'sensitive family man' were overlapping components of the Reagan revolution, comprising on the one hand a domestic regime of an economy and a set of social values dependent on the centrality of fatherhood."[13]

Reagan represented the new man both in his movie roles and his role as president.[14] As a savvy actor, he was master of his own post-Hollywood image. He embodied his Hollywood legacy as the affable and trustworthy lead with an added swagger, masculine decisiveness, aggressiveness, and stoic strength. He was often depicted as invincibly masculine, riding horses and chopping wood in typically macho attire: jeans, boots, and cowboy hat.[15] As actor and director of the national script, Reagan cast himself as the hero of economic recovery. Tax cuts for the wealthy, military build-up and decreased spending on social welfare programs were intended to invigorate the economy and reduce the size and presence of the government in everyday life.[16] Like Reagan's can-do willful assumption of office, the mood of the day was best captured by the vigilantism of the early Westerns—incidentally Reagan's favorite genre—in the moral hero who takes it upon himself to demand justice for the whole town.[17] Though Reagan was faulted by some critics for immigration leniency, the ethos of his administration and the campaign leading up to it informed this new round of border Westerns. Reagan had been widely quoted as encouraging the militarization of the border; "The simple truth is that we've lost control of our borders, and no nation can do that and survive."[18] He implies that the survival of the nation rests on regaining control of the borderlands, which was a key impetus behind the 1986 immigration law. The border guard became the new cowboy of the American frontier, the walking allegory of a hobbled national economy and pride, and precursor to pronouncements that a beat-down and bruised America "will stand tall again." Who better to fill this rising cultural demand than Charles Bronson?

BORDER JUSTICE . . . BRONSON STYLE!

The advertising copy for *Borderline* (1980) brings Bronson's reputation as a vigilante to a new genre while exploiting the political, social, and actual risks associated with the borderlands: "Bronson's on the border . . . and there's no turning back!" Suspense is created in the uncertainty about the male border guard's safety in the "dangerous" borderlands from which "there's no turning back." David Maciel describes *Borderline* as the "first major Hollywood movie on the theme of Mexican immigration," and notes its affinity to the Western and "genuine sympathy for the exploitation of undocumented workers," though he adds that "the social message is never made clear, nor is the dilemma of Mexican immigration really addressed."[19] The film, in a typical Hollywood

For Thousands It Meant Freedom...
For Some It Meant Death.

LORD GRADE presents
CHARLES BRONSON
in
"BORDERLINE"
Produced by **JAMES NELSON**   Directed by **JERROLD FREEDMAN**
Written by **STEVE KLINE** and **JERROLD FREEDMAN**

2.2 Promotional material for *Borderline*.

liberal veneer, offers moments of sympathy—carefully administered by
the benevolent border patrol—that are eclipsed by the larger ideology
of immigrant phobia. In the end, *Borderline* treats undocumented immigrants as a national scourge of infinite and relentless supply.

The tagline of *Borderline* suggests a disturbing mystery at the center
of the plot: "Charles Bronson stars as a no-nonsense U.S. border patrol
officer stationed between San Diego and Tijuana. When his best friend
and partner is murdered during a routine stop, Bronson begins a secret
manhunt that leads to surprising places." The "secret manhunt" reveals
two related surprises; first of all, the man behind the biggest immigrant
smuggling operation is an ex-marine *and* he has major corporate backing
that distributes this smuggled labor power. Second, Bronson's partner
and a young immigrant have both been killed by the "evil" ex-marine
and Vietnam veteran. The border guard and the immigrant are united
in this risk since both wage their lives in their contact with the border,
but our attention is guided solely to the patrolman's death. Maciel notes
that the minority characters of the film are indeed secondary to the
Anglo protagonists: "The undocumented workers, the subject matter

of the story, are the least developed and least known aspect of the film. They have no names, personal histories, motivations, nor feelings. The reasons for their ordeal or circumstances are never revealed."[20] This is the primary marker of the 1980s Hollywood border narrative: the ostensible migration narrative that becomes a thin veneer for the real story about the demise of the Western hero.

The subplots of both *The Border* and *Borderline* involve an immigrant woman who longs to reunite with her lost child. The border cop is willing to aid in this reunification even beyond his official duty and often in direct violation of the law. Yet the cultural imperative to honor and protect the family as the primary social unit reflects a long history of immigration policy based around family reunification. Eithne Luibhéid describes these policies as part of a larger imperative of social control: "Family reunification provisions constructed women's sexuality not just as heterosexual but also as procreative within a patriarchal framework. Consequently, they reified women's sexuality as a form of property that men owned, controlled, and competed over, and that was most appropriately channeled into marriage and reproduction."[21] The attitude of the male border patrol officers to the Mexican women fits this model of patriarchal and protective sponsoring that is deemed both individually heroic and socially responsible police work. Female immigrants embody the moral imperative of migration to restore the family unit, while male immigrants are bent on destroying it, typically through trafficking in drugs and other contraband.

In *The Border*, after the two border patrolmen round up a group of undocumented crossers in the desert, one suddenly breaks free. Charlie (Jack Nicholson) captures the guy and Cat (Harvey Keitel in a precursor to his role in *Bad Lieutenant*), his partner, cruelly roughs him up. Charlie, mystified, admonishes Cat while the other relatively "innocent" immigrants register shock—most notable on the face of Maria, Charlie's favored charge. Cat then rips open the guy's shirt to reveal a large amount of concealed drugs and addresses Charlie's rookie-cop hesitation: "Ever see this before? They push this in grammar schools, Charlie, ten-year-old kids getting hooked on this shit." Based on the same anxiety that will later drive *Traffic* (2000), Cat is vindicated in his use of excessive force since the drugs will rapaciously force a new pre-teen market rather than, for instance, meet a native demand for leisure use among adults. We identify with Charlie in his initial confusion about his new job as border patrolman; Charlie's tough lesson is our lesson to be learned, and

2.3 Charlie (Jack Nicholson) meets Maria (Elpidia Carrillo)
during a routine roundup of undocumented immigrants in
The Border.

his acculturation stands in for our own. He will learn that most roundups are empty routines, kickbacks are the only way to make a living,
violence is the most efficient form of communication, and most laws
promote ineffective governance. Behind Charlie's rapid acculturation is
a subtle division of the immigrant population that serves a dialectic
of good and bad identification, between innocent immigrants (typically
female) who represent the industriousness and family-centered values
of the Reagan ideology and male "evildoers" of globalization gone awry
who run drugs and take jobs from Anglo-Americans. The virtuous female immigrant's innocent gaze converges with that of Charlie to the
subjection of the bad guy border crosser; even the immigrant public of

which the United States is largely comprised can find a model for identification that achieves the proper narrative aim.

Cat's bullying is justified because he cares about protecting North
American schoolchildren from evil, but ultimately, Cat is rendered the
bad cop to Charlie's good cop. This is evinced in another scene: when
Charlie is picking up his uniform Cat encourages him to get it fitted and
to match it with a pair of expensive cowboy boots, the cost of which can
be deferred with credit. Yet, Charlie decides to "take it just the way it
comes off the rack," signaling his refusal of credit-based consumerism
and eschewing corruption of the uniformity of law. The scene is an allegory of the border patrol unit. Charlie's partner, Hawker, remarks, "You
know it's funny what you can see in a man, just in the way he wears his
clothes; a uniform is supposed to make everyone the same, that's what
the word means, uniform, but if you . . ." when he is suddenly cut off
by boys throwing rocks at the car. We never hear the end of his speech
since he is killed shortly thereafter, but the idea left hanging gains a
visual explanation through Charlie's dilemma in the story. Does he
follow the uniform code of the law or reshape it to better fit personal
desires for economic gain? He will be drawn into Cat's corrupt and subjective interpretation of the law for financial gain, but not entirely for
self-interest. He is simply trying to please his wife and maintain domestic tranquility, which means capitulation to her consumer desires;
he needs the money to fund the ratcheting up of his wife's consumer
lifestyle. The blame for Charlie's actions is placed on the consumer-
susceptible Anglo woman whose greedy desires put the entire border
region and national security in jeopardy. The overworked and weary cop
will be redeemed with the heroic rescue of his wife's visual and moral
opposite, the humble and victimized Mexican woman.

In these 1980s versions of the border film, we are drawn into sympathy with the good but corruptible agents and made to understand the
motives behind their corruption. They take kickbacks and retain seized
goods and money because they are overworked and underpaid, and often capitulate to the consumer demands of their spouses. Or they are
simply capitulating to the culture of the border patrol units, as a pair
of patrolmen in *Flashpoint* admit: "We skim a little bit off the top from
time to time just like everybody else." They cross professional ethical
lines with the women they police because, after all, they are sensu-
ous and human. These violations pass with little narrative repercussion

2.4 Charlie and his pleading wife Marcy (Valerie Perrine).

while the evil corporations, the Vietnam vets, the mean Feds, the drug runners, and the immigrant "job takers" are marked unambiguously as bad guys.

BAD GUYS AND BUDDY COPS

Borderline, The Border, and *Flashpoint* are participants in the buddy cop genre made popular by later films like *Lethal Weapon* (1987), *Bad Boys* (1995), *Money Train* (1995), and *Men in Black* (1997). Like *Bad Boys,* border cop films engage a racially homogenous masculine dyad, unlike interracial buddy narratives symptomatic and dismissive of black-white racial tension, which Cynthia Fuchs has described as a denial of the reality of racial tension or which Ed Guerrero has described as the protective custodianship of the white cop for his African-American charge.[22] The racial likeness of the border cop buddy films does not obviate the racial dialectic typical of the cop genre; rather it serves a different, perhaps more pernicious aim: the racial division in border films is drawn across national boundaries, where Anglo buddy cops bond against racial invaders from south of the Rio Bravo.

In the border zone buddy narrative, the partners mirror each other through the external feature of race (white), yet each represents a different stage in the formation of the border patrolman; their difference is marked by a combination of age and experience often typified by the young rookie cop and his older seasoned partner. Theirs is a tutelary relationship in which the older partner will mentor the rookie, instructing him on the specifics of the job; like Hawker with Charlie in *The Border*, the experienced cop enables the new cop's acculturation. The typical heterosexual difference that energizes most Hollywood plots is grafted onto this professional stage difference. Moreover, the intensity of their friendship and devotion makes them the most fascinating couple in the narrative, although not for long, because, inevitably, the cop couple will be broken up so that the work of the narrative can be accomplished.

Typically, one member of the partnership is killed, leaving the remaining cop to avenge his death. The death of the cop signals the return of the vigilante, the exceptional figure who will act alone, outside of the law and according to a unique code of moral good. This turn of events clears space for the absolute suturing of the viewer into the empty space left by the dead hero. In the murdered buddy revenge story, we, by occupying the place of the absent partner, collaborate in the search and destroy mission to defend national propriety and sovereignty. The spectator becomes the new buddy and all that this entails, including complicity with the remaining protagonist and tacit adherence to the ideology of U.S. exceptionalism, in which the United States is deemed a superior moral and political example for the rest of the world, through the code of vigilantism.

Like *The Border*, *Flashpoint* (1984) dramatizes the rookie/ingénue and older/experienced cop hierarchy between the older jaded cop, Kris Kristofferson as Bob Logan, and his youthful charge, Treat Williams as Ernie Wyatt. The younger Wyatt is idealistic and maverick, angrily rankling authority with a sense of moral rectitude, fairness, and justice; he is the unmistakable namesake of the legend of Western mythology Wyatt Earp, famous for his righteous valor. Logan is quiet and conservative; he follows his father's dictum, "If you can't get out of it, get into it." But Logan idealizes Ernie Wyatt for his naïve idealism, describing him in laudatory terms: "Yeah Ernie's different. He's about fifteen years younger for openers. He still believes in god and country and his job, duty, the Raiders. He's got a lot of integrity, he's a real straight arrow. They don't make'm like that anymore, he's the best man in the unit." Wyatt evokes Logan's nostalgia for the lost ideals of his youth and the "brave young notion that you can still do something about it," a description that recalls the activist ethos of the civil rights era,

2.5 Buddy border cops Treat Williams as Ernie Wyatt and Kris Kristofferson as Bobby Logan in *Flashpoint*.

which will return in the phantom remainders and clues to the assassination of President John F. Kennedy buried in the borderlands desert. But the activist resonance of this reference is abstracted from its sociohistorical context. The return of J. F. K. is not a reminder of the civil rights struggles of women and peoples of color, but rather signifies government corruption, federal involvement in an assassination plot, and ongoing efforts to conceal it. Thus, J. F. K. connotes the oppression of big government, which might also be evinced as legislation that protects marginal groups to the detriment of these Anglo cowboy heroes.

Though Logan and Wyatt represent the law, they are also "just like us," with foibles and flaws that make them accessible for viewer identification. In fact, the officers are introduced to us as "regular guys," unmarked, exposed, and vulnerable in the locker room before they dress. Wyatt lolls around in a tequila-induced hangover, then lands naked and slack-jawed on a bench and Logan covers him in a shirt. We are not entirely sure what their roles are until the camera closes in on the patch on the shoulders of their uniforms that inscribes their identities (to our surprise): U.S. Border Patrol.

After they dress, Logan and Wyatt saunter tardily into a meeting of their unit where the head officer chastises them and the rest of the

racially homogeneous (all white) patrolmen convened for being ineffi-
cient and unproductive: "What it comes down to is that for the past two
years Del Lamo has had the piss-poorest record of any United States
Border Patrol sector in the sovereign state of Texas." The remark is met
by these proud underachievers with clapping and cheers. Mr. Lacy, a
federal agent shipped "all the way in from Washington, D.C.," puts an
end to the frivolity; he steps up to introduce new "illegal alien" tracking technologies ("he himself devised") that would increase efficiency
and, in a phantom return of Fordist mechanization, render human labor
obsolete while subordinating the remaining officers to the new technology and to the Feds who control it.

The Feds, invariably portrayed in Hollywood as cold and severe au-
tomatons of power, are depicted as the real oppressor. This was a commonplace theme in the 1980s; Susan Jeffords notes that heroes like
Dirty Harry and other vigilante types would "defy government policies"
to "rescue citizens from their leaders."[23] These heroes were men "pit-
ted against bureaucracies that have lost touch with the people they are
to serve, largely through the failure of bureaucracies themselves to at-
tend to individual needs."[24] As noted earlier, one of the major themes
of the Reagan administration was the promise to decrease big government and its unwieldy bureaucracies. In *Flashpoint*, when the officers
protest their downsizing, they are told, "This is a bureau decision—you
don't have any choice in the matter." In a narcissistic refraction of the
policing gaze, the object of the border patrol reorganization, which is to
say the "victims" of the new tracking devices, are not the immigrants
who remain invisible, but the patrolmen who will be eliminated. The
injustice falls upon the patrolmen who displace the undocumented immigrant as the objects policed by the government. The immigrant is
elided and displaced in the Republican critique of big government.

The new technology is a scanning and detection system with "geo-
sensors" buried in the desert that are "so sensitive they will pick up the
coins in a man's pocket," to which rebellious young Wyatt responds,
"They haven't got any coins in their pockets, that's why they're trying
to cross the border," causing yet another round of cheers and laughs from
the rest of the officers. They continue to laugh as the Fed explains how
the computerized graph, similar in complexity to early video games like
Space Invaders, traces the "imaginary illegal alien" across several quad-
rants on a matrix. Wyatt then asks the federal agent Mr. Lacy how the
geo-sensors will affect the officers, and the response (delivered in stilted

and official diction) directly addresses the film audience/U.S. public: "There won't be a need for so many agents on patrol. That means considerable savings for the taxpayer." Though we, the audience, are the taxpayers, the address fails to resonate since our affections are aligned with the border patrolmen, whereas in *Borderline*, being addressed as taxpayers resonates for the implication that the immigrant objects of border patrol are culpable for the hemorrhaging of taxpayer dollars. Yet we seem to not mind when those dollars are associated with the patrolmen, who are good and humble Anglo-Americans, and are spent so that they might keep their jobs. This is in keeping with the larger ideological mandate of Hollywood border narratives for more, not fewer, agents patrolling the border.

Wyatt vociferously challenges the federal agents brought in to reorganize their border patrol unit, while Logan makes sidelined wisecracks or merely postures his resistance with folded arms. The older Logan was once like Wyatt, but has lost all of his youthful rebelliousness and naïve belief in the possibility of effecting change. For instance, when the partners discover a million dollars in stolen or misappropriated funds in the desert, Wyatt wants to do the "right" legal thing, while Logan would rather take the money and escape across the border—in typical border film fashion, the border marks the limit between order and corruption and escaping to Mexico signifies impunity. The radical Wyatt is killed trying to "do the right thing" and Logan "takes the money and runs," leaving the system intact and returning the story to its generic conditions. Logan is more adept at maneuvering in the system for his self-preservation and self-interest, which are the reigning values of the conservative plot. But, Logan has changed in the course of the plot to finally occupy Wyatt's critical position, at least in theory. Logan intends to stay and investigate the J. F. K. assassination mystery and follow procedure by reporting the violations of the federal agents. Yet he has to choose between snitching on the corrupt Feds and getting killed, or taking the money and allowing the secret of the federal links to J. F. K.'s assassination to remain hidden. He chooses to take the money and save his own life, but the film ends with the ominous threat of the return of the repressed: "I'll be back."

Unlike in the earlier border narratives, in *Flashpoint* there is no representation of immigrants, who are tellingly referred to as "imaginary illegal aliens" in connection with the electronic tracking system. In place of the immigrant is the liberal hero and voice of the immigrant cause,

Ernie Wyatt. His mission as a border patrol agent is to put an end to the traffic of undocumented immigrants by a single purveyor, prominent businessman Pedroza. In one scene, the only of its kind, Wyatt investigates a crash in which a van carrying twenty-one undocumented immigrants is hit by a water tanker while running a red light. Pedroza owns the van, but he denies any involvement in the matter. Wyatt delivers a speech meant to appeal to Pedroza's sense of ethnic and racial solidarity, echoing a civil rights era ethos of race-based social justice: "You stand here lying to our faces with that white piece of shit lawyer in your pocket while they pull your people out of here in plastic bags . . . you pick up wetbacks in Chihuahua and pack them in anything on wheels. You promise them freedom and you sell them death. You are a fucking assassin. You are a fucking butcher! Your own people!" Wyatt's heroism is underscored by his empathy for the "imaginary illegal aliens," yet a major blind spot in this portrayal is his use of denigrating terms to describe Mexicans. Also, this critical account is never developed, and this is the last we hear of the immigrant predicament. As with the rest of the border stories, the Mexican plight is a mere backdrop to the cowboy heroism of the Anglo lead, and the only Latino in the entire plot, Pedroza, is depicted negatively as ruthless and corrupt. The immigrant struggle has only a passing mention in the film; it is overshadowed by the ongoing victimization of the border patrol by the federal government.

Flashpoint captures the main topoi of 1980s border films: the buddy cops, the identification and sympathy between the patrolmen and the patrolled, the victimization of the border guard by a powerful and over-large federal government, and the deleterious forces of a new economy. Similarly, *The Border* depicts border guard oppression as a symptom of the new, globalized reality of the 1980s. Jack Nicholson is Charlie, the well-intentioned good cop saddled with a bad wife who lives beyond her means. The tagline reads: "Charlie (Jack Nicholson) and his wife Marcy (Valerie Perrine) are two people caught in the turmoil of conflicting values. Marcy is consumed by her middle class materialism—regardless of cost. Charlie's goals are decidedly more profound. As a border guard along the Rio Grande, he has to choose between loyalties to his job and country, his wife, and his compassion for human suffering." Charlie almost capitulates to Marcy's rampant consumerism, which would mean capitulating to the corrupting forces at the border, yet he is redeemed by his idealization of a Mexican immigrant, Maria, who inspires him to be heroic and virtuous. *The Border* instrumentalizes Maria to represent

Charlie's conflicts so that he might work through his own personal dilemmas, impasses, and professional ruts. Hardly a fully developed character, Maria is a screen for the "good values" of the border guard who longs for her pre-industrial simplicity, unsullied by the tandem advances of late capitalism and civil rights era feminism. Maria is not just a projection of Charlie's character; there is also a curious elision between the two. He assumes her role and status in the story as a victim of globalization, initiating an enduring legacy of the Hollywood border film.

The Border associates Maria and Charlie from the beginning. Both migrate to the border region of El Paso, Texas, for better economic opportunities. In the beginning, we witness the reason for Maria's departure (an earthquake that kills the father of her baby during its christening), the subsequent journey that she, her brother, and the baby make to the border region, and their various attempts to cross over. Her journey is marked by the opening soundtrack, a country song about the borderline and reaching the "broken promised land." The lyrics articulate Maria's position, but we associate the male singer more readily with Charlie's misery. In a scene that precedes Charlie's departure from Los Angeles to El Paso, he sits alone, miserable and misunderstood, drinking a beer in the dark while his wife sleeps peacefully. His anthem begins playing, a song about disillusionment: "It's too late / to turn back / are you living in a nightmare, / are you living in a dream?" The song with lyrics that we might also associate with immigrant disillusionment with U.S. culture continues to play as the film cuts between Maria's journey across the border and Charlie's trek to El Paso, clearly establishing their congruity. Their connection and equivalence is firmly established as the borderlands are drawn into full relief. But the visual narrative establishes a complementary difference between Charlie and Maria upon their arrival to the borderlands. When Maria and her brother reach the border, they look out from the rocky desert of the southern side, populated by a solitary goat, toward the northern city. Their arrival at the border signals a return to the classical Western division between Anglo civilization to the north and Mexican barbarism to the south.

Unlike the border guard, the undocumented immigrant is always an object of the law who rarely moves beyond the juridical domain associated with the frontier. For instance, *The Border* and *Borderline* feature many scenes of Anglo agents with almost no comprehension of Spanish booking undocumented immigrants. We recognize the officer-couples as the subjects of the narrative discourse because they interrogate the immigrants and speak to each other about their professional dilemmas; in short, they interpret their worlds together and make themselves understood. The immigrants, by contrast, are mute objects of the officer discourse; they remain ciphers both within the narrative and beyond it. The majority of male border-crossers are never fully humanized subjects, but are meaningful as signs of the cops' sacrifice and noble good. Border films of the 1980s depict these officers as maverick individuals and humane bearers of the law, whereas the undocumented immigrants are subhuman and massified by the joint features of race and working-class clothing. The migrant is only a docile body, arrested, booked, examined, and subject to an endless procession and repetition of arrests and retreats. The subjection of the immigrant reassures the viewer that the border zone is under control and that border agents are always on hand to protect against the conflicts and crises of national identity.

1980s-style border films play on society's unconscious associations and inchoate fears of borderlands by invoking the bottom line, the cost to the taxpayer. Taxpayer dollars are wasted on ex-military officers gone bad, especially those trained for anti-communist purposes—e.g., wars in Central America and Vietnam—while undocumented immigration is represented as the most costly federal expense. These films turn "compassion fatigue" into economic distress, but they don't leave the viewer at loose ends. Instead they offer an easy solution in the elimination of the "imaginary alien." Much of the fear surrounding Mexican migration was projected onto crude economic market concerns about the deleterious effect of immigration on the health of the economy through unemployment rates, the cultivation of scourge-like informal economies, and the cost of public services and subsequent increase in taxes. The government encouraged and magnified these Reaganite concerns to deflect from the massive hemorrhaging of tax revenue on defense spending and military build-up in the 1980s. Thus, the defense of the border shifted from being just a problem of the borderland states to becoming a major, if not *the* major, national issue of the 1980s.

Borderline depicts the national context of the border patrol issue to create a sense of national cohesion. In order to convey the vast impact of the issue and to emphasize the expanse of U.S. boundaries, the Feds ship an agent from New York City to a San Diego border patrol unit. Sending just one agent all the way from New York seems counterintuitive, but works allegorically to shift the problem from a state to a national level. The culture shock of a New Yorker in California, as well as any mythic bicoastal antagonism, is immediately neutralized by the common goal of stemming the "hemorrhage" of "illegals" into the United States. Though the story takes place in San Diego, it foregrounds the national dimension of the immigration issue. One of the guards marks this nationalism: "Sleep tight, America, your tax dollars are hard at work."

The characters of *The Border* and *Borderline* express bewilderment at the constant shuttling of immigrants into and out of the imagined space of "America" as if all the action were a deflection from the national state of affairs, i.e., an exhausting waste of effort, time, and taxpayers' money. Yet this movement of relentless exchange is crucial to the idea of the United States as a coherent entity. Far from meaningless or a waste of resources, this police work is a flexing and firming of the national musculature and a sign of a vigorous national corpus; moreover, the cessation of border flux would mark the end of the attractions of the U.S. economy. The repeated roundups are not pointless, but the stuff of identity formation, a process that is both dialectical and infinite. National identity is formed against these outsiders, who are tossed out by the border agents and exiled to the edges of the nation and beyond.

BORDER UNCANNY

The borderlands are zones of the uncanny, full of buried pasts that threaten irruption across their serene space. The return of the past carries something unforeseen and exiled from national consciousness, but present nonetheless: a mysterious piece of history unearthed in the desert (*Lone Star, Flashpoint*), hidden censors (*Borderline*) or border guards with secret pasts. The guards are themselves a symptom of this national dumping ground; they are part of the list of historical detritus that has drifted to the borders of memory, the enigmas that resist interpretation, including the J. F. K. assassination, Vietnam veterans, and marooned ex-military officers. Guarding the border is a loose metaphor for guarding history, keeping secrets, staving off the unresolved stuff of the past, and making it remain at the edges of national consciousness.

The signifier "Vietnam" is the most lucid apparition of repressed history. In *Borderline*, a guard explaining to the new rookie, Jimmy Fante, the state of police activity on the border says, "We're in the middle of a damned invasion," recalling the phobias of "communist invasion" that justified the Vietnam War from which many of these characters are fallout. *Borderline* features the sinister Vietnam veteran bent on destroying

2.6 The border patrolmen unearth secrets in the desert that offer clues about the John F. Kennedy assassination.

U.S. national integrity. He uses his military knowledge and technology to import thousands upon thousands of undocumented immigrants for a big corporation. His Mexican-American assistant intones, "You're pretty smart for a white guy," to which he responds, "Uncle Sam spent a lot of bread in 'Nam teaching me how to be" (another aside to the already enraged tax-paying viewer). In films of this era, Vietnam veterans were figures of the inassimilable remainders of history; they represented a divided nation unable to come to terms with the devastations of war and its misguided ideological motivations. In popular culture veterans might be represented as disillusioned with the government, disaffected, and politically withdrawn, as well as angry, volatile, and vulnerable to illicit and outcast ventures.

In *Flashpoint*, the Fed's new immigrant tracking system is part of the technology of full-scale war. In fact, one of the officers remarks, "We've tried those sons of bitches in 'Nam, didn't work then, ain't gonna work now." Vietnam is not a shining coordinate of U.S. history. Border films made the Vietnam War relevant to 1980s moviegoers by restaging the war as one between border crossers and border control; eschewing final aims, border films represented this war as not one of wholesale success but of small victories (in the form of roundups of undocumented immigrants) in a process infinitely deferred, one that presented the dynamic formation and reassertion of national identity.

Flashpoint and *Borderline* unravel the enigmas of the disaffected Vietnam veteran and bring this wayward character back into the fold; failing this, the veterans face elimination and exile. Logan in *Flashpoint* is a Vietnam veteran who "dropped out" to become a border cop. His reasons for "copping out" are political, whereas the ex-marine in *Borderline* refuses the noble role of veteran for unknown reasons. Logan's resume, delivered to us by the FBI agent, reveals an impressive career that ended with the Vietnam War: "Logan, Robert E.: born 6/8/41, graduated West Point, 1963, 'Nam Green Beret hero, three Silver Stars, recommendation for the Medal of Honor, had the world by the tail at twenty-four and then all of a sudden, poof, he up and quits." Logan's self-exile in the desert is the post-military version of the 1960s "dropout" who left his golden career when Nixon was president, Logan claims, not for the "pressure, but the politics." The following dialogue between the FBI agent and Logan sounds not unlike the typical argument between the conservative suit and the liberal dropout:

—This whole fucking nation is politics. You work for the border patrol, a division of the Immigration Bureau, which answers to the Department of Justice, which is directly responsible to the Congress of the United States, now you don't think that's political? You think you've beaten the political system because you're hiding out at the bottom of it?

—I don't work for the system, I work for the law.

—You work for the same law that pays all our salaries, the law of supply and demand. Think about it, whiz kid. Your fucking job depends on those wetbacks and if we didn't have them, we'd invent them, otherwise how would your department justify the millions it gets from Congress each year? It's the American way, pal. Supply and demand and when the supply is lacking, create it. Shit, every morning I get up and I thank God for drugs and murder and subversion because without them, we'd all be out of a job.

Here we turn again to the rhetorical strategy so pervasive in the 1980s: the continual repetition of the same to the point of exhaustion. Both parties, representing the larger state and the local police force respectively, are part of the same over-taxed system. Neither has enough staff or resources to make any effective change in the flow of undocumented immigration. But in a twist not explicitly drawn in the other films of the era, the positions and livelihood of both characters are absolutely dependent on the continual production of policed bodies. Their shared engagement in the bad faith system created by the forces of advanced capitalism is what ultimately unites them.

Into this contest between the politically withdrawn and disaffected border cop, representative of "the people," and the enfranchised conservative, representative of "the state," enters a new villain that eclipses this ideological impasse and national disunity: globalization. This is the moment when the processes of governance and the mechanisms of state control are superseded by the workings of international capital and the law of supply and demand. The film disabuses the border unit of its total separation from the U.S. government, while casting a unifying net over Vietnam veterans and those who were against the war. These border films show that those on different sides of a conflict—border agents and immigrants, Vietnam veterans and war protesters, the government and the people—share the same concerns. Border narratives gloss these oppositions to heal the rifts caused by past traumas, particularly the Vietnam War. Lawrence Grossberg describes this rapprochement between the people and the nation as an effort by the Reagan era New Right to redefine the nation on their terms.[25] Gil Troy, in his critical analysis of the cultural politics of the Reagan era, also describes the 1980s as a time of "great reconciliation" between opposing factions.[26] In the border films of the era, the individual and the state are drawn into the same metonymy of the nation, and their difference is neutralized by their common subjugation to the market. In *Borderline*, the market is sustained by the transnational trade in undocumented workers and the agencies created to regulate and police this trade.

In these border films, our sympathies are aligned with the populist figure of the border agent who, during a time of incredible affluence, is overworked and underpaid. The main stars are a pair of buddies, one of whom loses his life on the job, leaving the lone ranger hero to accomplish the moral mission of the narrative with his new partner, the viewer, in tow. The combination of tragedy and humble circumstances elicits our full affective engagement with the oppressed hero. The crises faced by the border cops, the continual roundups with no resolution, and the evasive and relentless return of the undocumented immigrant make his position noble and heroic. The continual refrain of the genre during this era is the need to reinforce control of the border and the relentless pursuit of undocumented immigrants, leading to the exhaustion not just of the border agents but also of our compassion for immigrants. The focus of the plot shifts entirely to the unhappy circumstances of the border agent, completely eclipsing any liberal discourse about immigration and the struggle for survival of the immigrant. In the final scenes of these films, the immigrant functions merely as a backdrop for our reawakened sympathy and compassion for an entirely new population of oppressed peoples, the border patrolmen.

BORDERSPLOITATION

What are we in for when we watch these stories? From our current vantage some twenty years later, we can see that these stories are boosterish and boorishly nationalistic. Some might claim that these films are forgotten relics of the 1980s in their B-grade plots; indeed they are rendered obsolete by virtue of their low genre status. But it is the very obsolescence of these films that attests to their historic specificity. Their locality is a sign of a time in history, now past, that we would, perhaps, like to forget. What makes these border films so passé and so trite that they cannot live beyond their short moment in history? Quite plainly, the idea is that we are better now. We have progressed beyond the parochialism and political blind spots of the 1980s, and we see clearly from the panoramic vantage of historical high ground. Yet this sentiment obfuscates the legacy of these plots. Each film plays out the same drama and the same topoi again and again, as if the work of the first incarnation was left unfinished and the border were a national wound that refused to heal. The borderlands are containers of traumatic material and unassimilated histories repeated endlessly in the dreamwork of Hollywood cinema. The current slate of border films and television dramas—*Extreme Prejudice* (1987), *Deep Cover* (1992), *Traffic* (2000), *Kingpin* (NBC, 2003), and *A Man Apart* (2003)—reopen the trauma of Hollywood film and television border images. The United States is again heroic, and though Latinos are represented with greater nuance, this is not achieved without the sacrifice of reactivating a Hollywood history of the dark mythology of the borderlands that intensifies phobias about external threats to national health and "homeland security."

THREE

THE "NARC" IN ALL OF US
BORDER MEDIA AND
THE WAR ON DRUGS

"No country in the world poses a more immediate narcotics threat to the United States than Mexico."

—U.S. DEPARTMENT OF STATE (1996)

"Our borders constitute the first line of defense in protecting the American people from terrorists. Last July I
met with border security agents and other federal and local officials during my visit to the border, and I promised
them we would address this national security crisis. The
Republican Congress has responded to the American
people's demand for a secure border by increasing the
physical barriers and infrastructure along the border and
by providing state of the art monitoring technology. I
look forward to the President signing the Secure Fence
Act tomorrow."

—SPEAKER OF THE HOUSE J. DENNIS HASTERT
(R-IL) COMMENTING ON WHITE HOUSE SIGNING
OF THE SECURE FENCE ACT (OCTOBER 25, 2006)

O n February 10, 1986, just two months before Reagan signed a national security directive designating
international drug trade a national security threat,
Elliott Abrams, then assistant secretary for inter-
American affairs and in 2005 appointed deputy national security adviser to President George W. Bush,
gave the talk, "Drug Wars: The New Alliances against Traffickers and
Terrorists," before the Council on Foreign Relations in New York City.
Abrams hoped to move the "drug problem" from the cultural realm of
television news programs and Friday night dramas to the more serious
domain of international policy as it comes to bear on national security
and the "well-being of the American people."[1] He described the United

States as the victim in the drug trafficking networks that lead northward and suggested that defending national security meant "defending ourselves against drugs."[2] Tracing use patterns of cocaine from the drug's origins in Bolivia, Peru, and Colombia to its destination in the United States, he cited a popular television show when he claimed, "Something of the traffic always stays behind: this is not a Miami vice alone."[3] He drew the association, then already commonplace, of the Colombian revolutionary forces, known as the *Fuerzas Armadas Revolucionarias de Colombia* (FARC), and drug trafficking in order to promote the need, described in the title of the talk, for "new alliances against traffickers and terrorists." The association of traffickers and terrorists since the mid-1980s has not lost any of its original force; rather, I argue, this association has achieved geometrically expanding proportions.

In his speech, Abrams rallies for collaboration across the Americas, but ends with a stridently moral and nationalist assessment of the "drug problem": "This is not just a health problem, not just a foreign aid problem, not just a police problem. It is a moral challenge and a national security matter. It threatens democracy in our hemisphere and children in our homes. Let us treat it with the seriousness it deserves."[4] This language and rhetoric about the messianic duties and moral obligation to protect the homeland and hearth captures exactly the same sentiment that enthralls audiences of Hollywood drug trafficking films, recalling, for instance, the dramatic scene in *Traffic* (2000) when drug czar Robert Wakefield, fresh from the Washington war on drugs, returns home to find his teenage daughter with a serious drug addiction. This reverberation of sentiments—that the drug war is waged across the hemisphere, on the streets, and in the home—resounds with what Abrams contends in his speech: "There is a bit of 'narc' in all of us now."[5] Though by "us" he is referring to all high-ranking officials in the hemisphere, he uses this inclusive term to indicate the pervasiveness of drug trade across local, national, and international political spheres. The term "narc" has many different meanings depending on its context of use: it generally refers to narcotics agents, but by the 1980s, it became a popular term for those who acted as cops by snitching on anyone deemed culpable of a narcotics offense. Here it carries both meanings; it refers to the stretching of the jurisdiction of narcotics agents to all levels of state control and the imperative for all of "us" to take on the role of policing and enforcement and thus to take part in the war on drugs.[6]

Rather than an indication of a lack of serious attention, the continuing media presence of drug issues is a sign of a wide cultural permutation with endless power to shape public perception.[7] The drug trafficking television shows and films from the 1980s to the present are fundamental in bringing out the "narc" in all of us, mostly by forging identifications with those on the frontier of the U.S. war on drugs: undercover cops, DEA agents, border patrol, and Texas Rangers. Hollywood media actively supports and extends the war on drugs by putting each viewer squarely in the moral world of the enforcer; this "narc hero" is characterized by his or her deeply "American" values of righteousness, enterprise, autonomy, and initiative. In this chapter, I explore some popular examples of Hollywood film and media that generate a "narc" sensibility in the viewer: *Extreme Prejudice* (1987), *Deep Cover* (1992), *Traffic* (2000), *Kingpin* (NBC, 2003), and *A Man Apart* (2003). In all of these media, in either the main plot or a subplot, there is a good but maverick cop, the "narc" stand-in who works alone on a moral mission against a Latin/o American drug empire deemed a nightmarish symptom of late capitalism. This chapter departs somewhat from the others in that I pay attention to the pervasiveness of the "war on drugs" across Hollywood film as well as television. There are a couple of reasons for this; primarily, drug policies heavily influence the messages of both popular Hollywood film and television, most apparently thanks to the work of drug czar General Barry R. McCaffrey in the 1990s. Also, television shows like *21 Jump Street* (Fox 1987–1991) and *Miami Vice* (NBC 1984–1989) influenced "narc" media in ways that superseded Hollywood films of the genre.

Like the border patrol of the 1980s border films, the hard-bodied heroes of drug trafficking films provide cultural redemption from the moral degradation of globalization in the form of the Spanish-language and Latin/o American version of the corporate entity, or what the television series *Kingpin* calls "la corporación," an organization ruled by a ruthless Latin/o American drug kingpin who produces and traffics in contraband with blatant disregard for the rule of law and the boundaries between nations. With the possible exception of *Traffic,* these narco-border films target Latin American nations as producers and suppliers of drugs while relieving the United States of responsibility for its role as a consumer nation in the perpetuation of drug trade. These films present a solitary narc hero who transcends government corruption on both sides of the border, but who nonetheless endorses a unilateral drug control policy lead by Washington.

The narc hero is the cinematic counterpart of the ideal viewer, whose values and judgments are continually put into play in the unfolding of the story. The audience enjoys a privileged vantage onto the arrests, collateral damage, treachery, and deceit on both sides of the war on drugs. The narc hero is the last man standing, the lone cowboy with a clear moral mission in the midst of borderless free trade or globalization without boundaries. Many of the Hollywood cross-border drug trafficking films contribute to a battle of perceptions between the United States and Latin America. These films intensify inter-American drug war offensives by establishing a higher moral ground from which the U.S. narc can point fingers. Even as the dynamics of the drug trade change, the tropes and ideas driving the war on drugs as represented in Hollywood remain the same.

THE POLITICS OF CONTRABAND

During his tenure as president between 1969 and 1973,[8] Richard Nixon waged an "all out global war on the drug menace,"[9] which included a number of high profile initiatives to reduce drug trade by cutting off supply—most notably the 1969 Operation Intercept that mandated searches of all people and vehicles crossing the border into the United States from Mexico; this campaign was cancelled after just seventeen days due to international tensions and few apprehensions of contraband.[10] But it began a dynamic of U.S. coercion and Mexican compliance and an emphasis on curtailing supply rather than reducing demand.

In 1972, Nixon backed the war on drugs with real force by consolidating four government agencies into the Drug Enforcement Administration (DEA). The U.S. narcotics control strategy has since maintained an emphasis on producer nations over consumer nations, implementing policies that threaten and undermine the sovereignty of nations in the southern hemisphere in the name of U.S. national security. The phrase "war on drugs" is a metaphor; it does not refer to an actual war or warfare with a designated or organized enemy, but it does refer to the U.S. government's emphasis on militarization rather than other, more socially driven goals. Coletta Youngers and Eileen Rosin argue that this "narrow focus" is a consequence of viewing drug trafficking as a national security and border defense issue rather than a consequence of the social or economic conditions of both producers and consumers.[11] The very phrase, "war on drugs," generates the idea of an enemy rather than a set of conditions and a complex dynamic in which many different players are complicit. Narco-trafficking Hollywood border films tend to locate a clear enemy in the Latin/o American drug traffickers and the corrupt state that colludes with or harbors their efforts. Much of drug war efforts have focused on interdiction at the border; in fact, Tony Payan notes that the war on drugs has coincided with the borderlands since its inception. For instance, the first action of this war mentioned earlier, Operation Intercept, was a foundational and symbolic event signifying the focus on the border as well as the impossibility of closing U.S. borders to international drug trade.[12]

By the 1980s, the war on drugs was not just headline news, but also a major event of popular culture. Curtis Marez examines the myriad forms of media—Hollywood movies, documentaries, memoirs, novels, television shows, *narcocorridos*, and rap music—that trace this period of the intensification of the war on drugs in the 1980s and 1990s. These media were part of a concerted attempt to expand the rhetoric and ideology of the war on drugs. Marez argues that media images about the war on drugs helped to "generate powerful ideas about state power, foreign policy, and transnational capitalism" that became a primary point of reference for political relations across the hemisphere.[13] For drug czar McCaffrey, the media was the main source of cultural currency in the campaign against drugs. As a result of his efforts, mass media had a tremendous impact on the direction and execution of the war on drugs to the point that the war on drugs is now inseparable from its mass mediation.

By the mid-1980s, changes in drug trafficking dynamics were reflected in films like *Extreme Prejudice*, in which Colombian cartels—after the success of the initiatives of the South Florida Task Force and perhaps also in part thanks to bad publicity from *Miami Vice*—searched for new routes for shipping contraband into the United States.[14] The U.S. law enforcement agencies' crackdown in the Caribbean basin led some Colombian cartels to shift their focus onto the U.S.-Mexico border.[15] Following this move, *Extreme Prejudice* (1987) begins its work on the border. The borderlands provided a perfect stage for the political dramas of the war on drugs for a number of reasons. For one, the setting put the issue back onto the iconic topography of the United States, the mythic southern frontier of Western lore. The borderlands are "America," whereas Miami, for many, belongs to elsewhere, not only for its position in the Caribbean basin but also for its reputation as the capital of and its extensive transnational links to Latin America. The border is a militarized zone crawling with Texas Rangers, border patrol, DEA, and

3.1 Maria Conchita Alonso as Sarita, the object of competition between men in *Extreme Prejudice*.

various other agencies of control and enforcement of the national line, so it is the perfect place to examine other histories of U.S. interventions and national security as a military objective.

Extreme Prejudice, one of the first drug trafficking films released after Reagan's declaration of the intensification of the war on drugs, forges an association among drugs, the border, and national security that had characterized the war on drugs from its inception. In fact, filmmaker Walter Hill risked convoluting the storyline in an effort to make this grand scheme apparent. Briefly, the film is about two Anglo guys who used to be best buddies, but have parted ways: Jack Benteen is now a Texas Ranger, while Cash Bailey became a drug kingpin operating out of Mexico. They are also linked by another aspect of their past: Jack is involved with Cash's ex-girlfriend, Sarita (Maria Conchita Alonso), who reprises the Western role of the Mexican woman who mediates between two Anglo men—as in *My Darling Clementine* (1946), *High Noon* (1952), and *Vera Cruz* (1954). Maria Conchita Alonso will return in *Kingpin* to a similar role as the object of competition between men.[16] Jack and Cash are fated to meet along the border where the latter does business, laundering money through Texas banks and delivering contraband to the United States.

When *Extreme Prejudice* hit the theaters, the drug war along the border had yet to be fully militarized, but the military lingo in the title was certainly an exhortation to this end. The title reminds viewers of a similar mandate in the Vietnam War era saga *Apocalypse Now* (1979); in *Apocalypse Now* a wayward military officer is to be "terminated with extreme prejudice," while in *Extreme Prejudice* this command is issued by a crooked ex-major against a purported "deep cover DEA agent" gone bad. Later, the film *Clear and Present Danger* (1994), a reflection of George Bush Sr.'s militarization of the drug war, uses similar military language to justify waging an illegal war in Colombia, where the drug trade is depicted as a "clear and present danger" to U.S. national security.

Though the title *Extreme Prejudice* refers to a military imperative of uncompromising elimination of the enemy, it has an eerier significance within the context of Reagan's revved-up war on drugs. The film continues many of the terms set by the earlier 1980s border films preoccupied with immigrant traffic, but by the mid-1980s, cross-border drug trade began to supplant and contain the issue of U.S. migration. Like *The Border*, *Borderline*, and *Flashpoint*, *Extreme Prejudice* tells the story of two men on different sides of the law and the national boundary that represents this division. The film is a modern-day Western after Peckinpah, but lacking the moral ambiguities often found in Sam Peckinpah's work, *Extreme Prejudice* depends on the moral legacies of the classical foundations of the genre. The tagline states: "*Extreme Prejudice* delves into the classic battle between good and evil. It's a bold, modern Western that delivers a powerful punch." In good Western tradition, the audience is squarely on the side of the narc, the good cop whose history of intimate friendship with the drug lord recalls the similar dynamic of outlaw Pike Bishop and his friend-turned-enemy Deke Thornton of Peckinpah's *The Wild Bunch*.

The reference to *The Wild Bunch* draws upon a significant association. For Richard Slotkin, *The Wild Bunch* (1969) is a veiled reference to the demoralization of the United States after the My Lai massacre in the debacle of the Vietnam War.[17] The existential meaninglessness of the final shootout and the irrational and relentless violence of the entire film reflect a cultural disillusionment with the rule of law. *Extreme Prejudice* similarly begins with references to the historical detritus of Vietnam and other U.S. interventions. The men who comprise what they believe is a special paramilitary operation are all ex-soldiers who conceal their identities because they were all wrongly presumed dead by the U.S. armed forces; these men hail from special operations in Vietnam, Laos, Hondurus, the Philippines, Turkey, Lebanon, Germany, and Panama.[18]

Early 1980s border films like *Borderline* replay the trauma of the Vietnam War in the borderlands, yet *Extreme Prejudice* revisits it as the hemispheric war on drugs, to a decidedly different end. The film is pitched to an audience who believes the government has "lost control of our borders," in the words of Reagan's famous declaration—a loss of mastery that is a consequence of time, money, and energy spent on military interventions elsewhere, particularly Vietnam. Many of the special agents of the commando unit headed by Major Hackett were last stationed in Saigon or in regions of political insurgency that could be likened to Vietnam.[19] In these border films, the drug trade is rarely depicted as systemic and deep-rooted, but rather as an operation run by a single powerful kingpin, the toppling of whom signifies victory in the war. In a manner reminiscent of the psycho-dramatic repetitions of the Alamo, the Vietnam War, through its remainders—veterans and technologically advanced "space age" equipment—is restaged in a drama that ends in victory. Thus, "winning" the war on drugs resignifies other losses in U.S. global wars, so the final vanquishing of the enemy on the border and the successful defense of the national line seal U.S. dominance in the region and the world.

Extreme Prejudice opens with each ex-soldier from a different part of the world arriving at an air terminal in the border city of El Paso. These men form a highly skilled private army under the leadership of ex-major Paul Hackett, whose unidentified body, according to army records, was found during the evacuation of Saigon in 1973. What Hackett introduces as their secret government assignment is actually Hackett's personal mission to expropriate the fortune of a drug lord with whom he has done illegal business. The redeployment of the military for private gain is a favorite trope of the border film and reflects the plot of a major television show of the era, *The A-Team* (NBC 1983–1987), in which Vietnam veterans team up to provide their services to civilians. This entrepreneurial use of military training not only taps into public fears about the misappropriation of armed forces, but also is part of the outlaw version of capitalism associated with cross-border traffic in contraband—like the Vietnam veteran in *Borderline* who uses his military expertise to transport undocumented immigrants. These border media partake in the abiding Hollywood trope of Vietnam veterans as potentially dangerous for their special training and disaffection from the government, as in *The Stone Killer* (1973), *Magnum Force* (1973), and more recently *No Country for Old Men* (2007).[20]

The Ranger and the major will eventually agree to "slip over the border" together to bring Cash to justice, but Jack remains "freelance"; it is this relative autonomy, like that of all the cowboy heroes before him, that enables him to pursue his individual sense of justice in the face of government corruption—an abiding Hollywood critique apparent from the 1980s to the present. Jack works alone; his mission seems uncomplicated by the presence of superior officers, support staff, or the limits of jurisdiction. He exhibits the Western version of outlaw heroism as a lawman who breaks the rules to serve a greater sense of justice. Like Lieutenant Colonel Kirby Yorke of *Rio Grande*, Jack crosses out of his jurisdiction to seek his quarry. This role of the "lone Ranger" allegorizes the unilateralism of the United States in its foreign policy of intervention, justified as an imperative of national security. Like Colonel Yorke and many of the narc heroes in these border films, Jack experiences no legal repercussions from going beyond his duty and jurisdiction; instead he is personally rewarded with the love of a woman.

Jack is determined to persuade his nemesis, kingpin Cash Bailey, to abandon his drug empire. With this aim, Jack arranges to meet with Cash at "twelve, noon," a reference to high noon maverick morality. To underscore this point, Jack's sidekick promises to put on a good show, to which Jack replies that it will be a "real Western." Like the Confederate and Union soldiers of *The Undefeated* or *Vera Cruz* who represent the two halves of the United States, Cash and Jack, the estranged and polarized intimates, reunite outside the United States in Mexican territory. *Extreme Prejudice* relegates the messy conflict of national disunity beyond the boundaries of national identity, staving off potential crises of self-definition. Cash arrives dressed in pure white to Jack's black, a visual confirmation of their opposition. Acknowledging their past friendship ("We rode the river together"), Cash proposes they join forces, trying to lure Jack with the promise of a huge pay raise, "tax-free." Jack responds, "You can buy me, Cash, hell you always could, but you can't buy the badge. One without the other ain't no goddamn good." He is resolute and unwavering in his moral position. He implores Cash, in a phrase reminiscent of then first lady Nancy Reagan's similar exhortation ("Just Say No"), to simply "quit selling dope," a simple moralism

3.2 Cash Bailey (Powers Boothe) and Jack Benteen (Nick Nolte) used to be best friends, but Jack became a Texas Ranger and Cash became a drug kingpin operating out of Mexico. Cash is dressed in pure white to Jack's black, a visual confirmation of their opposition.

that is completely removed from the socio-economic complexities of drug trade and consumption. But Cash responds feverishly, "You don't understand, they want it, Jack! They like the stuff!" This scene refers to a long-standing dynamic in the bi-national war on drugs on sustaining drug traffic in the region, or what Tom Barry (with Harry Browne and Beth Sims) has called the "finger pointing or chicken-or-the-egg arguments over the relative influence of U.S. demand versus Mexican supply."[21] The border symbolizes the separation of producer and consumer nations as the defining division across the Americas. *Extreme Prejudice* inculpates the United States as a consumer nation in the global drug trade, but redeems it as the nation leading anti-drug efforts in the hemisphere, and depicts it as either unaided or hindered by producer nations. Cash suggests that the Mexican government is completely corrupt and complicit with the drug trade, as evinced when he claims that he has "bought off nearly every politician."

Extreme Prejudice depicts the U.S. government just as poorly as its neighboring state, though for different reasons; the government, symbolized by the evil trinity of the DEA, CIA, and FBI, invades the Texas Ranger unit to oversee border drug-curtailing activities, first as fake "DEA" agents, then later as an FBI agent loaded with ludicrous bureaucratic mandates—that is, with lots of forms to fill out. Hackett, as an ex-commanding officer in the military posing as a DEA agent, represents the deceit and manipulation of the government, but once we realize he is a fake, the critique loses some of its traction. In his solitary single-mindedness, Jack initially refuses to cooperate with the ex-major Hackett posing as a DEA agent, but will work with him if Hackett can promise that Jack's requests will be fast-tracked. The government, Jack claims, has been too slow to respond, refusing to release classified information and delaying important operations for fear of offending foreign governments. The DEA/CIA/FBI is the designated oppressive force bent on delaying, disrupting, or otherwise undermining the individual in his or her execution of justice, free enterprise, and pursuit of self-interest or happiness.

During this era, the vilification of the DEA/CIA/FBI was a common popular cultural reference for a public weary of government corruption; federal agents signified the evils of "big government" and thus were corrupt, cruel, bureaucratically oppressive, and therefore the real villains in many Hollywood films. These depictions were in keeping with Reagan's plan to reduce the size of the government, as outlined in his inaugural address to the nation on January 20, 1981. He states that "government is not the solution to our problem; government is the problem" and that "all of us together, in and out of government, must bear the burden [of self-rule]."[22] This ideology of self-rule, initiative, and enterprise became the dominant ethos of popular political culture, iconized by vigilante figures like Jack, the humble, "all-American" Texas Ranger who shows America that he can execute justice on his own without the help of the government and its agents.

In the film, Jack, still unaware of Hackett's criminal enterprise, travels freelance with the commando team to Mexico on a "paramilitary operation" in search of Cash Bailey. According to the ex-major, Cash Bailey himself was on a deep cover DEA mission in Mexico when he turned his knowledge and connections into a drug empire (a trope that returns in *Deep Cover*). Hackett tells the commandos to pursue Cash Bailey with the mission of "termination with extreme prejudice" and that there are no "friendlies" beyond their immediate company, implying that the Ranger is also subject to this command. Like many young soldiers, these men have no idea of the real ideology of the commanding officers; they are simply following orders. But things change when the subordinate officers defy orders in a move that both reflects the counter-cultural ethos of the Vietnam War era and the actual practice of sub-ordinates murdering their corrupt, incompetent, or dangerous officers during the war.

Jack is left on his own to face Cash, who had earlier warned him not to turn things into the Alamo, an overt reference in which Jack, with his patriotic heroism, represents the Texas standoff against the odds. But this time, in keeping with the border Western's triumphant historical revisionism, Texas (and Jack) will win, but not until the scene collapses into a bloodbath reminiscent of the last scene in *The Wild Bunch*. The final shoot-out, in Hollywood but not Peckinpah style, eliminates all the contradictions and problems of the story; entrepreneurial and cor-rupt Vietnam veterans and the detritus of Vietnam as well as the North American drug lord and thus the U.S. role in inter-American distribu-tion of drugs all meet their demise. After evoking the myriad complexi-ties of managing the border region, the film offers a fantasy resolution where the hero gets the girl and restores international order. The mes-sage is clear: big government and its agencies are imperious and corrupt and the real redemption belongs to the incorruptible individual lawman. Jack dramatizes the virtues associated with U.S.-based entrepreneurial capitalism: the crushing of an "evil empire" typical of anti-soviet rhet-oric, the emphasis on individual "self-rule" rather than government-sponsored programs and policies, and the idealization of initiative and enterprise.

After the shoot-out, Cash's second-in-command steps into the power vacuum left by his death and claims triumphantly that there will be no more working for gringos, since Mexico "needs the money." This scene will later be replayed in the border *narcotraficante* film of Robert Rodriguez, *El Mariachi* (1992), with a gringo drug lord who, like Cash, is marked by his white suits and whose death in the final scene puts the business back into the hands of the Mexicans. This acknowledg-ment of the need for Mexican-owned and operated businesses seems like a gesture of fair-minded diplomacy on the part of the filmmaker, but the overall picture of Mexico lacks such grace. *Extreme Prejudice* relinquishes U.S. responsibility in the perpetuation of the drug trade, emphasizing a long-standing political position in the Washington war on drugs: the drug trade originates in Mexico and is solely a Mexican responsibility. In fact, the film represents Mexico as cultivating Cash Bailey's operations, offering an enabling context of lawlessness and corruption in which Cash operates with impunity. After he kills one of his henchmen, Cash claims, "It's a damn nice country here. I like it. Man can get away with anything long as he keeps paying his friends." Moreover, there are no Mexican law enforcement agencies collaborating on the various U.S. missions taking place in Mexico because they are all in cahoots with Cash. Cash Bailey's miniature empire seems to coexist peacefully with the nation it occupies.

In *Extreme Prejudice,* Mexico is the perfect location for the renegade operations of a deep-cover agent gone bad, where his decadence and moral lassitude are represented as cardinal features of the local character. The United States does not come off as cleanly as it does in a film like *Traffic,* where most of the bad guys are Mexican. But, in *Extreme Prejudice* all of the transgressive North Americans, including renegade major Paul Hackett, his commando unit, and drug kingpin Cash Bailey, are eliminated in one long gun battle. Like other drug trafficking films of the border genre, this film addresses the man apart, the lone Texas Ranger who, like Gary Cooper in *High Noon,* will act according to an unwavering sense of moral duty that represents the North American spirit.

Extreme Prejudice only obliquely refers to one of the major preoccupations of the war on drugs—the idea of the corruption of the deep cover agent and the intimacy of the police to the policed. *Deep Cover* (1992) delves deeper into the psychology of the undercover cop to examine the differences between the criminal mastermind and the moral crusader. It captures many of the tropes of the undercover cop film, especially of the proximity of the cop to his or her patrolled constituency. The only difference between the enemies, the film suggests, is that the cop has chosen to be "good" and law-abiding and the criminal has chosen to be "bad" and break laws. This reflects the moral philosophy so prevalent in narco-traffic border narratives, succinctly articulated in *Extreme Prejudice* by the wise old county sheriff: "Right way's the hardest, wrong way's the easiest." These cop narratives offer a facile Hollywood "do the right thing" morality tale that leads the viewer into properly identifying with the moral labors of the "good" cop, whose values will be challenged but ultimately upheld. *Deep Cover* links the street crack trade to the international drug trade, not as symptoms of socioeconomic conditions, but as signs of corruption and greed with deep roots south of the border. The conclusions are clear and unambiguous: both must be eliminated with extreme prejudice. Moreover, the film marks the shift from the border to urban centers of drug trade, yet the national line is always a point of reference, and the truly bad guys—the drug kingpin and his cronies—originate from the unspecified location of "Latin America," beyond the frontiers of the United States. Because the film was made in a post-Noriega scandal era, it depicts Washington as complicit with and protective of Latin American kingpins at the expense of local markets targeted by the drug trade, specifically those located in African-American communities.

Deep Cover is a cop bildungsroman tale in which we examine why and how the main character becomes a cop and the origins of his moral crusade. Of course, the story begins with the symbolic center of the war on drugs, the family, while emphasizing the legacy of the drug trade and drug abuse in the African-American community and the deeply racist roots of U.S. drug policy. Yet the critical perspective of the film is often overwhelmed by stereotypical images that undermine its anti-racist discourse, a discourse reserved only for the African-American characters. Depictions of crack houses and of crack-addicted Latinos and African-Americans are too abundant and uncontested, portrayed in a manner that falls neatly into dominant discourses about racial degeneracy. Along the same lines, *Deep Cover* depicts the Latin/o Americans as primitive and rapacious; for instance, when drug lord Felix Barbosa makes a lascivious comment about a white woman, his white sidekick remarks apologetically that "he can't help it . . . it's in his nature." But, unlike the Latin/o Americans, the African-American community, through the main character, will achieve redemption. The anti-racist discourse in the film is limited to a critical analysis of the African-American role and position in the war on drugs, whereas Latin/o Americans are relentlessly degenerate, cruel, and corrupt; most often they are ruthless drug lords who, with the complicity of Washington, are bent on destroying African-Americans.

Deep Cover opens with an analeptic and slow-motion shot of addicts smoking crack in a crack house, then cuts to a calm winter Christmas scene set in Cleveland in 1972 to create a mood in which "aberrant" resides intimately with "normal" domesticity. The internal voice-over of the main character accompanies this scene with an explanatory narration in "Night Before Christmas" style: "So gather round as I run it down and unravel my pedigree: my father was a junky." The narrator Russell Stevens, an African-American boy of about ten years old, listens to his father's warning not to be like him, then watches as his father attempts to rob a liquor store and is shot while holding the bloodied money. The child swears that the same fate will not befall him, but the narrator's ominous tone suggests otherwise. After another cut, we are in Cincinnati twenty years later, where the same boy is now an adult police officer being questioned by a racist white superior officer, Carver, who asks, "What is the difference between a black man and a nigger?" Two black officers have already failed this test, one by not knowing the answer and the other by reacting violently. Officer Russell Stevens (Laurence Fishburne) responds, "The nigger is the one that would even answer that question," and qualifies to become an undercover narcotics cop "on loan to the DEA." He passes thanks to his ability to anticipate racist stereotypes, which is taken as a sign of his authenticity and "street credibility." Moreover, the DEA's racism is treated as a matter of course, the stuff of a neutral test of aptitude where the rational maneuvering through a racist system is a sign of mettle and grit. This white and black dynamic constitutes the dominant epistemic order of the film; that is, there are two competing systems of knowledge that correspond to the film's dual aesthetic. One is coded white, dominant, and universal, which is represented by Carver, the DEA, and the Feds. Carver, for instance, knows everything before it occurs, which gives him the illusion of omniscience and omnipresence—he claims to be "god." When Stevens asks if he has ever killed anybody, Carver responds that he "went to Princeton to avoid all that shit." The "other" order of knowledge is urban, local, and coded as African-American. African-American characters are closely identified with popular and street culture through hip-hop visual and verbal aesthetics and references to Hollywood films and genres. For instance, a drug dealer, Ivy, regularly quotes from Arnold Schwarzenegger films, marking his violence with phrases like "Hasta la vista, baby," and "I'll be baack." Stevens represents the skepticism and anti-racism that mark this order of knowledge. Stevens' cardinal pose in the film is that of a disaffected and stoic distance. His removed status enables him to create a critical distance from the federal institution for which he works.[23] Like Texas Ranger Jack of *Extreme Prejudice*, Stevens uses this distance as his salvation from "big government," and his skepticism and critical distance are the Hollywood signs of his superior moral position. In all on-screen meetings between Stevens and Carver, the commanding officer appears in hazy and diffuse light while Stevens is fully lit to convey his moral clarity and sense of purpose.

Stevens is the reconstructed "snitch," the Hollywood narc whose efforts are not in the service of the war on drugs, but in reexamining its conditions and objectives within an analysis of black-white racial relations, in which Latin/o American drug traffickers are adjuncts of the white agenda. The anti-racist discourse of the film begins to take hold from the first interview scene and slowly develops until we no longer trust Carver or the entire DEA. The film captures an era in which high-level corruption was common knowledge—after government ties to Manuel Noriega had hit the press and scandalized the public. *Deep Cover* represents the African-American community's distrust of the government and systematically reveals why this distrust is justified. As the audience comes more and more to identify with Stevens, it becomes clear that the traffickers and the state that supports them are complicit in the spread of drugs that destroy African-American communities. African-Americans are sacrificed to the drug war in a manner that reflects widespread social indifference about racial oppression. When Stevens shoots and kills a rival black dealer, he realizes that nobody cares, and that he could continue murdering African-Americans without reprisal, just as the government is doing by enabling the transit of "crack" into the inner city.

Stevens initially declines the offer to be an undercover cop since he claims no immediate relation to the drug world. Yet we have already been given visual information to the contrary in the film's opening sequence in addition to the racist implication by the DEA that simply being African-American guarantees entrée into the world of drugs. Carver, the DEA agent, tells Stevens that he "score[s] almost exactly like a criminal" in his psychological profile, especially high in the areas of "rage" and "repressed violence," and that while undercover, all these faults will become virtues. Stevens only has to follow one rule: "Don't blow your cover." By breaking this rule in the end, Stevens marks his final disaffection from the "system."

From Stevens' first appearance in the interview with Carver, the camera seems to hang on shots of his stoic expression and pensive but penetrating gaze. These intimate shots lead into the internal voice-over narration addressed, at points, directly to the audience—one of few racialized male internal voice narrations besides that of *American Me*, in which the speaker builds an analysis of his place in a racist system. The narration creates intimacy with the audience who are privy to the secret codes of the deep cover operation. Stevens carries the privileged vantage in the film; his expressions gauge the narrative mood, and for much of

3.3 In *Deep Cover*, Russell Stevens (Laurence Fishburne), an undercover agent "on loan to the DEA," is marked by his stoic expression and penetrating gaze.

the film he lends the viewer insight into the drug world on the streets from the perspective of an insider. The voice-over guides the viewer from Stevens' work as deep agent to his descent into fully occupying the role of drug dealer, but it also brings the viewer squarely back into the moral mission of the drug war when he ultimately regains his cop persona. The narrative, after a short waylay, builds toward the creation of the African-American narc hero, who is deeply critical of a corrupt and racist system.

Stevens is instructed to go after the "big guys" in a long chain of command leading back to Latin America; never is a single nation in the Americas singled out, but rather the whole of Latin America stands in for a few possible countries of origin. Carver pinpoints Felix Barbosa, who is "like a middle level executive" who "supplies the guys who supply the guys who supply the street." Barbosa in turn gets his stuff from the number one importer of the West Coast, Anton Gallegos. Gallegos is successful because his uncle Hector Guzman is an "influential Latin American politician" who helps him smuggle the product into the country. Carver tells Stevens to get the nephew in order to "smear the uncle," as he points to a pyramid-like chart of the proto-corporate drug empire—a similar layout will reappear in the short-lived television series *Kingpin*. Stevens inquires whether his final aim is to inculpate the politician Guzman, a Manuel Noriega–like figure, but the commanding officer evades the issue, suggesting a complicity of the U.S. Feds with crooked "Latin American politicians." This scenario reflects the dynamics of high-level corruption on the part of the United States, which had been protecting real-life Panamanian dictator Manuel Noriega from investigation for his involvement in drug trafficking since the 1960s.[24] The U.S. government used Noriega as an intelligence source to snitch on those whom he allowed use of the Panama Canal to transport drugs, but the government later indicted him for doing so; Samuel I. del Villar concisely describes this debacle as the "DEA-CIA-Justice-State-White House-Noriega entanglement."[25]

Stevens quickly becomes a big-time dealer by collaborating with a rich white lawyer and drug trafficker, David Jason (Jeff Goldblum). He achieves this success to his utter dismay: "I hated doing what I was doing, but I was good at it. Being a cop was never this easy." Stevens echoes the simple moral philosophy of the county sheriff from *Extreme Prejudice*, who contends the "right way's the hardest." Unlike *Extreme Prejudice*, which appeals to the morally righteous Anglo male viewer, *Deep Cover* is a drug narrative aimed at viewers on either side of the war on drugs, especially African-American viewers. It opens up a discourse about transformation and rehabilitation through personal will in a post-self-help era; it promulgates the idea that anyone can turn from being an object of the war on drugs—a drug dealer or consumer—to an active subject or narc hero of the war on drugs, opening up a narrative space for the emergence of characters like ex-gang member turned DEA agent Sean Vetters of *A Man Apart* (2003).

3.4 Stevens quickly becomes a big-time dealer by collaborating with a rich white lawyer and drug trafficker, David Jason (Jeff Goldblum).

Stevens moves quickly into the center of the drug empire, becoming Jason's partner in his apocalyptic scheme, like an illicit pharmaceutical company, to produce an opiate that will make people more efficient and better workers without side effects. They consult a "scientist" who produces the molecular model of cocaine, which through some variation and the addition of another molecule becomes the super drug that for five million dollars can be produced for the whole West Coast at "thirty cents a pop," although "the world'll cost more." This recalls a similar scheme later in *Kingpin* in which the main character is introduced to a new drug, liquid heroin, whose properties point to the future of the drug trade because the drug are so easy to produce and deliver that its ubiquity and global dissemination are ensured. Of course, both of these scenarios reflect the mid-1980s marketing of "crack," in which cocaine was mass-produced for greater profit to expand operations beyond a middle-class and often affluent market to those with less disposable income, specifically consumers in inner cities and racialized ghettoes. "Crack" was much cheaper than powder cocaine and much more addictive, which led to an epidemic of chronic users among the most socially marginal groups and increased crime and inner-city violence.[26]

The symbol of the 1980s public health panic that fueled public sentiment in the war on drugs was the "crack baby" and all that it implied about the genealogy of drug addiction. The crack baby, always African-American, was a symbol that distilled centuries of discourse about racial determinism. Just as Stevens is beginning to lose faith in the deep cover operation, Carver uses crack babies to remind him why he is on the streets and adds that a whole generation of "your people are being destroyed before they're even born because these guys, Barbosa, Gallegos, and Guzman, are bringing that shit into this country." The anti-racist discourse of the film aimed at critically framing the African-American position in the war on drugs sacrifices Latin/o Americans in an overly simplistic analysis of the drug trade—where eliminating the source commandeered by evil Latin/o American kingpins would resolve the problems plaguing the African-American community. Any passing allusions to U.S. involvement in the drug trade are eclipsed by the portrait of Latin/o American ruthlessness and corruption. This simple notion that cutting off the supply from Latin America would decrease the collateral damage of the street drug trade dominated by people of color from the lowest socioeconomic bracket had become the standard discourse of the war on drugs. Of course, this simplistic scenario obviates a discussion of the real dynamics and conditions that create and sustain the drug trade.

Stevens discovers that the DEA is actually protecting the Latin American kingpin Guzman so that he can "run for president down there someday." Stevens is outraged: "What is he, the new Noriega? He helps you fight communists, you let him bring drugs into the country to sell it to niggers and spics and you use me to do that shit?" He becomes so disillusioned by the corrupt police system that he refuses to continue colluding with it. Stevens, who was never seduced by the drug trade lifestyle, suddenly finds refuge in it. He quits the police force and takes his first hit of the drugs he has been dealing. At this point, he relinquishes his police badge and becomes an actual drug dealer. The viewer follows suit and briefly abandons the moral safety of the police story, but not for long. As in many Hollywood "narc" films, Stevens truly becomes a dedicated narc when he works alone and beyond the limits of the law as a vigilante hero.

Before Stevens reverts back to his moral position, he and Jason meet with Guzman—the corrupt Latin American politician who "goes fishing with George fucking Bush"—to propose funding of the super drug. This new drug, Jason claims, is "completely synthetic, therefore no growing, no refining, no peasants, best of all, no international borders, no customs agents," to which Guzman replies, "You racist Americans, you just want to cut us poor Hispanics completely out of the market," in a rare moment of recognition of racism directed at Latin/o Americans. But Jason neutralizes this remark by claiming that the globalized market does not recognize national boundaries, only wealth: "No Mr. Guzman, I think you know that there's no such thing as an American anymore, no Hispanics, no Japanese, no blacks, no whites, no nothing, it's just rich people and poor people. The three of us are all rich so we're on the same side." The lawyer expresses the triumphs of globalization as those of complete indifference, echoing the politics of U.S. free trade imperialism, the consequence of which is greater inequity between rich and poor nations.

The meeting at this point is foiled by the only good cop left, the lone narc haunting the margins of the plot. This African-American cop, nicknamed the "Reverend," believes that drug trade and street crime are consequences of "evil." Though he is a good cop, he is an exemplary sacrifice to critical racial discourse that targets corrupt institutions. Yet, when the "Reverend" is shot, Stevens regains his critical racial awareness and returns to his moral position as "snitch." Stevens' individual struggle between following the letter of the law and succumbing to corruption is depicted as part of a larger problem in the police force. The internal division within the police force between corrupt and honest cops is eclipsed by the greater moral division across the Americas that separates North from South, emphasized by the fact that there are no honest or justice-seeking Latin/o Americans anywhere in the entire plot. The film associates Latin/o Americans with corruption across the hemisphere, corruption that negatively affects African-Americans. For instance, when a crooked Latino cop needs some busts to seem legitimate, one of the drug kingpins offers a Jewish lawyer, but the cop claims to need some "spades," since politicians like "the dark faces, so they can scare the suburbs into voting Republican."

Stevens is forced to cover up all the corruption he witnessed and praise the DEA in exchange for the release of Betty, his money launderer and budding love interest. He follows these orders, but at his congressional hearing he offers an incriminating video of Hector Guzman, "friend of presidents," meeting with drug dealers. *Deep Cover* criticizes racist state and federal institutions and agencies, though it does not fully address systemic social conditions relating to racism and the drug trade. In the course of the narrative, we as viewers undergo several critical transformations in identification that lend insight into the ambiguities and complexities of the police system. We begin squarely in the realm of the cop, a firmly established moral position that, in characters like Jack in *Extreme Prejudice,* rarely wavers. Yet, as Stevens gets deeper into his cover, the boundary between his cop persona and his drug dealer cover begins to blur. Against our expectations, Stevens does not cross this boundary because of some internal predisposition, weakness, or greed; rather, he becomes a full-time dealer out of disaffection from the corrupt and racist police system. Stevens exposes the link between high-level state corruption and street cop corruption within the U.S. war of indifference against African-Americans. By the end of the film, Stevens reverts back to his moral position and becomes the lone narc who takes on the racist system corroborated by the Latin/o American drug trade. He strikes a deal with the state, receives exoneration, and gets the girl, Betty. But, the ending of the film is ambiguous. When asked by Carver what he did with the money appropriated from the drug lords, Stevens responds with the same answer to the racist question that begins the film. By withholding the money from the DEA, he has finally gotten one over on the system that had used him for its corrupt purposes.

In the final voice-over sequence, Stevens lets the audience in on a secret, informing us that he took eleven million dollars in drug profits and now is in a quandary: if he keeps the money, he's a criminal, but if he returns it, he's a fool. He inculpates the audience, closing the gap in identification between him and us: "It's an impossible choice, but in a way we all have to make it. What would you do?" The film ends with the image of Stevens placing a rose and a fistful of bloodied bills, reminiscent of those in his father's hand in the opening scene, on the gravestone of his neighbor, Belinda, who died of a drug overdose; this image gives us no clues about how he resolves the closing dilemma. Yet we identify with the only police special agent not inculpated in the high-level corruption between the U.S. government and Latin American leaders; this obviates a more sustained critique of these relations while foregrounding the ideal narc hero for our consumption. The moral and ideological messiness of the story is superseded by the individualist fantasy of Stevens getting the girl and the money and taking off into the sunset, or in the dictum of the genre, "making a run for the border."

A few years after the depiction of government corruption in *Deep Cover*, on February 6, 1996, General Barry R. McCaffrey was sworn in as the new drug czar, the director of the Office of National Drug Control Strategy. He promised to introduce more effective means of control and prevention by doing away with the obsolete language of the "war on drugs," emphasizing treatment of the "cancer" of addiction, and he described his efforts in less grandiose terms as "anti-drug." McCaffrey was determined to launch an aggressive campaign using Hollywood film and media culture and other outlets of mass media—radio, video, print journalism, and Internet—to send anti-drug messages. To this end, he began a major advertising campaign in 1997 and intensified efforts to encourage and mentor Hollywood directors and writers to incorporate anti-drug themes and storylines. He wrote a series of articles for various nationwide periodicals that outlined his platform and proposals for eradicating drug use. Choosing the appropriate community of readers at the center of the entertainment industry, McCaffrey wrote an article for the *Los Angeles Times* on January 2, 1997, that called on the "mass media to honor the highest ideals that make the creative arts the repository of our collective cultural heritage."[27] He exhorts the media industry to take up the anti-drug cause: "The news and entertainment industries owe it to our youth to portray realistically the dangerous consequences of illegal drug use. Writers and producers of comedy series might think about the impact of subtle 'wink and nod' acceptance of illegal drugs as well as blatant pro-drug messages that put teens at risk."[28] Later, his methods came under attack as violating the First Amendment and Federal Communications Commission (FCC) regulations; he would reward major television networks for adding anti-drug content into programming by releasing them from federally mandated advertising airtime.[29] By the middle of 2000, McCaffrey, after public criticism from the television scandal, strategically shifted his target to the Hollywood film industry, disingenuously claiming, "As powerful as television is, some experts believe that movies have an even stronger impact on young people."[30] He proposed the use of workshops, briefings, and conversations rather than financial incentives to persuade the industry to adopt anti-drug content and themes.

Traffic, released the same year that McCaffrey turned his gaze entirely to Hollywood, benefited from the persuasive spin of the media drug czar.

3.5 *Traffic*'s drug czar, Robert Wakefield, bears similarities to real-life U.S. drug czar General Barry R. McCaffrey.

Traffic's fictional drug czar, Robert Wakefield, is clearly modeled on McCaffrey. Yet Wakefield is a more amiable and softer Hollywood version that must have pleased the delicate ego of the real drug czar who, according to insiders, spent an inordinate amount of time and resources on his public image.[31] After McCaffrey's term came to an end, the position relapsed to its former low profile on the landscape of popular culture.

Traffic plays off the then drug czar's straight talking, no-nonsense approach to enforcement, but it uses the Hollywood machine to leverage an objective lost in McCaffrey's campaign: the cooperation of Mexican officials. The film cites a well-known corruption scandal involving the Mexican drug enforcement chief, who was discovered to be in cahoots with Amado Carrillo Fuentes, the biggest cocaine trafficker in the country, just days after drug czar McCaffrey had praised the chief for his successful and admirable work in his anti-drug campaign.[32] The same scenario is replayed in *Traffic* as a seeming indictment of the drug czar. But, in a manner that would speak to McCaffrey's faith in the power of media, the film imagines the collaboration of the Mexican policeman Javier, played by U.S.-based Puerto Rican actor Benicio Del Toro, in U.S. anti-drug efforts, making the Latin/o American borderlands native to the narc hero.

3.6 *Traffic* features a pair of Mexican cops, Javier (Benicio Del Toro) and Manolo (Jacob Vargas).

Traffic departs somewhat from other films of the drug trafficking genre in the way it foregrounds Mexican law enforcement at the border. To emphasize this new vantage, the film opens in the desert, twenty miles southeast of Tijuana, with a pair of Mexican cops, Javier and Manolo. As in *Touch of Evil*, we will soon learn that the real moral hero is the Mexican cop, but in this case his moral crusade is hitched to the machinery of the U.S. drug war. The idea of the righteous hero alone in a sea of NAFTA-esque corruption derives from a U.S.-based cowboy mythos, but in this case it masquerades as Mexican to fulfill the larger political agenda of expressing the need for better cooperation of Latin American governments in U.S.-backed and based drug control programs. Though Mexico had been cooperating with the United States for decades, the popular impression was that of Mexican reluctance to participate in the war on drugs. This was a false impression; ever since Operation Intercept in 1969, the Mexican government has been coerced to "cooperate." In fact, Operation Intercept was a successful attempt to apply pressure to Mexico and resulted in the creation of the U.S.-lead transnational effort, Operation Cooperation.[33]

From the very beginning of *Traffic*, there is little room for moral ambiguity; the whole first part of the film is a series of arrests and apprehensions of everyone involved in the drug trade. However, there is a nod to the ambiguities of the liberal drug culture of the 1960s when Wakefield's wife, a relic of this era, claims to have "experimented" with everything. She is depicted as morally weak and misguided for wanting to allow her daughter, already an addict, to explore and figure things out for herself, but there is no such messy liberalism for Mr. Wakefield. Any moral ambiguity about illicit drugs is quickly eclipsed by the message that drugs are bad and drug dealers—mostly black or Latin/o American—are exploiting and dehumanizing Anglo-Americans.

The overall attitude toward Mexico is immediately apparent in its visual register. Director Steven Soderbergh himself explains that he shot all scenes in Mexico through a "tobacco filter" and then oversaturated the film, which gives Mexico the look of the Old West. For Richard Porton, the effect is that Mexico "becomes a miragelike, evanescent realm where life is cheap and morality is infinitely expendable."[34] He cites a similar analysis by Catherine Benamou in which she argues that *Traffic* poses a postmodern United States against a premodern Mexico, "which has presumably never been able to draw the line between the law and lawlessness."[35] The Mexican government's backward attitudes about drug control confirm this portrait of Mexico as backward. The U.S. drug czar Robert Wakefield soon discovers that nobody is doing anything about drug control in Mexico, and that they have no position that corresponds to his. Wakefield thinks that he might have found his counterpart in General Salazar, not knowing that Salazar is involved with a Tijuana cartel. Salazar is not only ruthless, but also cold-hearted, unlike the empathic and deeply committed Wakefield. During an interview, Salazar admits to having no treatment program, suggesting that when addicts overdose, they receive their "treatment." The trafficker informant Eddie tells us, "In Mexico, law enforcement is an entrepreneurial activity," and that NAFTA makes everything easier, echoing every sentiment that drives the Hollywood line. Yet there are problems on both sides of the border; the Mexican government is mired in institutional corruption, whereas the United States is mired in bureaucracy and due process in a holdover from the Reagan era critique of big government. For instance, Carlos, a major U.S.-based kingpin, is captured by DEA agents but released on what seems like a technicality when the only witness against him is murdered. If Mexico is corrupt, the United States is too law-abiding.

Although there are no targeted "enemies" in the war on drugs, *Traffic* depicts Mexico as the real enemy. This attitude dates back to 1969, when the United States, angered by Mexico's refusal to consider crop destruction as a viable anti-drug measure, enacted Operation Intercept (mentioned earlier as the first battle in the war on drugs), the largest ever search and seizure operation along the border. The search created epic traffic jams and a near standstill at the border that gravely affected commerce and productivity for the borderlands region, particularly for many Mexicans on their way to work on the other side of the border.[36] Ted Galen Carpenter called the operation "an exercise in international extortion, pure and simple and effective, designed to bend Mexico to our will."[37] Mexico took just two weeks to capitulate to Washington's demands and allowed the paraquat marijuana eradication project to take place.[38] The United States thus began a series of games of intimidation that targeted and played out along the border.

The ideal narc, the only character who we find trustworthy and unwavering in his commitment to justice, is Javier, a poorly paid and humble Tijuana cop. He is not a corrupt narc like Manolo who wants private gain for information he holds, but exhibits just the right amount of remorse for selling out his compatriots to the U.S. government, a transgression that is eclipsed by his internal moral rectitude. *Traffic* is ostensibly about the war at home, but projects the narc sensibility onto the Latin/o American character, one who as a border resident encompasses both spaces: he is bilingual and travels readily in both Mexican and U.S. cultures. Within the logic of the film, the ideal viewer is not the Anglo family whose position against drug trafficking has been well established and confirmed across popular media and culture, but the transnational Latin/o American whose cultural fluidity and access is a valuable commodity in the war on drugs. Javier gives up his coveted information because he believes that it is the "right thing" to do. He is the new cowboy on the frontier, the "American" hero who stands up for what he believes is right. But, more importantly, he does so in a way that privileges the role of the transnational American narc to encourage and promote collaboration across the Americas. The ideal described by Elliott Abrams, assistant secretary for inter-American affairs, of complete integration of the policing agencies across the hemisphere in the war on drugs is finally imagined in *Traffic*.

Kingpin (NBC 2003), written and produced by David Mills of *NYPD Blue* fame, is slightly different from other Hollywood media of the same genre for its post-*Sopranos* ethos of using outlaw protagonists as the primary agents of the narrative. Many of the major actors of Latino cinema of the 1990s appear in *Kingpin*, giving it the illusion of being a Latino cultural production, yet really the show contributes to a longstanding Hollywood association of criminality and Latinos. The series traces a family of Mexican drug traffickers based in Ciudad Juárez who run *la corporación* as they change leadership and deal with internal tensions and struggles for power. The only law that the family-run business of drug trade abides is the law of higher returns in the cold-hearted pursuit of profit, a pursuit that transcends ideological, sexual, national, and racial boundaries. After a series of shifts in power, the patriarch of the drug family is established in the character of Miguel Cadena. We almost forget that Miguel is the head of a major cartel; he seems to comport himself with diplomacy and business savvy and acumen. He runs *la corporación* like, well, a corporation. Nonetheless, the actions of his ruthless brother Chato remind us at every turn that this family traffics in a NAFTA-esque scoundrel capitalism. As we follow the life and operations of Miguel, we also follow other competing storylines about DEA agents, undercover cops, and street dealers. The moral lesson is always just below the surface, and the privileged perspective belongs to the cops, especially DEA agent Delia Flores.

The pilot episode of *Kingpin* opens in the desert on the Mexican side of the border. Like *Traffic*, it opens by exposing the collusion of drug traffickers with the state, represented in this case by the governor of Ciudad Juárez. Ernesto, the new kingpin replacing his exiled father Jorge, has crackpot dreams of building a tunnel from this region into the United States, a plan upon which the more prudent Miguel casts aspersions. These tunnels along the border region symbolize popular anxieties about various kinds of "underground" plots against the United States. The series deliberately exploits the various unconscious associations of the borderlands with hidden secrets and transgressions. The pilot moves swiftly among the many regions and players of the drug trade— from Ciudad Juárez to Houston, El Paso, Mazatlán and Colombia—to suggest a wide circuit of connectivity. The pilot episode ends with the song "Walking in the Rain" by Grace Jones, as the

DEA agent, Delia Flores, who was shot by Ernesto earlier, recovers and Marlene, Miguel's gringa wife, snorts lines of coke in her darkroom. The series reverses the Western typology of the pious blonde Anglo-American woman and the transgressive Latina, but this reversal serves the larger narco-border narrative ideology of the ethnic or racialized hero on the frontlines of the war on drugs. Delia's role is part of a genealogy of racialized narc heroes that derives from Stevens in *Deep Cover* and Javier in *Traffic* and that leads directly to Sean Vetters of *A Man Apart*.

The series grafts many of the nightmare rollbacks of workers' rights onto the drug trade version of neo-liberal capitalism, in which factories move below the border to seek cheaper wages and longer work hours. In this case, the owner of a methamphetamine laboratory along the border demands a major increase in production, and when one of the workers asks if there will be more workers to aid this process, the boss replies that in fact, there will be one less employee, and asks the man to leave. This cruel scenario plays on fears about downsizing, disposable workers, and the increased burdens on remaining workers as features of a competitive, bottom line–driven global market. While playing on these fears, the show disabuses the North American public of them at the same time. This kind of outlaw capitalism is represented as limited to Mexico so that the viewer's outrage might be deflected onto a more suitable foreign object.

Kingpin thematizes the games of retribution initiated by the United States against Mexico, referring especially to the 1985 incident in which the United States government acted out its frustrations with Mexico, using the border as a stage for political payback. In 1985, when real-life DEA agent Enrique Camarena, on assignment in Mexico, had been too successful in his investigation, he was murdered, allegedly by one of Mexico's major drug lords. The United States, angered by the slow pace and incompetence of the Mexican legal investigation on this matter, retaliated with Operation Intercept II, which slowed down checkpoint operations at the border for millions of Mexican workers who crossed it daily to work in the United States. This, of course, enraged the Mexicans who lived and worked on the border.[39] Camarena's murder occasioned a vigilante cowboy response on the part of the United States DEA, which put bounties on those involved in the crime, resulting in a number of kidnappings, and threatened extradition to the United States for the perpetrators.[40]

In *Kingpin*, the general of the Mexican army, under pressure from the U.S. government to avenge the death of a DEA agent, blows up the maquiladora-like methamphetamine laboratory. But in the logic of the series, the United States is more victim than aggressor. The U.S. role in this offense is eclipsed when the general admits to pandering to the United States and offers to do the same for the Cadena family, demanding three million dollars a month for the secure transport of contraband. The corrupt general is a stock character of the Hollywood narco-trafficking film, again recalling General Salazar of *Traffic* who is in cahoots with the Tijuana cartel. As in *Traffic*, the Mexican state is depicted as the real enemy in the war on drugs.

Kingpin takes the same route that most narco-traffic media take; cocaine addiction finds its way into Miguel's house and family and claims his white wife, Marlene. Miguel sends her to a rehabilitation clinic that puts her to work cleaning a kitchen, the worst possible punishment for the wealthy leisure class. Marlene is miserable in her group therapy. She claims that drug addiction is a choice and refuses the twelve-step mantra that she is powerless over her addiction, which gets her into a big brawl with the other fallen housewives. This refusal of the twelve-step mantra signals a cultural shift around the discourses of rehabilitation and recovery. By the year 2000, many major popular magazines— including *Vogue, Elle,* and *New York Times Magazine*—ran articles that were critical of the recovery discourses of the 1980s, and the number of twelve-step centered clinics had diminished by half.[41] Marlene reflects this transformation; she refuses the rhetoric of "disease" in lieu of that of free choice, in keeping with the moral logic of the narco-border narrative. Her character provides a powerful testament to the North American glorification of the will of the individual, the same will that is at the center of the entrepreneurial spirit of capitalism. She exhibits this spirit often as she pushes Miguel to take a more commanding role in the family business, until he becomes the undisputed kingpin. But this ambitious drive poisons the entire family. Miguel and his wife and son are haunted by nightmares, which serve as cautionary mini-narratives about the return of traumatic memories and the psychological damage associated with involvement in illicit activities. The family is destabilized by *la corporación,* and the series ends with the unraveling of each member of the extended family. Although the short-lived series is ostensibly about a drug trafficking family, the Cadenas never set the narrative moral terms. Instead, the exemplary figure is Delia Flores, the narc DEA agent.

Like a true narc, Delia forges on relentlessly with an investigation, even when she is told not to continue, until the "bad" guys are caught. She acts alone, according to an internal sense of duty and justice that is not determined or limited by her job description. She is the exemplary narc, and her character provides the moral backbone and message of the series. She seems to be modeled on the female therapist Dr. Jennifer Melfi of *The Sopranos* (A&E 1999–2007), who is unconnected to the larger network of family and business relations and who provides a proto-feminist reservoir in the midst of an often misogynist plot. Delia occupies a position typically reserved for the male hero; we witness her riding on horseback alone across the desert, an allusion to the border genre's abiding symbol, the male cowboy. She exhibits the vigilantism of the cop cowboy when she takes justice into her own hands and operates as a renegade agent. When she gets transferred to Houston, she takes the initiative to infiltrate a private club to investigate a drug ring and, like many border heroes before her, she crosses the line by going against orders from her superior officers. In familiar ends-justify-means logic, this individual pursuit of justice will lead to the only successful operation by the DEA in the series.

Kingpin was extremely short-lived, perhaps because it was too risqué for network television, but it succeeded in continuing the tropes of Hollywood drug war media. The Cadena family portrait conveyed the impression of the decadence and internal dissolution of the Latin/o American *corporación*, which, had the series continued, would have lead to its total devastation at the hands of the DEA. *Deep Cover, Traffic, Kingpin*, and *A Man Apart* all present the new agent of anti-drug warfare as the agent of color, the solitary narc hero who takes down *la corporación* with insider ethnic, linguistic, or racial knowledge—knowledge that the Anglo heroes lack. The mediated war on drugs targets ethnic audience identification with these heroes while it presents the image of collaboration across ethnic/racial and national lines; this, in turn, would suggest that the National Drug Control Policy is effective across the hemisphere.

SUPPORT OUR TROPES

Popular perceptions of the war on drugs are overwhelmingly negative. Few Americans across the hemisphere believe that the United States has made any progress, and the facts and figures of the drug war only confirm the public's worst fears. All manners of production and consumption show dramatic increases over time, and the role and function of the DEA have been under serious scrutiny. The government, it seems, has run out of ideas. In *Traffic*, when drug czar Wakefield gathers the heads of various agencies engaged in the war on drugs, he asks them to "think outside the box"—the annoying refrain of the new creative thinking discourse. As they sit encapsulated in a plane thousands of miles removed from the practical realities below, Wakefield tells them to consider new ideas regardless of viability or cost. The silence is uncomfortable, but the message is clear: all possibilities have been exhausted. But, only a few years later, a new idea emerged on the horizon of popular culture. *A Man Apart* uses many of the same tropes and themes as the war on drugs media that precede it, but it changes the protagonist DEA cop to an African-American ex-gang member. The good-guy/bad-guy schism of films like *Extreme Prejudice*, *Traffic*, and *Deep Cover* is enfolded into the character of Sean Vetter, played by bi-racial muscleman Vin Diesel. Diesel's character puts heroism and faith back into the DEA agent; he is good, but not self-righteous. Unlike characters in drug trafficking films of the 1990s like *Deep Cover*, Diesel makes the character and occupation of the DEA agent seem appealing to urban youth. As a mixed-race actor racially marked as a light-skinned African-American, he bridges the split racial imaginary of the war on drugs.

A Man Apart begins with flashes of images of cocaine, drug-related murders, and headlines from the war on drugs. The opening shot swoops in from the Pacific Ocean to the San Diego border while DEA agent Sean Vetter informs the audience in voice-over: "Mexican cartels have 1500 miles of border between them and the greatest drug-consuming nation on earth, separated by a fifteen-foot-high fence which starts at the Pacific Ocean and travels the distance of four states." The next shot takes us to a warehouse where Latino workers cut cocaine. The voice-over continues: "They flood our streets, day after day, week after week at an average of twenty tons a month. Now that's enough to provide a line of cocaine for every man, woman, and child on this planet." This opening sequence is perhaps the most compelling of the entire film by linking the border to a paranoid vision of the worldwide proliferation of cocaine. The film degenerates quickly into a hyperkinetic series of massive shoot-outs and chase scenes lorded over by Diesel, the overly muscled and volatile super–DEA agent.

A Man Apart opens with a major deal that goes down in south central L.A. The voice-over describes the drug's origins in Colombia, then the image switches to the Mexican flag in Tijuana, establishing the link among Colombian and Mexican cartels and the cocaine's destination in south central Los Angeles. This is a commonplace of drug trafficking stories like *Kingpin, Deep Cover*, and *Traffic*; all establish a similar national and racial dynamic. The next scene features Colombian drug lord Memo, who exploits opportunities presented by Mexico's northern border towns; in his first appearance he gives a speech in which he expresses gratitude for the ratification of the North American Free Trade Agreement (NAFTA). Like *Traffic, A Man Apart* holds NAFTA responsible for the proliferation of drug trade.

By 2003, sixteen years after the release of *Extreme Prejudice*, the themes, tropes, issues, and ideas in drug trafficking media had not changed. Yet, by the late 1990s the dynamics of the global traffic in drugs had changed completely. The nonprofit policy, research, and advocacy organization known as the Washington Office on Latin America had been studying and monitoring the impact of U.S. policy and the war on drugs across the hemisphere with the aim of "increased public and policymaker debate on drug policy issues and, ultimately, a shift toward alternative policies that are both more effective and more humane."[42] The editors of the organization's manifesto, Coletta A. Youngers and Eileen Rosin, begin by disabusing readers of many of the fundamental beliefs about drug trafficking dynamics in the Americas. For example, they point out that the market distinction between the Latin American producer and the U.S. consumer is no longer a viable model.[43] The United States is a major producer of marijuana and crystal methamphetamine and illicit drug consumption has risen sharply across Latin America and the Caribbean.[44] They argue that there are "fundamental flaws in the supply-side approach" to the war on drugs, embodied in the image of the Latin American drug producer that has become a cardinal feature of the Hollywood film and media culture. Most films stake out the Latin/o American kingpin whose elimination is a major part of the narrative resolution, and *A Man Apart* continues this facile plot structure.

Sean Vetter's anti-narcotics unit is one of the most successful because it is comprised of agents from the streets who "don't look or act like cops." As the head of the DEA gives a speech about shutting down cocaine distribution in Southern California, we see images of the takeover of a cocaine refinery in Mexico by another more deadly entity under the leadership of the cold-blooded and ubiquitous "Diablo." As part of the terrorizing campaign that signals new leadership in the drug trade, a gunman enters Sean's house and murders his wife, thus inaugurating a revenge narrative. Vetter rallies the rest of the agents around him with the idea that the new organization that is taking over everything will flood the West Coast with cocaine, which he warns, in the tired rhetoric of the drug war, will "come into their fucking homes." His police brutality method of dealing with suspects gets him suspended from the force. But, like any good old American Hollywood hero, he does not let this stop him from delivering the bad guys to justice. The final half of the film is pure chase and gun battle as we follow Sean as he tries to extract information from various characters about the whereabouts of "Diablo." His dialogue lapses into the refrain of "Answer the question!" shouted in menacing tones. In the end, he avenges his wife's death, eliminates the kingpin, and is restored to the DEA unit by his superiors. This simple film is part of the media that serve the larger purpose of restoring audience faith in the long-derided professional narcs, the DEA. Sean Vetters gives credence to the notion that the war on drugs is successful. Yet, the war on drugs has been called "America's longest war" and a sign of America being "addicted to failure" for its lack of efficiency and effectivity.[45]

Hollywood film and media culture sets viewer expectations and responses and suggests connections among drugs, border control, and terrorism that continue to shape the cultural agenda into the present. These modern Westerns achieve resolution by eliminating the remainders and reminders of U.S. wars of intervention, particularly Vietnam, and by knocking off the Latin/o American drug kingpin. A major plotline in all of these films and media involves the work of a narc hero, someone who acts alone and according to an internal moral imperative to bring down drug trafficking kingpins, suggesting that deep-rooted and complex drug trade issues are readily "solvable" through the U.S.-sponsored war on drugs. This contradicts the popular conception that the war on drugs has been a phenomenal failure, a hemorrhaging of funds that has merely intensified drug trafficking–related violence and increased production and distribution across the Americas. Hollywood drug trafficking films do not address changes in dynamics across the Americas that severely undercut the division between producer and consumer nations. The war on drugs is not reframed, but reinvigorated with the redeployment of the same tropes.

A Man Apart (2003) puts the drug war into the action genre; as the title suggests, the man apart is the consummate narc warrior, but this time he is an African-American ex-gang member who uses his rehabilitated street savvy to bring down drug lords. As with all the heroes of Hollywood films, the impetus behind Sean's relentless pursuit of the "bad guys" is personal, originating in the family but becoming the aim of an honest and noble citizen. This radically reconstructed DEA agent represents the new way, the new narc hero in the reconfigured and renovated image of the war on drugs.

FOUR

URBAN FRONTIERS

BORDER CINEMA AND THE
GLOBAL CITY

" . . . every state is a border state, and almost every city
is a border city."

—SPEAKER OF THE HOUSE J. DENNIS HASTERT IN
A PRESS CONFERENCE ABOUT THE PERVASIVENESS
OF THE NEED FOR INCREASED BORDER AND
IMMIGRATION CONTROL AS AN IMPERATIVE OF
NATIONAL SECURITY (OCTOBER 2006)

n March 2006, Angelinos staged the largest demon-
stration in the history of the city against a bill that
would further demonize undocumented immigrants
and those who granted them employment, and build
a fortress-like wall along the border. The whole nation focused its gaze upon the city as various news
programs turned their attention to the issue of immigration and the borderlands. Los Angeles became the epicenter of the immigration debate
not only for its large Latino population and its employment in the shadow
of the Hollywood media industry, but for its proximity to another mythological construction, the border between the United States and Mexico.
Many critics have described Los Angeles as a border city that harbors the
border as part of the experience of its topography.[1] The idea of Los Angeles as a border city is not meant to diminish the trauma of border crossing
or the disorienting experience of entering a new territory or a new nation-
state, but rather to explore the various real and symbolic effects of the arbitrary designation of borders and boundaries. The border emerges in the
city as a symbolic boundary and a complex of operations, especially in
the technologies of surveillance that reach northward and link up to the
policing agencies within the city. Border policies target areas of the city
that have their own economies and mythoi of sovereignty; abandoned by
the city proper, they become tantamount to separate national entities.

Luis J. Rodriguez nicely captures this urban respatialization in his collection of short stories, appropriately entitled *The Republic of East L.A.*

Many critical Latino films based in Los Angeles link the national borderline with divisions across the city— *El Norte* (1983), *Born in East L.A.* (1987), *Stand and Deliver* (1988), *American Me* (1992), *Mi vida loca* (1993), *My Family/Mi Familia* (1995), *Star Maps* (1997), *Bread and Roses* (2000), and *Real Women Have Curves* (2002)—crystallizing the association of the divided city with border and immigration policies built on typologies of inclusion and exclusion and other schizoid dyads of colonialism: citizen and alien, "legal" and "illegal," white and "of color," developed and underdeveloped, First and Third World, and civilization and barbarism. These films challenge the polarization of Los Angeles and expose the exclusion and denigration of Latinos, Chicanos, and Latin American immigrants in the largest border city of the Southwest. The perceived boundaries among neighborhoods become national boundaries. Often those living in these neighborhood republics are represented as objects of police and INS surveillance and control, while middle-class Anglos are objects of police protection. Several of these films explore the literal separation of Latino neighborhoods from the rest of the city. For instance, in *El Norte*, Rosa, upon her acclimation to Los Angeles, is mystified by the absence of Anglos until her friend informs her that they can be found sequestered in their own neighborhoods. The Chicano residents of east L.A. or Echo Park are subject to discriminatory surveillance by the police, e.g., in *Mi vida loca* and *American Me*, or recent immigrants live in constant fear of the INS, e.g., in *El Norte*. These films deploy stories of identity formation and cultural conflict within narratives critical of the disparities and divisions rendered by uneven disbursements of public funds and the fracturing economies of globalization. One of the primary ideological aims of Latino cinema has been to expose inequities, which supports and enables the different though tandem purpose of imagining different urban dynamics.

I examine several critical Latino films that draw characters across the border and into Los Angeles to trace the effect of international political agendas on local circumstances. While these films explore the various divisions and borderlining experiences of the city, they also defy the mythos of the split city and expose the dynamics of power in globalization. I begin with two films that explore the journey into Los Angeles from Mexico from different periods in recent history: *El Norte* (1983) as representative of the conditions of border crossers in Los Angeles in the 1980s and *Star Maps* (1997) as a film that examines the "boom" in Latino culture from the perspective of an aspiring actor in the city of dreams. Finally, I examine a film that engages the issues of border films like *El Norte* and *Star Maps*, but that takes a very different course. *Bread and Roses* (2000) guides the audience through the various steps of labor activism for undocumented immigrants. While it is also concerned with the polarization of urban space and labor markets, *Bread and Roses* offers possible escape from the vicious cycle of poverty and invisibility for Latinos and other immigrants in the city.

CITY OF DREAMS

The border had become an impasse of national politics by the early 1980s, giving rise to a wave of border films that dramatize and work through anxieties about immigration in the popular imaginary. Among such films, *El Norte* stands out as a classic of major independent cinema that depicts border crossing and the subsequent everyday experience of the border in the global city. Written by Anna Thomas and Gregory Nava and directed by Nava, *El Norte* (1983) received wide critical attention. It won an Academy Award nomination for best original screenplay, was named an "American Classic" in 1996, and has been targeted for special preservation by the Library of Congress. The story, based on the Mayan creation myth *Popol Vuh*, follows the travels of two young Guatemalans through Mexico to the United States. They aspire to the free upward mobility promised by the media-induced mythos of *el norte*, "the north," yet the reality they find is one of stark division and stasis; they live and work in the peripheral zones of the iconic and cinematic Los Angeles. *El Norte* explores the hidden workings of split economies. It reveals the real political, socioeconomic, and psychic costs of divided cities by bringing the simulated realities of mass media to their logical end, thereby sacrificing each character to the disorder of the city.

By the 1990s, the nation's immigration policy had become increasingly phobic. The 1993 Operation Blockade in El Paso, an intensive short-term border surveillance exercise, served as a model for other border cities. In 1994 California voters passed Proposition 187, dubbed the "Save Our State" initiative, to deny public benefits to undocumented immigrants. A new federal law in 1996 provided for increased sanctions on undocumented immigrants and restrictions on legal immigration.[2] Border ideology shifted into a more intensely polarized and complex debate.

During this same period, Latinos were struggling for equitable and fair representation in film and television after years of being typecast negatively. In the late 1980s, the consolidation of what Chon A. Noriega and Ana M. López call "the Latino filmmaking 'canon'" or "Hispanic Hollywood" created new opportunities for Latino representation in mainstream media.[3]

This double reality of immigration and widening representation is reflexively analyzed in *Star Maps*. Like *El Norte*, it depicts the alluring images of North American media as they come to bear on the spatialization of Los Angeles. The title alludes to the tourist maps of movie stars' homes, though the story takes place beyond the exclusive neighborhoods of the stars. In *Star Maps*, Carlos dreams of becoming the next major Latino star, but the racist ideology of the corporate studio system renders this dream delusional. Moreover, his only shot at landing a role requires that he, as a Chicano, traffic in a fetishizing racial fantasy about Mexican men. *Star Maps* shows how racialized populations are implicated in the colonial and globalized sexual economy of Los Angeles and how this scenario is refracted through the mass mediation of Los Angeles' dominant industry, Hollywood.

Bread and Roses depicts the realities of free trade globalization from the bottom of the urban labor market. Rather than contributing to the divided topographies of city cinema by adding another link to the larger symbolic interface of the city, the film forgoes fantasy by providing lessons in labor organizing. Like *Norma Rae* (1979), it is the story of a woman's evolution of political consciousness through the labor movement; but unlike the story of the eponymous Norma Rae, Maya's story has deeply transnational features. In *Bread and Roses*, Maya immigrates to Los Angeles from Mexico to work with her sister at Angel Cleaning Services, a non-union operation paying its workers less than living wages with no benefits. Maya falls in with a union activist and quickly becomes a leader in the Justice for Janitors campaign, an actual movement organized by the Service Employees International Union (SEIU). The film offers some realizable solutions to the problems posed in *El Norte* and *Star Maps*; it illustrates the potential for direct action activism in the city, making it part of a dramatically appealing story.

SCHIZOPOLIS

A city may divide for numerous reasons: settlements of capital that alienate the core from the periphery, polarized labor markets, divisions between "good" and "bad" neighborhoods, uneven disbursement of public funds leading to uneven development and levels of public services, designated shopping and entertainment zones, and secured and unsecured neighborhoods.[4] The term "schizopolis" refers to a schizo-city—a split city that has internal borders that divide its inhabitants. Like border policy, the urban divide recalls typologies of inclusion and exclusion and other cultural schisms.

With the publication of *The Divided Self* in 1959, long before what many mark as the postmodern cultural turn, R. D. Laing made a radical claim against the norms of his profession of psychiatry and psychoanalysis. He interpreted schizophrenia as a symptom of culture, a "special strategy" for coping with an unlivable situation. In this view, being "schizo" expresses the contradictions of technocratic capitalist culture while it exposes the social and moral norms that delimit sane from insane. In a preface added in 1964, Laing writes:

A man who prefers to be dead rather than red is normal. A man who says he has lost his soul is mad. A man who says that men are machines may be a great scientist. A man who says he is a machine is "depersonalized" in psychiatric jargon. A man who says that Negroes (sic) are an inferior race may be widely respected. A man who says his whiteness is a form of cancer is certifiable.[5]

This reading of the schizo state is a critique of the forms of social and political power that define the norms of wellness while creating the conditions of illness. In 1961, Michel Foucault made similar claims in his archaeology of the asylum, entitled *Madness and Civilization*—a book enthusiastically reviewed by Laing. Both writers define wellness as an ideological norm gauged by one's embeddedness in a dominant sociopolitical reality.

Drawing on the Heideggerian sense of inhabiting place, Laing traces the shift from a "sane schizoid way of being-in-the-world" to a "psychotic way of being-in-the-world," displacing his analytic frame from the clinical to the existential.[6] He revises the term "schizoid" to describe the split between the subject and the world and the split within the subject:

Such a person is not able to experience himself "together with others" or "at home in" the world, but, on the contrary, he experiences himself in despairing aloneness and isolation; moreover he does not experience himself as a complete person but rather as a "split" in various ways, perhaps as a mind more or less tenuously linked to a body, as two or more selves, and so on.[7]

Laing's emphasis on place anticipated what urbanists like David Harvey describe as the dominant ethos of late capitalism in the metropolis.[8] Harvey explains how the schizo condition of urban late capitalist culture fosters psychic dissonance and disorder. The global cities are sites where modernist versions of order break down, syntagma and system dissolve, power is dispersed, and the new order of the day is alienation, fragmentation, and discontinuity. Part of the schizoid reaction to the city emanates from its contradiction with the culture left behind in the suburbs, in the exurbs at the outer edges of sprawl, in the provinces, and in smaller cities and towns of other nations. The despair created by this dissonance is most intense for those who immigrate into the lower economic strata of the city. Trapped in undercapitalized neighborhoods isolated from the center, they face the hostilities of various combinations of discrimination due to race, ethnicity, class, sexuality, and gender. Living in the schizopolis, depending on where you live and work or how you experience these chasms, means having to make sense of this incomprehensible paradox. For some this effort exacts heavy psychic costs.

FAULT LINES

Our expectations of major global cities are guided in part by their media-induced mythos. Cities shape and transform us through various kinds of interactions and designations contingent upon where we live, work, play, shop, belong, and feel safe or unsafe. Mike Davis describes post-liberal Los Angeles as a militarized space of permanent surveillance riddled with barricades protecting the well-to-do against the dangerously invidious underclass.[9] Imagine coming to the city with the dream of free mobility, only to find that parts of the city are off-limits to you—from gated communities to shopping malls—and that you are under permanent security surveillance and profiled as part of a criminal class. The result can be a deranging alienation of self-conception from social being.

For recent arrivals to the city, the disturbing effects of the urban experience are intensified by the disorienting transitions inherent in immigration. In a study of the psychic impact of immigration, Carola

Suárez-Orozco and Marcelo Suárez-Orozco describe the process of displacement as isolating and alienating; immigrants may be bereft of resources, and their accustomed coping strategies may no longer function. In the shift from predictable to unpredictable contexts, immigrants are often stripped of social and extended familial relationships, of a sense of social status and belonging, and of cultural competence and control. The distress of the new context can be intensified by traumas experienced in the country of origin—war, famine, poverty, and violence—and during the migration journey, especially for those undocumented immigrants who must cross the highly militarized border zone separating the United States and Mexico.[10]

In "Journey Beyond the Stars," an introduction to a volume of essays about the "Third Worlds" of Los Angeles, Deepak Narang Sawhney ponders the deep economic and social divide that afflicts Los Angeles and wonders how such a wound might be treated.[11] Various therapies are possible, from micro to macro applications, and from diagnosing the cause to treating the symptoms—that is, from profound economic restructuring to transforming the skin of the city, the top layer of image and fantasy that sells a utopia of prosperity. The answer lies in finding a middle ground, a bridge that would address the split and relax the borders that maintain separation and exile.

One way of creating a bridge of this sort would be to enter into the "imagotopia" of Hollywood by engaging its dominant storylines while adding a new dimension to its romanticizing gloss. Such a task is accomplished by bridging First and Third World cinemas to expose the interconnectedness of the First and Third Worlds to wider audiences. Another remedy, suggested by José Luis Gámez in his work on cultural commemoration in East Los Angeles, is to reclaim the center from the internally colonized periphery, or in other words, to reterritorialize the center of the metropolis from the outskirts through creative critical practices.[12] Noriega describes Enrique Hank López's strategy of maneuvering the "schizo-cultural limbo" of being between nations and national identities as a hyphenated American; his strategy acts as a model for democratization that is critical of assimilationist discourses.[13] Noriega concludes, "López forgoes a stable location or 'home,' instead working between these many spaces, claiming the identity as a strategy of citizenship and not as the measure of his identity, which remains open-ended."[14] Each strategy suggests the excavation of a complex historical memory as a means of re-inhabiting and redeploying cultural schisms.

NORTH BY SOUTH

In the middle of *El Norte* (1983), the main characters ride a north-bound bus through Mexico to Tijuana, a trip that is a commonplace of the border film genre. *Star Maps* (1997) and *Bread and Roses* (2000) begin a little later in this familiar journey, as the bus and van, respectively, approach the final destination of Los Angeles. In *El Norte* and *Star Maps*, the male characters fall asleep and dream, but their dreams are as different as their reasons for migrating. One has a nightmare induced by the cause of his hasty departure, while the other has a wish-fulfillment dream inspired by the promise of Hollywood. Border films engage this split imaginary—the dream of economic success against the nightmare of economic exploitation and social injustice, or the "American Dream" against its hidden reality. These reveries toward and across the liminal space of the border anticipate those inspired by the dreamscapes of Los Angeles. The main characters of both films are depicted crossing the border with dreams of a better life, only to be borderlined and broken down by Los Angeles. Each character is traumatized and tyrannized by the culture of the city, and each film reveals how the global schizopolis divides and destroys psyches. *Bread and Roses* teaches us that you can do something about it.

These films are examples of the borderized image of the city as an effect of the imagined and real bifurcation of the Americas. They are part of the genre of Latino border films, a genre that thematizes cultural contact and displacement across a north-south divide. *El Norte, Star Maps,* and *Bread and Roses* are border films in another way as well: they are films on the border between New Latin American cinema and Chicano cinema. They can be viewed as part of the forged alliance of Chicano and New Latin American cinema, a cinematic movement constituted in 1967 at the Latin American Film Festival in Chile dedicated to creating social awareness and political change.[15] At the sixth meeting of the Annual Festival of the New Latin American Cinema in 1978, this new alliance was made explicit within the political program of the organization:

We also declare our solidarity with the struggle of Chicano cinema, the cultural manifestation of a community that combats the oppression and discrimination within the United States in order to affirm its Latin American roots. This reality remains almost or entirely unknown by most of our people, or reaches them through the distortions of the imperialist news media. Yet today the Chicano community has its own filmmakers and films, and demands of us the commitment to strengthen the cultural-historical ties that join us together, by contributing to the dissemination of their films, their experiences, and their struggles.[16]

El Norte, in particular, contributes to this alliance through its narrative structure, which embodies the continuity among Central American, Mexican, and North American cinemas. The film's three segments correspond to the trajectory of the main characters' journey of exile: origin (Guatamala), passage (Mexico), and destination (Southern California). These cinematic relations are inflected in the contact among Mexicans, Central Americans, and Mexican Americans, yet the film criticizes this utopian continuity by revealing the fault line in the Latino community between recent arrivals and Chicanos. Chicanos and Latin American immigrants are represented as divided by the urban culture of survivalist competition that takes precedence over collective struggle. For instance, Latin American immigrants mock a Chicano worker for his sense of superiority, his lack of Spanish language skills, and his Chicano self-identification. The same Chicano calls the immigration service out on Enrique, the recent immigrant, with the goal of claiming his job in his absence. These struggles within underprivileged ethnic/racial communities reveal how limited urban resources create jealous competitions that drive intra-community rifts even deeper while they work against a totalizing image of Latinos.

Christine List finds the imagined continuity of Latin American and Chicano cinema overly optimistic.[17] Writing about *El Norte* after its release in the United States, List found the film to be contrary to the leftist tenets of the New Latin American cinema for its use of the popular narrative formula of melodrama—which Joel Oseas Pérez describes as afflicting the film like *una gripa severa,* "a terrible cold."[18] Melodrama captures the struggle of the individual within a story of pathos rather than one of political consciousness; it features the politics of tolerance rather than of confrontation. The film exploits the simplistic values of good versus evil within a linear plot that neutralizes the political events in Guatemala and the relationship of the United States to Mexico. The film elicits sympathy and pity for the characters because of their unfair treatment in a cold and cruel world. List notes the pernicious market-driven reasons for such an ideological gloss:

The film clings to the melodramatic form and its reductionist treatment of social issues. Thus, it discourages a more penetrating analysis of prolonged impoverishment in the Third World, especially the implications of U.S. monetary aid and economic investment. Consequently, the film also avoids confronting/alienating the upper-middle class audiences which populate the art house cinemas and subscribe to cable Arts and Entertainment television. It is this audience which (perhaps unknowingly) invests in the companies that lobby the government to keep the Guatemalan army supplied and trained. And it is this same audience that profits from the submissive work force with which impoverished Central America provides them.[19]

Leftist filmmakers and critics focus on form as the means of liberating content from its ideological mask, using experimental techniques that eschew narrative pleasure and upset audience expectations. A problem with leftist filmmaking, especially in the United States, is its appeal to a rarified audience with specialized tastes and its tendency to alienate mass audiences. Kathleen Newman, writing about another melodramatic epic feature of Latino cinema, *American Me* (1992), draws on state theory to explore how the micropolitics of film image and sound impact the dominant political organization of the state.[20] She propels the debate beyond the impasses of positive representation and liberatory narrative form by turning to the reterritorializing potential of image to address social inequities and imagine social equality. In a similar fashion, José Luis Gámez analyzes how Chicano cultural productions offer a means of understanding processes of urban differentiation while they also contain strategies for reinhabiting space in East Los Angeles. Likewise, the images of *El Norte* expose the failures of a major global cosmopolis to imagine hospitality for political refugees of Central America and the economic divisions that cause even more displacement and distress.

Though a film might be formally normative, it has the potential to disrupt on an unconscious level through the image. Stanley Cavell, recalling Freud's dream work, considers film to be like a dream; any film is only what we remember it to be and any memory is likewise subjective, inchoate, and full of gaps that we fill with our own expectations, personal ideologies, and projections.[21] For this reason, the most powerful images of any film might form the frame of meaning and interpretation; detail and nuance are forgotten to the foregrounding of the image with impact. These surprising or captivating images have the potential to disrupt the flow of narration. The ideological course of *El Norte*'s classical narrative is blocked and reversed by the devastation of the film's familiar images. The familiar or tantalizing image of the Guatemalan countryside or the Los Angeles skyline draws in even the most Hollywoodified viewer, but added to this repertoire of memorable images are those of the dehumanized coffee workers or the Mexican barrios of Los Angeles. The melodramatic emphasis on split values, of good versus evil, intensifies the schizo-affective rifts that structure both the narrative and the city.

El Norte may follow Hollywood generic conventions, but according to Mario Barrera, the explicit reference to *Popol Vuh* creates a multilayered interplay of "theme, message, and myth." This, according to his analysis of story structure in Latino films, propels *El Norte* beyond the "ordinary" or, by extension, beyond the normative.[22] Likewise, Lucila Vargas describes these multiple levels of meaning as the bases of a dual spectatorial address split between conscious and unconscious levels through narrative and image, respectively, so that whether you like it or not, the film is working its sociopolitical message into your psyche. The two dimensions are linked and harmonized by what Vargas describes as *un círculo doble*, "a double circle" of circular images and narrative cycles. The circularity of time and events, the images of tires, the moon, the sun, the cement mixer, and the tunnel all work to create a sense of the organic unity of time and space and of image and text.[23] The economic and political reality of the story's urban destination is also split, especially in the depiction of transnational space within the globalized city of Los Angeles. The brother and sister, Enrique and Rosa, have fled repressive military-backed landowners in Guatemala and are traveling through Mexico to Southern California. As they cross the border and arrive in Los Angeles, it appears as if they have dragged the border along with them. They face the same fear of *la migra*, the Immigration and Naturalization Service (INS), in the city as at the border crossing, and they find Los Angeles to be internally split between little Mexico on the urban outskirts and the Anglo neighborhoods. Their story is an explicit critique not of the macropolitics of a deleterious free trade, but the micropolitics of dual treatment of this trade—that is, the dual treatment of the movement of goods versus the movement of people across borders.

EXODUS

El Norte begins in Guatemala with a series of images of the idyllic Guatemalan landscape, where mist partly veils mountains that rise behind a lush, verdant valley. This picturesque scene of apparently untouched mountainsides is offered as a tourist's postcard of life before the onslaught of industrial capitalism. Suddenly the ideological gloss of the postcard image is destroyed with the irruption of a surprising and even shocking element. The dreamlike imagery gives way to the image of hands picking coffee, and a close-up of the mountainsides reveals stooped workers toiling in the fields, depersonalized and faceless beneath their straw hats. A shotgun blast signaling the end of the workday triggers a procession of disembodied feet.

Thus a fantasy scene is ruptured by the reality of native subjugation to an export-oriented economy. Reality becomes the stain, the sullying element that destroys the cohesive and hermetic form of the fantasy— the beautiful and untouched countryside that satisfies the tourists' gaze. This tacit critique registers as an irritation; the image would be captivating if it weren't for the presence of the workers, whose toil reminds the viewer of the irksome labor that generates the products of leisure. These workers are not Juan Valdez, the advertising icon who joyfully selects every bean for the pleasure of the North American consumer. As we watch, the coffee travels, unhindered, from the countryside of Guatemala to a restaurant in Los Angeles. This displacement parallels Enrique's transformation from agrarian to industrial worker and his journey from laboring on the coffee plantation to serving coffee in the city. However, unlike the coffee, Enrique is not a welcome presence in the city.

The opening scene sets up the critical structure of the film, which accomplishes its critique through negative images that expose one side of globalization—a reality that upsets the viewer-as-tourist expectation created by the opening shots. This scene and others like it constitute the film's nightmarish other side, in which these momentary lapses make the viewer realize that the dream is not a dream, but real. The film is both an entertaining suspension of reality and a reminder that there is no wholesale escape from this reality. In this way, El Norte destroys even the most familiar and comforting skylines, landscapes, and cityscapes, an effect that deters the viewer from falling into a numbing Hollywood haze.

The story exposes the centripetal forces of late capitalism that draw people to the global city. It is thus a story about the forced mobility of globalization. Zygmunt Bauman describes globalization in terms of the split status of mobility determined by whether you can travel or not and why you travel. Globalization "divides as much as it unites"; it presents the world as a global village and as a single place, yet at the same time it deepens divisions between the haves and the have-nots.[24] Bauman asserts that movement is inevitable even if you stay put, since even the landscape of home is in constant flux. Whether movement is cybernetic, intellectual, or supersonic, it signals the expansive possibilities of globalization from above. Yet there is movement that is constraining and unfree, an economic exile that is both cause and symptom of freedom. The border-crossing immigrant so often depicted in the 1980s represented this terrifying unfreedom created by globalized wealth. Hollywood border films fence off this engulfing and shaming other from the U.S. psyche with renewed borders and boundaries, but *El Norte* refuses such happy oblivion.

El Norte does double duty; it exposes the forced exile imposed by U.S.-backed regimes in Central America while it critiques the economic inhospitality of a Mexico hobbled by debt to the United States. The film dramatizes the impossible predicament of Central American migrants in the 1980s. For Enrique and Rosa, fleeing their village is a matter of self-preservation against the death squads that roamed the Guatemalan countryside during what is considered one of the worst eras of human rights violations in the country. Technically, the Refugee Act of 1980 gives persons fearing persecution the right to political asylum in the United States. But in reality, the U.S. government seldom grants refuge to those fleeing right-wing regimes backed by Washington. Furthermore, access to the law's benefits requires full enfranchisement within a middle-class sociopolitical structure.

In part one of the film, Enrique and Rosa face a rural counterinsurgency force determined to seek out and massacre civilians suspected of supporting an insurgency. The film represents insurgency as a limited effort by poor villagers to recover land that was expropriated by army-backed landowners. However, even these efforts depend on organization of the poor and are viewed by the army as suggesting affinities with the larger guerilla movement. The film does not make such affinities explicit, although it does suggest that the organizers cannot remain "neutral" in the country's civil conflict. The army kills Enrique and Rosa's father, played by well-known Mexican actor Ernesto Gómez-Cruz, and takes away many others, including their mother, with the ominous orders to get rid of *esa mierda*, "this shit." Knowing that they will be sought out and murdered in turn, Enrique and Rosa flee north, passing themselves off as Mexicans to avoid being sent back to Guatemala. It is not surprising that they do not choose to stay in Mexico; by 1980 the

Mexican economy had been devastated by debt, unemployment, and a stagnating agricultural sector.[25] The country is hemorrhaging emigrants northward, and Enrique and Rosa are caught up in the flow.

Nor is it surprising that the young Guatemalans choose the United States as their destination. The film reveals their godmother's desire to visit the United States, inspired by a ten-year romance with *Buenhogar,* the Spanish language version of *Good Housekeeping.* "The north" is the subject of dinner conversation fueled by stories from friends and, more forcefully, by the images in magazines and on television. These images instill a series of expectations and fantasies about equal access to wealth and success—about a country where everyone, even the poor, drives a car. To a curious Rosa flipping through the pages of *Buenhogar,* "high-tech" kitchens and modern appliances are signs and synecdoches of the "good life." These images complement the picture of prosperity created by the Reagan regime: tax cuts that lead to increased spending, big government expenditures for military fortification, loosening barriers to trade, and the creation of mega-corporate conglomerations.

Part two of *El Norte,* titled "The Coyote: Mexico," offers a split image of Mexico very similar to that of Guatemala in part one. The scene opens with a panoramic view of a countryside dotted with wildflowers against a blue and partly cloudy sky.

Suddenly a truck noisily cuts across a road traversing this country scene. Mariachi music plays on the soundtrack as we hear the cursing of the driver, agitated by a sudden flat tire. Unfortunately, while the representation of the cursing Mexican is meant as comic relief, this one-dimensional characterization of Mexicans and Mexican-Americans is complicit with stereotype and the comic formula for how to "act like a Mexican." Joel Oseas Pérez notes that one montage sequence of run-down shacks in Mexico juxtaposed against clean middle-class homes in the north is iconic of the negative filmic discourse that contrasts Mexican underdevelopment with U.S. prosperity. Yet the film goes one transnational step further by exploring the difference between the mythos and actuality. When the bus reaches its destination of Tijuana, the scene shifts to a post-industrial Mexico in rapid decay. At first, the visual impression of Mexico is purposefully abject to create a critical counterpoint to the visual depictions of Los Angeles, but it is a counterpoint that will turn into continuity and complementarity. Enrique and Rosa will come full circle as the border town they hastily and gladly abandon becomes visually indistinct from their destination.

After a grueling journey through rat-infested sewage tunnels, part two ends with the pair on the cusp of Southern California, bordering San Diego. Their coyote, or border crossing guide, tells them they will reach Los Angeles the next day. This announcement inspires a dreamlike hovering pan of luminous nighttime Los Angeles with overwrought triumphant music resonating with a redemptive tone: Los Angeles as the promised land.

Part three, "The North: Los Angeles," maintains the visual analogy of the first two sections. Los Angeles is a place of tall palm trees set against a deeply colored sunset. A closer shot reveals the telephone cables cutting across the trees and pulling back to reveal the decrepit and shanty-like Lazy Acres motel. Enrique and Rosa experience a transnational Mexican Los Angeles, one hidden from the dominant spaces of the city, a place where the whole day can pass without the appearance of an Anglo-American. After narrowly escaping *la migra*, Rosa and a new friend make their way to a Mexican diner in the Mexican-American section of the city. The street signage is in Spanish and the storefronts and population are entirely Mexican. An astonished Rosa remarks, "Do you know where the gringos are?" to which her Mexican-American friend responds, "You don't think that gringos want to live with Mexicans, do you? They live in their own neighborhoods." The border reemerges as a symbolic blockade within the city, marking distinctions between neighborhoods that recall national boundaries.

The dual zoning of the city follows the inclusion/exclusion typology of immigration policy in relation to Latin Americans. Though a tangible place, the border is also a symbolic zone created to suture the gaps of North American national identity against the infiltration of "unwanted" immigrants. Immigrant phobia in California gathered considerable force during the Reagan and first Bush administrations. The Immigration Reform and Control Act of 1986 aimed to stop the flow of undocumented Latin American immigrants into the United States and to penalize employers who hired them. The push to restrict immigration peaked in 1994 with California's Proposition 187, which sought to deny undocumented immigrants access to all public social services including public education. Nicolás Kanellos describes the immigration and immigrant phobia in California as "Hispanophobia" aimed specifically at Mexicans and Central Americans.[26] Fears about Mexican immigration into California inspired a stepping up of boundarizing exclusion and border patrols aimed at deportation of immigrants by the Immigration and Naturalization Service (INS). No other national, ethnic, or racial-ized group has undergone the mass deportation experienced by Latin Americans in the United States. Yet immigration policy as it relates to both Asians and Latin Americans exhibits a push-pull ambivalence in which immigrants are invited and necessary and yet excluded from full social, political, and economic integration. The exclusion of the popula-tion that meets the fundamental labor needs of the city is reflected in the design and ongoing construction of the metropolis. For instance, in *El Norte* each character takes on employment that is basic to the larger operations of the employing agency and the city. Thus a construction company employs Enrique to lay the foundations of new middle-class homes that he may never have the means to occupy.

DUAL TIME ZONES

The Los Angeles of *El Norte* is a global city, but its globalism is one of concentrated wealth alongside criminalized and persecuted immigrant workers. This is conveyed in the split images of each place where action takes place within the city, showing the class-conditioned experience of urban space. The presentation of the underrepresented space or im-age is the other side, the stain of the normative viewing expectation. In the restaurant where Enrique initially takes a job, the workspace—the frantic kitchen—is set against the serene and somber dining room. This division of labor and leisure has racial, ethnic, and temporal implica-tions; the Anglo patrons enjoy a slow-paced, leisurely meal while the Latino workers sweat in the kitchen. Likewise, the space of the city is divided between zones of labor and leisure. The Mexican-American neighborhood has a hustle-bustle atmosphere, while the wealthy neigh-borhoods are tranquil. The split scenes in the city visually accord with the establishing shot in Guatemala. *El Norte* reveals the hidden secret of ideology—the labor behind the commodity. The North American au-dience of coffee drinkers gets full exposure to the workers picking cof-fee beans in the Guatemalan countryside, and restaurant diners see the workers in the kitchen. The products of labor emerge as a fragment of some other reality that persists in another narrative frame, another part of the city, and another national economy.

El Norte sacrifices Enrique and Rosa to the schizopolis to make its critique legible. After the northern progression through various polar-izations and contradictions, each character's mental state is negatively affected by the conditions of late capitalism. However, their sanity

4.1 Rosa (Zaide Silvia Gutiérrez) and Nacha (Lupe Ontiveros) are confounded by modern technology in *El Norte*.

deteriorates in different ways. The INS drives Enrique from his job and leaves him unemployed. His only opportunity for employment is in Chicago, which seems ideal except that it means leaving Rosa, who has become hospitalized with typhus. Enrique eventually decides not to take the job, a decision that mystifies his would-be boss. Enrique refuses the careerism of the Anglo urban norm that values individual success over family or community ties. Though momentarily redeemed by choosing to remain, he lapses back into the lunacies of capitalism by willfully forgetting his father's warning not to be reduced to the disembodied arms of labor. In the end Enrique capitulates to the borderlining economies of the city by aggressively competing for work as a day laborer.

Rosa Linda Fregoso reads *El Norte* in terms of a divergent articulation of gendered subjectivity that corresponds to an aesthetic split between Euro-American realism and Latin American magical realism. Magical realism has always been interpreted as a critique of modernity's relentlessly linear course, posing instead an organic circularity and unity more closely linked to the processes and mythos of nature. Director Nava posits woman as closer to nature, with representational affinities to magical realism, while man represents culture and enlightenment realism. Rosa thus embodies organic pastoral traditions whereas Enrique finds his place in western culture.[27]

Indeed, Rosa embodies the critique of the culture of globalization. Her hallucinations might be interpreted as a symptom of the schizoid conditions of the city. She is the one who notices the urban rift of the polarized neighborhoods and divergent ways of living. Though typhus from a rat bite is the ostensible source of her altered physical and mental state, her realizations of the traumatic and traumatizing ruptures of the city are literally deranging. Her warning to Enrique not to think about the paradoxes of their journey lest he go crazy forecasts her own fate. She hallucinates on various occasions, always in a nostalgic desire for a simple past, but even these hallucinations are sullied by the contradictions of her present reality. In a fevered vision, for instance, she sees her mother making tortillas while commenting on the contradictory U.S. economy where you make more and spend more. Rosa, unable to accept the abjection of an urban economy that would keep her assembly-lined and sweat-shopped, loses her will to live and dies of typhus. The global city ruins rather than redeems her as she had hoped. Her sacrifice is a testament to the unlivable conditions of the city for those on the other side of the border that separates wealth from poverty. Rosa and Enrique cross the border with dreams of a better life, only to be borderlined and broken down by Los Angeles.

NEW DESPAIR-ITIES

Like Nava, Miguel Arteta often thematizes Los Angeles in his work, using the city not just as a backdrop, but also as a significant and signifying space. Both filmmakers made distribution deals with Fox Searchlight Pictures president Lindsay Law, who has expressed his commitment to Latino cinema. Arteta's *Star Maps* works the schizopolis from its symbolic and mythological landscape, Hollywood. The border reemerges in the city as a split between center and periphery, but also as a boundary and barrier that keeps Latinos and other racialized groups from emigrating to the center of the city-based but globally impacting media production. Charles Ramírez Berg contends that this exclusion and subjugation can be traced to the very foundation of the film industry in Los Angeles, the consolidation of which displaced the original inhabitants of the land. The cinematic erasure of the original mestizo Californios by Anglo-Americans parallels the expropriation of land from Mexicans. Moreover, Hollywood filmmakers created the myth of the superior Anglo by casting Mexican-Americans as the "Californian other" within a discourse of dehumanizing anti-Mexican imagery and practices.[28] Ramírez Berg concludes that the film industry both reflected and sustained "Anglo California's discourse on race," which maintained "WASP power structures by segregating Mexicans socially, economically, and geographically."[29] This principle of divide and conquer, first in practice then in image, continues to shape the destinies of Latinos in mass media and beyond.

Star Maps is a film about a severely dysfunctional Mexican-American family. The father works for a large prostitution ring of Mexican-American youths into which he has drawn one of his sons, Carlos. The father is abusive and cruel, and his tyranny is the source of the family dysfunction. The mother has suffered a nervous breakdown and hallucinates the presence of Mexican comedian Cantinflas; another of the sons, Juancito, is mentally disturbed. The daughter, Maria, is the only seemingly stable person. Carlos has delusions of Hollywood stardom, yet his fantasy will remain just that, since the city, like the industry, has already mapped him out of its coveted spaces.

Carlos and the other kids employed by his father operate on various street corners all over the city, selling star maps as a front for the prostitution ring that provides Mexican boys to Anglo customers, both male and female. This setup re-imagines the sex zones of a city, often conceived as places ghettoized into red light districts, parks, neighborhoods, or specific areas where sex workers might be found. In this case, the boys' own bodily coordinates maintain divisions across the city as objects mapped by ubiquitous circuits of Anglo male and female desire.

The idea of the "star map" has various connotations; the term can refer to a map of film stars' homes in Los Angeles or to maps of celestial stars or the constellations. A constellation is a symbolic ordering that has nothing to do with the inherent meaning of star location or placement. When grouped in constellations, stars function as coordinates of arbitrary designs—a horse here, the Big Dipper there—that serve as mnemonic devices to scale the universe down to manageable images and icons. Hollywood stars function on the same logic; both are figures of the sublime—unreachable and unknowable, and yet are consumable in small doses as image. They seem to occupy a place beyond social realities as the coordinates of an ideal life. Yet movie stars are also points on our social map; they are symptoms of U.S. culture that say something about us and deserve a good reading.

The history of stardom offers a limited view of U.S. culture. There have been few non-Anglo stars who have not fallen into the fetishistic game of double or nothing, of being either exotic and eroticized objects or completely assimilated figures. The history of the Latin star in cinema is a history of ethnic typecasting—of male and female Valentinos, of exotic spitfires and vamps. Real stardom was almost invariably the preserve of the light-skinned. The new slate of starring roles for Latinos in recent Hollywood cinema—as wedding planners, FBI agents, and good cops, among others—seems to mark a transformation in the definition of the Latino star. But this easy shift is suspicious. *Star Maps* addresses this issue in part by exposing the traumatic split that characterizes Hollywood and stardom, a split doubled and deepened by racialization. The split involves an ambivalent existential status: the star gains recognition not as himself or herself but as a character; he or she gains status but loses specificity. The stakes are higher for ethnic actors and actresses who might take roles that compromise not just their personal integrity, but also that of the group they represent.

SPLITTING IMAGE

Star Maps opens with the familiar image of a northbound bus traveling from Mexico to Los Angeles with a load of Mexican nationals—though in the case of Carlos, the trip will take him home. He is returning from a stint doing community theater in Mexico, where his mother sent him to escape the clutches of his pimping father. The small taste of recognition has sparked a desire for fame that is visually complicit with the immigrant desire for a "better life." We see the bus on the cusp of the city, moving in from the south with the city center just beyond. Though the bus is in transit, this is the fixed perspective of Los Angeles for Carlos, a perspective from below and outside. While on the bus, Carlos dreams that he is swamped by the adoration of fans asking for his autograph. We realize this is a fantasy when we see Carlos open his eyes to a quiet bus and the camera fixes on the article that inspired the reverie. The article proclaims Antonio Banderas to be "el nuevo Valentino," installing Banderas as a symbolic point of departure in the story within a legacy inherited from Rudolph Valentino, the Italian immigrant actor first associated with the idea of the Latin lover. Banderas, now well known in the United States, began his career in Spain as part of the main repertoire of actors in Pedro Almodóvar's gender-bending camp classics. Banderas was often cast as a clueless character whose youth, inexperience, and pretty boy looks marked him as an object of male and female desire—reminiscent of the rumors of bisexuality attributed to Valentino. When Carlos casts an identificatory gaze on Banderas, we immediately form the symbolic connection that links Carlos with the visual legacy of imported Latin lover and boy toy.[30]

Carlos' desire to be an actor is limited by the prearranged schema of Hollywood that is mapped not just across the movie stars but also across the city. The star map emplots our story, yet it lacks topographical detail or precision. Instead it shows Los Angeles in cartoonish simplicity, with Hollywood central and all else peripheral. The opening shot shows Latinos working on street construction and on the street corners while media stars are securely ensconced in their homes or otherwise safely screened. Stars' homes are not just points of reference, but constitute the grid that organizes urban space along a deep economic and sociocultural fault line.

Behind the city map is a story about the cartography of history—the micro-legacies of family and the larger legacies of culture. Carlos works under a double patrimony corresponding to two controlling fathers: his sadistic father, Pepe, and the legend of classical Hollywood, Valentino. Pepe guides the economic logic of Carlos' quest for fame; he consents to introduce his son to the "right" people only if Carlos works for him as a prostitute. Carlos is forced to trade his body for a shot at stardom; yet, in the legacy of Valentino, even stardom—if he can attain it—requires that he traffic in his body. The results of Carlos' quest clash with his expectations. He lands a walk-on part in a major soap opera, an opportunity provided by one of his johns, a soap star named Jennifer. But the role calls for him to play an undocumented worker who says things like, "I am like a matador with my leaf-blower," before being seduced by Jennifer, the older Anglo female lead. Though he had aspired to be a leading man in the mold of the Latin lover, in reality he plays the part of a fetishized sexual object. Disenfranchised labor in the city has a symbolic counterpart in supporting and typecasting film and television roles that add sexuality to stereotype—not, in the end, greatly different from the prostitution ring Carlos abandons for the soap role. In an impasse reminiscent of Enrique's fate as disembodied labor, Carlos can't seem to transcend his fate as fetishized and prostituted object. He is a victim of the schizoid split of the Hollywood system: the immigrant fantasy that anyone can become a star against the reality of racial denigration.

TOUCHED BY AN ANGLO

Though seemingly an upgrade, a role as a Latin lover would not offer the redemption Carlos seeks, nor would it be far removed from the role he plays. The Latin lover is fundamentally about Anglo women's ascension to sexual agency through the sacrifice of a racialized male object. Miriam Hansen notes how Valentino's role as a star was symptomatic of a historical shift in gender roles in the United States. During World War I, with the scarcity of male bodies to perform traditionally gender-specific labors, women were integrated into the workforce and subsequently gained new equity in marriage. With this new emancipation, women became desiring subjects who cast their gaze onto the desirable and racialized body of the Latin object, Valentino. Yet the position of women as agents of desire was ambivalent; a female character would be allowed to look, but her desiring gaze also defined her negatively as a tramp or loose woman. During this moment of cultural upheaval, the ethnic male body became a site of cultural work-through for the gendered sexuality of the heterosexual Anglo-American woman.[31]

Such is the case for the soap star Jennifer, who uses her fetish for "poor Mexican boys" for the emancipation of her desires. She and the other Anglo, female customers of Pepe's ring need the Mexican kids to mediate their desires for their significantly older and wealthy husbands. Women gain agency as subjects of desire as long as this process colludes with a phobic discourse that relegates the ethnic or racialized body to a lesser status, that is, as an object-to-be-looked-at, which for feminist film theorist Laura Mulvey designates a compromised subject position.[32] In the case of *Star Maps*, the male and female johns and also the television industry instrumentalize the boys as pure and abject physicality. The Latin lover is a symptom of a newly unrepressed female desire; he is a transitional object preceding a "real" object, the Anglo male. His lesser status is a testament to the women's new independence. (Would Lucy have been such a central character without the ancillary and supporting role of Ricky?) The return of the racialized male body signals a cultural moment of upheaval and disquiet. Carlos wants to be a star, but he only lands secondary roles that support the norms inaugurated by classical Hollywood. *Star Maps* links this moment to the cultural landscape of film when Latino actors in particular get roles that are hard-won but

4.2 Carlos (Douglas Spain) meets Jennifer (Kandeyce Jorden), a soap star, while working on the corner as a hustler in *Star Maps*.

that contribute to a cultural amnesia about the historical role of Latinos and Latin American immigrants in the U.S. culture and economy.

The desire to be a star, like the public desire for stars, is also a desire to conceal or transcend an unhappy reality—as is the case for Carlos. His desire for fame goes beyond fantasy and approaches delusion. For instance, in one scene he sees himself on the cover of every major periodical and industry rag and in another he delivers his throwaway lines as if they were classical theater. He has what Laing calls a "special strategy" for coping with unlivable situations—a strategy he shares with his delusional mother.[33] Her hallucinations of Cantinflas constitute the narrative norm of mental illness. She is medicated, housebound, and incapacitated. Moreover, as in the case of Rosa in *El Norte*, the mother's illness is the site of social critique, which is evinced in part through her identification with the critical figures of Cantinflas and other icons of Mexican popular culture, to whom she pays homage with newspaper clippings and posters. Like Rosa's hallucinations that demythologize modernity, Cantinflas' distinctive humor targets the contradictions and unhappiness created by modern urban life. Likewise, Carlos' mother articulates the reality of Carlos' predicament; when he tells her he dreams of being an actor and a star, she intuitively misreads this dream as a *pesadilla*, a "nightmare." Yet, like Enrique, Carlos turns his delusion into one that is endorsed by social norms, in this case the norms of Hollywood and the star industry—that anyone can become a star. But within the logic of the story, fantasies of stardom are deemed schizo for someone who falls outside of the Hollywood image of the movie star.

Carlos is deeply disturbed; his family trauma, manifested as memories of a scene of paternal violence, keeps returning and interrupting his life. When he has a traumatic block, he stops whatever he is doing, leaving the other characters mystified about what ails him. Yet the audience is privy to the traumatic scene, screened for us as a slow-motion flashback in muted tones. We see Carlos as a young child who has locked himself in a car to escape his father's tirades and abuse. Pepe then smashes the window and pulls Carlos from the safety of the car into his dangerous clutches—foreshadowing the father's later endangerment and abuse of his son. These momentary lapses stop the film from moving forward smoothly while they bring the flow of images to a traumatic impasse. The narrative refuses to pass over into pure entertainment and instead offers these moments of critical reflection for the viewer.

In the end, when Carlos realizes that Pepe has taken his small soap role, he explodes. Cruelly, Pepe shouts, "When you want something, you take it." Upon hearing this, Carlos loses his mind and beats Pepe nearly to death. The film ends with a violent breakthrough: Carlos walks away from the studio and his father to wander the streets of Los Angeles. Though he has broken from his father and the industry, he is still trapped in the inhospitable city. We know that his movement is not free; we know his path in the city is already mapped. We are left wondering what kind of future he might have and what kind of future Hollywood might designate for him and other minorities within the mass media.

THE GLOBAL SOUTH IN THE SCHIZOPOLIS

Bread and Roses refers to a famous landmark protest in 1912 in Lawrence, Massachusetts, where mostly female immigrant workers fought against poverty wages. They gathered on New Year's Day carrying banners that demanded: "We want bread and roses too." Director Ken Loach pays homage to those whose work and struggles paved the way for a new era of activism. *Bread and Roses* is not just one of the few dramatic feature films about labor activism, but it is also a major promotional advertisement and showcase for the globalized labor movement. It attacks two central loci of power in globalization—corporations and the media—and challenges the divisive urban dynamics created by these institutions.

Though *Bread and Roses* would fit comfortably into the Latino film genre for the presence of actors who have earned their reputation in this genre, it reaches across other immigrant cultures and other dispossessed peoples: African-Americans, the working class, and those facing age and ability discrimination in the workplace. It has been hailed as a socialist-realist film that uses some nonprofessional actors in a manner found more often in neo-realist New Latin American cinema (*Rodrigo D: No Future, City of God, Pixote*), though the film employs some professional actors that a Hollywood audience might recognize—e.g., Adrien Brody and George Lopez—along with actual union organizer Rocio Saenz. *Bread and Roses* inherits the dilemmas of previous Latino films, yet offers new solutions drawn from global solidarity movements. Critic Peter Matthews claims, "*Bread and Roses* can't be called one of Ken Loach's greatest works, but the fact is that virtually no other director would think of attempting a film about the plight of non-unionized janitors in Los Angeles. While this may not sound like a terrific inducement for popcorn junkies, the keen sense of moral responsibility informing the production makes most current cinema look fatuously self-absorbed by comparison."[34] A number of filmmakers and directors have treated such ideas in their films, most notably David Riker in *La Ciudad/The City* (1998), but the key difference between Loach and other filmmakers is his sense of political engagement and activist didactics as dramatic entertainment. The film goes beyond others of the same type by depicting all the steps and possible pitfalls of labor activism in what Leonard Quart and William Kornblum call the film's unusual mix of "entertainment, political polemic, and . . . Introduction to Organizing 101."[35]

Other stories of politicized awakening in the city, like that of Ana in *Real Women Have Curves*, might present a collective agenda, yet this is often eclipsed by narratives of individual success and escape. For instance, Ana encourages her female coworkers to undermine conservative ideas about feminine propriety and she speaks out against the devaluation of their labor, but her final triumph is personal and individual. Or in the case of *Mi vida loca*, the women of Echo Park work together and organize to get their due, yet their efforts are not connected to any larger political agenda. They organize within the community, which is a necessary step towards larger political visibility, but there is little thought to what lies beyond Echo Park.

BREAD AND ROSES, TOO

Bread and Roses begins with Maya's dangerous traversal of the border on foot and subsequent van ride to Los Angeles. Maya's sister, Rosa, greets her upon her arrival, but without the money to liberate her from the coyotes. Angered, the coyotes refuse to release Maya and drive off, flipping a coin to determine who will get their way with her. However, they fail to anticipate the craftiness of their charge. Using her wit and savvy, Maya escapes the motel where she was taken hostage by pretending to help her captor lather up in the shower, taking his keys and his boots. When he realizes he's been conned, he curses her up and down, looking out the window as she waves his boots in defiance and runs away. Recalling the comedic Mexican border genre derivative of the Spanish picaresque,[36] this is a new and uplifting image; unlike the tragic siblings of *El Norte* or Jennifer Lopez's character whose desperate deportation marks *Mi Familia*, Maya gets away with it, makes us laugh, and reminds the audience that you can pull one over on the forces in power. This scene is a telling preface for the victories to come.

In some ways, *Bread and Roses* is a critical retort to films like *El Norte* from the perspective of the global south, offering a story equally tragic and melodramatic, but with a solution facilitated by the labor movement. It is an alternative to melodramatic narratives that end in suffering, without redemption or viable political solutions for the characters. *El Norte* ends with Rosa's death and Enrique's spiritual death in his capitulation to the capitalist machinery fueled by cheap labor. Though *El Norte* is one of the first films seen through the eyes of the immigrant characters within a larger critique of the dehumanization of capitalism and the exploitation of workers, its ideology resonates with those of Hollywood border films discussed earlier, like *The Border* (1982), with Elpidia Carrillo (the actress who plays Rosa in *Bread and Roses*) as Maria. Both *The Border* and *El Norte* contain stories of immigrant suffering and hardship, but neither links the individual stories to larger political or social movements.

The Border nicely captures the liberal agenda of sympathy for the individual immigrant, but remains ignorant of the larger issues surrounding the transnational movement of labor. At best, *The Border* maintains an ambivalent and contradictory attitude towards undocumented labor.

We are introduced to Charlie, a border agent with a heart of gold, when he is sent to a Los Angeles factory to pick up undocumented workers. The factory owner claims that the "unions are squeezing me, threatening to burn this place down" and that the "life and death" of his operations and "half the factories in Los Angeles" depend on keeping the wages inhumanely low. The union's outrageous demand is minimum wage, or $2.50 an hour, in contrast to the $6 a day he is currently paying. Charlie sympathizes and takes only two token workers in order to keep the factory running. Both the factory owner and Charlie share the sense that they are, as the coyote in *El Norte* claims, doing a "public service" by providing jobs; the contradictions of this scene are eventually eclipsed by the larger Hollywood ideology of the happy ending. Every possibly hot political issue stumbled upon in *The Border* is trampled by the success of the cowboy Charlie in reuniting a helpless immigrant with her stolen baby. Neither *The Border* nor *El Norte* offers solutions for the exploitation of undocumented workers.

THE BUS STOPS HERE

A major dividing line between the films of opulent Los Angeles and those depicting working-class and poor neighborhoods is that between scarcely represented public transportation and the car. The car captures the main tenets of neo-liberal culture: mobility, consumption, individualism, and privacy. It is the perfect example of the neo-liberal guarantee of abstract ideals like democracy and freedom through the consumer market. Moreover, the car divides and separates people. It sustains the social relations of class that create a divided city. The cinematic image of the city is split along this new axis, between images of the car-possessing and those of the car-free.

Stand and Deliver, Star Maps, Real Women Have Curves, and *Bread and Roses* offer a picture of the other side of car-dominant Los Angeles, the Los Angeles of public transportation. Recently, Los Angeles mass transit has become a central feature of the chase film genre—e.g., in *Speed* (1994), *The Italian Job* (2003), and *Collateral* (2004)—but more as an exotic form of the chase vehicle than as an alternate mode of travel. In *Crash* (2004), the bus is viewed as a creation of the white and wealthy to shame poor people of color, which is why, one character remarks, there are such large and exposing windows. George Lipsitz, writing about bus poet Marisela Norte, claims that no one wants to be on the bus and many think of it as "the transportation mode of last resort, as the crowded, messy, dirty, noisy nightmare lampooned in Los Angeles' own Weird Al Yankovic's parody of Queen's 'Another One Bites the Dust': 'Another One Rides the Bus.'"[37] However, Lipsitz admits that, for the poor, this attitude is a luxury. Norte revalues the bus as her main source of inspiration; her poems span the length of a single ride and incorporate the space, rhythm, and speed of her trip: "Every weekday, Norte rides the Number 18 bus from her home in East Los Angeles to her job downtown. She writes poems about the people, places, and things that she sees from her vantage point on the bus. For many years she let the length of the bus ride determine the length of her poems. When she reached her stop, the poem was over. Of course, given the unpredictable pace of bus service in Los Angeles, this meant that all forms of poetry remained possible, from the haiku to the epic" (512).[38]

Norte's notwithstanding, most depictions of Los Angeles public transportation have been negative, ignoring the historical and political conditions that gave rise to it. Public transportation evokes a model of a city plan with a socialist design—an accessible and usable city where mobility is guaranteed for all peoples, regardless of class. As demonstrated by the multicultural and racially mixed community of the bus in *Speed*, mass transit is the last place of contact in a city where people are otherwise divided among neighborhoods or sequestered in their cars. Janet Abu-Lughod has shown that a main difference between a global city like Chicago and Los Angeles is the latter's absence of a city plan at its origination (1999).[39] Chicago, on the other hand, in the 1909 plan, was organized on a grid that would theoretically forge equal access to all parts of the city; this grid was then supported by a large-scale transit system linking the outskirts to the inner loop. The bus and other forms of public mass transportation were designed to increase mobility for those who could not afford the various expenses associated with owning a car. In Los Angeles after the Watts neighborhood riots, the McCone Commission reported a link among joblessness in Watts, low rates of car ownership, and a lack of public transportation alternatives. The residents of Watts were exiled from the rest of the city where suitable employment might be found.[40] The uprisings literally put Watts on the mass transit map. In response to the commission's findings, the city initiated a bus program that increased the access of its most needy residents.

The depiction of mass transit in a car dominant culture aligns an alternate mobility with activist means of forging access and creating solidarity. In *Bread and Roses*, Maya's movement in the city is wide and adventurous, from her tour of the university with Ruben on moped to walking in the city, riding the bus, marching downtown, and occupying the semi-public space of the corporate plaza. In a city where not having a car limits one's access, Maya finds her way around on the bus. For instance, she takes the bus to Sam the union organizer's neighborhood to inform him that his clumsiness caused the,unceremonious dismissal of her coworker, a fact she insists on telling him face to face. Loach does not reassert the borderlining partitions of the city by showing people limited to particular neighborhoods or by associating mobility with car culture. This minor image makeover contributes to the perception that divisions in the city are surmountable and affirms the value of collective transformation and redistribution of power relations over the status quo.

CORPORATE COMMAND CENTER

In his films, Loach often grounds his critical stance against globalization in the places in which it is most heavily armored, consolidated, and diversified: major global cities, particularly British cities. Yet in *Bread and Roses*, following the trend of urban theorists, he immigrates and makes Los Angeles the target of social reform for an increasingly rapacious global capitalism. As an English filmmaker with a socialist-realist agenda, Loach had not hitherto ventured into the U.S. cultural terrain, but it is clear that he had many reasons to choose Los Angeles as the center of the new labor activism. *Bread and Roses* makes good use of the insurgent political heritage of the city along with its reputation as the center of global media and the location of corporate headquarters.

Los Angeles, according to Michael Dear and Steven Flusty—drawing on Edward Soja's precedent—is the best model for understanding and "explaining the form and function of urbanism in a time of globalization."[41] Globalization, Roger Keil claims, "led Los Angeles astray from the trajectory of American urbanism," causing a "redefinition of the very concept of the 'American city'" not just as a global city, but also as the seat of global justice movements.[42] Keil points to the rebellion of 1992 as the origin of decades of diversification of protest movements and struggles located in various global cities around the world; though the event was spurred by a black-white racial politics, a multi-ethnic and multi-racial coalition of peoples rose up in protest.[43] The rebellion became a beacon for urban-based political movements and presented an image of Angelenos as organic social activists. The Los Angeles model of global city development had imploded; before 1992 "there was little discussion . . . about how it was possible that a society as diverse as the one of Los Angeles had been able to sustain itself in the pressure cooker of globalization and restructuring without erupting into full-scale social violence."[44]

Bread and Roses draws on the unrest of 1992 and other activist legacies; for instance, it draws specifically on the publicity garnered by labor activists in Los Angeles for the victorious Justice for Janitors campaign of 1990, the dramatic Hotel Employees and Restaurant Employees (HERE) union battles against The New Otani hotel, and the success of UNITE HERE Local 11 president Maria Elena Durazo and her crew of Latino celebrities and legislators in bringing one of the largest private employers in Los Angeles, the University of Southern California, to its knees by demanding more secure contracts for its veteran catering and cleaning workers.[45]

Urban-based global labor movements differ from national and often nativist labor unions in their attitude toward immigrant and undocumented labor. The new transnational movements are a function and consequence of globalization and its new international workforce. The current president of the Service Employees International Union (SEIU), Andrew Stern, has argued that unions need to build institutions that are strong enough to match the power of global corporations, which means unions need to reach across borders and become global.[46] The new labor movement connects workers' rights to international human rights; it reaches beyond the nation-state to secure workers' rights, since the state guarantees no protections or rights for undocumented workers who might be mistreated, subject to dangerous conditions, or fired out-of-hand.[47] A human rights agenda allows workers to identify injustices and violations of rights and appeal to a larger international tribunal for remedies and change.[48] The linkage of workers' rights to human rights enables local movements to work both locally and globally at once, but this local work is necessarily city-based, not nation-based. This is a major shift from labor efforts of the past. Helene Hayes, in a remarkable history of the relationship between immigration policy and undocumented immigration, shows that support for nativist and exclusionary immigration policies has consistently emanated from nationalist U.S. labor unions and organizations. Organized labor was behind every piece of exclusionary legislation from the Chinese Exclusion Act to the "labor certification requirement" of the McCarran-Walter Act of 1952. But the greatest victory for labor was in the transformation of the language of immigration policy from that of labor, and the imperative to fill national work needs, to the language of the ideology of family and "family reunification," which refocused the national gaze back onto internal labor markets.[49]

Although *Bread and Roses* is a labor activist film, Loach does not endorse the labor movement wholesale; instead, he remains critical of organized labor's connection to larger state-bound institutions. In the film, for instance, Sam's boss chastises him for getting three injunctions in two days and threatening the economic viability of the organization: "What are you doing here? The lawyers are going insane. I'm trying to keep the executive board off your ass." His boss suggests that he change targets, to which Sam replies, "An easier target?" insinuating that the fight against the management of Angel Cleaning Services is not a good investment of time or money. Sam taunts, "Not going to have your forty million [dollars] to give to the Democrats next election?" His criticism underpins a reality besetting labor unions. Labor's influence and dependence on the Democratic Party has increasingly become untenable because, as Sam the renegade labor activist suggests, unions must sacrifice local city politics to national politics. The union's tie to the Democratic Party limits its political effectiveness and many perceive the relationship as little more than the hemorrhaging of funds to campaigning—the cause of the recent split of the SEIU from the American Federation of Labor and Congress of Industrial Organizations (AFL-CIO).

Loach does not belabor the critique of union corporatization; he instead foregrounds the collective struggle of the workers in their local conditions. Sam leaves his paid position as union organizer to continue what seems like a losing battle against the building manager who employs the Angel Cleaning workers. In one scene, Sam interrupts the building manager's business lunch and as he announces how little the man pays his janitors (without lunch breaks), Sam eats a lambchop off the man's plate. This invasive, shaming move is above all effective. Like the cowboy vigilante hero of the old Western who breaks the law but is vindicated in the end, Sam achieves victory. As the Lower East Side Collective (LESC) in New York declare in their motto, Sam works "to make life miserable for bosses and bureaucrats" until they capitulate to workers' demands.[50] In the end of the film, Sam and Maya lead the workers in a march through the city toward the semi-public corporate plaza of the building that the Angel company's employees clean. The workers assert their sociopolitical membership in the city by demanding the recognition of their right to fair working conditions and insisting that workers fired for union involvement be reinstated. The film dramatizes the arc of this success through the narrative progression of events and their relation to urban space. In the beginning of the film, security guards force Maya out of the building's plaza, but by the end she and her coworkers successfully occupy this same contested corporate plaza space.

Like many activists, Loach locates corporations as the main center of operations of the city and as the source of split social formations. They are what Saskia Sassen has aptly called the "main spaces of authority in today's city," adding that the "vertical grid of the corporate tower is imbued with the same neutrality and rationality attributed to the horizontal grid in American cities."[51] That is, corporate culture is seen as impartial and precise and "ordered by technology, economic efficiency, [and] rationality."[52] Yet, corporations create an "amalgamated other" excluded from the elite day operations in the corporate towers, except perhaps as support staff.[53] *Bread and Roses* presents this "amalgamated other" as the invisible nighttime workforce that cleans the offices of the daytime professional class.

Sassen ponders how to remedy the split economies of corporate-backed urban formations: "How do we valorize the evicted components of the economy in a system that values the center?"[54] She approaches this question through politico-economic analyses of the city in which she herself discursively valorizes the "evicted components" by showing how they are integral to the operations at the center. These workers are crucial to the operations of the new global economic system, yet they are invisible. Sassen proposes a new perspective of global cities as a crucial "cogs" of globalization and as "command points, global marketplaces for capital, and production sites for the information economy," while they are also the sites of the invisible workforce who are "never represented as part of the global economy but are in fact as much a part of globalization as international finance."[55] This revaluation would help change the image-formation of the city; it would transform the ways we see and interpret the city and its inhabitants.

The invisibility of the Los Angeles workers allegorizes the larger marginality of the manual and service labor markets and the devaluation of labor in general. In *The Working Poor: Invisible in America*, David Shipler explains how consumers rarely factor the value of labor into the economic equation. In a striking example of this invisibility, he cites Tim Brookes' commentary on National Public Radio (NPR) in which Brookes expresses his outrage at the inflated price of popcorn at the movie theatre. Brookes does his own research on the "actual price" of the 5.25 ounces of popcorn, which he figures is 16.5 cents at bulk rate plus 5 cents for electricity and 1 cent for the bag, which netted the theater a $4.075 profit.[56] Shipler finds the ludic paradox of Brookes' analysis: "Evidently, the theater had the remarkable sense not to hire any workers, for Brookes gave no hint of having noticed any people behind the counter. Their paltry wages, which wouldn't have undermined the excessive profits, were absent from his calculation. The folks who popped the corn, filled the bag, handed the bag to him, and took his money must have been shrouded in an invisibility cloak. No NPR editor seemed to notice."[57] Surprisingly, even left-leaning and non-commercial NPR fails to recognize the importance and value of labor. Shipler makes visible this unseen labor force and offers solutions for further integration of the dispossessed into the mainstream of society.

In *Bread and Roses*, Maya rails against her status as invisible. She makes her presence known in a disruptive manner. For instance, at work she and a colleague are cleaning the entrance to an open elevator when some business professionals rudely step over them without acknowledging their presence. Her colleague, Ruben, asks if he has told her the story of the uniforms which *nos hacen invisibles*, "make us invisible." Maya subverts her apparitional status by pressing all the buttons on the elevator, to the frustration of the next batch of professionals who unknowingly walk into it. The prank is a satisfying diversion for Maya, but has little political effect since the professionals are mystified about its author. In another scene, she cons a gas station attendant and robs the gas station to help pay for her colleague's college tuition, perhaps thinking that without any legal record of her existence, she is untraceable. Though she helps her friend to achieve upward mobility, her actions give fodder to larger cultural phobias about the deleterious effect of immigration and the association of undocumented immigrants with illegality and criminality. She makes use of the insurrectionary antics of activism, but does not draw connections between labor organizing and political and legal visibility. Maya's reckless pranks against her status as invisible and undocumented serve no larger political agenda. These antics will become her downfall; they are in direct opposition to the political agenda of the labor movement: visibility. Invisibility, however, might be deployed more strategically; for instance, *A Day without a Mexican* (2004) exposes the consequences of the absence of the Mexican labor force in order to make their contributions visible. The main character Lila Rodriguez asks, "How do you make something invisible visible? You take it away." *Day without a Mexican* takes a different approach to the issue of the Mexican labor market in California as a whole while using Los Angeles as one focal point of the narrative. While *Bread and Roses* targets a specific aspect of the labor market in downtown Los Angeles, *Day without a Mexican* exposes the wide range of Latino occupations across every aspect of the culture of the state: from state officials, artists, and television anchors to farm laborers. Both films urge the political, cultural, social, and economic visibility of Latino labor in California, from the urban centers of power in Los Angeles in *Bread and Roses* to the larger array of contributions of Latinos in *Day without a Mexican*.

ACTIVISM 101

Bread and Roses is at moments dramatically didactic, using actual facts and figures from union work in which the contradictions of capitalism are played for high drama. "Justice for Janitors" union organizer Sam Shapiro first inducts Maya into the cause during a house visit. He shows Maya, Rosa, and her family how wages for janitors have steadily dropped from $8.50 plus benefits in 1982 to $5.75 without benefits seventeen years later in 1999. Sam plays to the type created in part by Tyne Daly as Alice the social justice worker in *Zoot Suit* (1981), or the union organizer Reuben, played by Ron Leibman in *Norma Rae* (1979), in which the union organizer is not from the ranks of those he or she is organizing in terms of race, ethnicity, and class. Loach exposes this tension when Rosa yells at Sam, calling him a "fat union white boy college kid," and throws him out of her house. Later, after another worker is fired for her refusal to rat out her colleagues, Maya asks Sam, "What do you risk? How much do you get paid?" We find out that he is paid quite little, but still twice what the janitors are making and presumably with benefits. He can't get fired for raising hell since his job is to protest companies and corporations that hire non-unionized workers; he is paid to take risks, whereas the janitors risk their jobs and their livelihood and often that of the extended family they support.

Ken Loach's position as a British filmmaker with a long curriculum of films addressing the concerns of the British working class is necessarily that of an outsider. He is not organically connected to the everyday politics of living and working in Los Angeles, nor is he connected to the film industry there. Critic Peter Matthews comments on his refreshingly naïve understanding and representation of the Hollywood elite: "A supposedly comical episode in which the exploited casuals invade a swank Hollywood party with their vacuum cleaners is so poorly staged it suggests that Loach has never been within miles of such an event."[58] The Hollywood party takes place in isolation; it is full of stars and their agents and lawyers, yet there is not even a hint of paparazzi. The scene of the arrival of the major industry players is eerily deserted and unimpressive. It reveals Loach's own alienation from the force field of Hollywood, which is perhaps his greatest virtue—his badge of sincerity. In this scene, the activists storm the Hollywood party to inform the showbiz elite exactly how little their agents, lawyers, and financiers are paying their janitors. This shaming encounter is so spectacular that it promptly makes the news. Cornered by bad publicity, the building managers have no choice but to capitulate to the demands of the workers.

Loach draws up an ending in which everyone wins but Maya. The bosses are publicly shamed into reinstating the workers and all workers receive health insurance and holidays. But Maya is found culpable of robbery and deported. The story ends as it began, with Maya in transit, but this time heading south. The answer, Loach suggests, is not in the creation of informal and subversive economies or in exploiting one's status as invisible, but in political engagement, the demand for recognition, and linking present struggles to their forebears. For instance, when those central to the protest are arrested, they give as their own the names of iconic Latin American revolutionaries: Emiliano Zapata, Augusto Sandino, and "Pancho" Villa.

THE PROLIFERATING BORDER

Much of Latino cinema from the 1990s exposed the unfair and inhumane conditions for Latinos in the city, the reality of a borderlining experience as an effect of globalization where, for instance, goods and capital freely travel across borders, but people do not. Los Angeles itself is a schizopolis where national border policies emerge in the city to limit the mobility of the urban underclass. Ken Loach's *Bread and Roses* is a labor activist film that reimagines the split city for those at the very bottom of the labor market. Loach imagines mobility as actual and symbolic, where movement across and around the city, into exclusive spaces and into better or more secure social positions, is the work of activism. For instance, in the beginning of *Bread and Roses* Maya is barred from entering the corporate building where Rosa works. By the end, the workers, including Maya, are occupying this space and protesting the unfair working conditions in the building. The story of the successful struggle for workers' rights is a powerful template for dramatic activist filmmaking, for imagining and presenting what some might deem impossible as possible.

In *Star Maps* and *El Norte*, the border that separates people and ideas by marking distinctions of type and kind is also a delineation between two states of mind: rational possession of one's faculties and psychic depropriation. Carlos and Enrique want success. They want to fulfill the dreams delivered by an increasingly ubiquitous Hollywood culture in which "making it" means making it onto the map of culture and gaining visibility, but only on the terms of an industry with deeply entrenched and eroticized racial fantasies and hierarchies. By internalizing this culture, these characters risk and endure an internal alienation. The borderizing psyche of the United States is as relentless as it is enduring; there is no fantasy, no dream, and no image beyond its colonizing reach. The border is part of an "American" lived experience, but it is part of a wide range of fantasies and ideas about U.S. national identity that destroy and divide psyches.

El Norte and *Star Maps* offer scandalizing yet cautionary stories for those on both sides. *El Norte* warns against full adoption of conservative American dream plots while it shames viewers whose touristic, colonial, and metropolitan gaze is cast on the Third Worlds around them. *Star Maps* pursues a similar purpose. It warns against the fantasy that anyone can make it, and make it intact, into the centers of U.S. popular culture, while it shames the colonial gaze that fetishizes, instrumentalizes, and consumes the colonized object. *Star Maps* exacts its critique in a more complex and nuanced manner than the earlier film. It is not just Carlos' Anglo male and female "johns" who lord over him, but also his sadistic father Pepe, the Anglo soap star Jennifer, and the entire film industry, including even the most liberal agents in Hollywood. The mapping of each character in the city is crucial to understanding the formation of racialized and sexual subjects and the restrictions on their movement. This process is wrought partly by the historical settlement of the city and the impact of globalization, which further entrenches the divisions that separate classes and communities.

Moving into the opportunity-ridden global city does not offer the films' protagonists a better life. Rather, the immigrant and racialized populations experience Los Angeles as uniquely deranging. The city doubly bipolarizes: literally in the split economy of the city, and symbolically in the seductive and deceptive images of a global city that is open and hospitable. The immigrant urban experience is a transnational disenfranchisement that cuts deeply into the operations of the city. This is the paradox of the global city: it is a major world center of economic, political, and cultural power, and yet as this power becomes more centralized, the socioeconomic structure of the city becomes more intensely bifurcated. The symbolic center of the city not only becomes more opposed to the periphery, but the periphery becomes more and more exiled from the city proper.

Moreover, the "global" aspect of the city refers more to the economy of a world system than to cultural inclusivity or a cosmopolitan embrace of the other, the stranger, or the immigrant. The city is spatially exclusionary; its internal boundaries reflect those of the nation ever more stringently. The global city reveals the problem of national borders and the various kinds of boundaries between nations, a problem that has more to do with exclusionary anxiety than actual economic or political benefit. In this era of globalization, large cities seem to diminish the presence and importance of national self-definition, yet symbolic dividing lines are intrinsic to the city and thrown into relief by the presence of the immigrant. The immigrant, having just crossed the border, is suddenly faced with a new border within the city.

Cinematic and televisual representations of Los Angeles, from the glamour and prosperity of gated communities to the poverty and urban blight of East and South Los Angeles, have long contributed to a divided visual experience of the city. These depictions reflect the split experience of the city; the two sides of town—the two types of depictions—exist separately, and never the twain shall meet. Rather than as a city doomed to Hollywood film and television representations of social divisions, we might reimagine Los Angeles as a powerful clearinghouse and meeting ground of the global south for the political agencies that seek just treatment for marginalized populations and fair terms for trade, labor relations, and immigration and international policy.

FRONTIER MYTHS ON THE LINE
BORDER CINEMA REDUX

Since the beginnings of cinema, Hollywood has depicted the U.S-Mexico border as a lawless place ruled by a dark mythology, and home to every illicit activity and industry. The cultural connotations of the borderlands are endless, from lacuna, fringe, outskirts, aporia, abyss, gap, or lapse in meaning to horizon, threshold, and boundary; borders suggest limits—the end and beginning of things or the edge to which you take things before the risk turns to crisis or sanity to madness. Crossing the dividing line calls forth what Jacques Lacan has called the "jouissance of transgression," or the limit experience in the thrilling exploration of the dangerous and forbidden, an experience that unhinges the subject and threatens to destroy a stable self-conception.[1] It is certainly no accident that the border zone has been the frontier of radical experience, where the United States citizen goes for underage drinking, exploration of various transgressive sexual acts and desires, gambling, and every vice forbidden by the standards of western morality. And it is not surprising that these outlaw practices converge on the border just below and beyond the national body. Hollywood border films play out the psychic drama of border transgressions that allegorize a larger threat to the integrity of U.S. national identity.

Hollywood border films have always been primarily about the maintenance of the integrity of U.S. national identity and the need to control the border to exclude foreign-born populations. The founding cosmopolitan idea of the nation-state as a hospitable terrain open to those seeking asylum and survival is no longer part of the complex of issues around immigration. Rather, public discourse about immigration is replete with post-9/11 concerns about its various hazards. The cosmopolitan idea of political unification of the Americas so prevalent before the turn of the century has transformed into that of a fortified North America waging a war on the border against an "invasion" from the global south, which includes all manner of criminalized immigrants, from purported terrorists to drug traffickers and agents of Venezuelan president Hugo Chávez. Border films and other forms of popular media reflect and promote a hostile shift in attitude against migrants and foreigners within an ever-increasing preoccupation with national security.

In many post–World War II border Westerns, the border is little more than an imaginary line in the desert or naturally existing river that functions as a major political referent for each side of the hemisphere. The vagueness of the boundary is significant since the border had yet to be fully defined due to cultural, political, and economic fluctuations after the Civil War. Many Westerns, like *The Wild Bunch*, show the difference between nations in makeshift signs indicating the limits of the United States; these are signposts of how effectively the United States has institutionalized control of the border, from early signage to the contemporary fortress-like barricade.

At the height of the Western genre, the border was a defining symbol by which audiences could explore and monitor the dynamics and tensions of U.S. relations to Mexico in particular and to the rest of the hemisphere in general. Border Westerns remythologize the major events of history toward a more favorable outcome for the United States. Many of the issues and problems that demanded resignification were themselves the major battles of history that led to changes in the territorial boundaries of the United States. For example, border films neutralized cultural tensions subsequent to the Louisiana Purchase by including French characters who become acculturated by an Anglo lead. Such is the case in *The Comancheros*, which features Frenchman Paul Regret, whom the morally upright Texas Ranger captain Jake Cutter, played by John Wayne, rehabilitates from his French decadence. Yet, the historical circumstances that led to changes in the size and power of the United States are not part of the overt narrative or story discourse. Rather, they are encoded in the stories in plotlines that follow a mythic historical line: all battles are won, new territories are swiftly integrated, racial and ethnic outsiders assimilate without complaint, and the cowboy, Texas Ranger, and cavalry continue to reign over the Southwest.

By the early twentieth century, the western frontier had lost some of its representational power to the southern frontier. The southern line replaced the western frontier as a major organizing symbol of popular culture because it defined the nation on different, more modern terms: the United States was now bounded, limited, and exclusive.

The postwar Westerns emphasized the imperative for U.S. intervention in Latin America as a source of hemispheric security, often played out against the ghost of the invidious French empire of Maximilian. The United States, in the form of cowboys, cavalry, ex–U.S. Civil War officers, and mercenary gunmen, wanders into Mexico to help Mexicans defend their land. By the 1980s, the tone of the border Western had shifted toward a new emphasis on the internal politics of national defense against an unwanted immigrant "invasion." These films were not outright Westerns in the strict sense of the genre, but shared in its themes. *Borderline, The Border,* and *Flashpoint* trade the Texas Ranger and cavalry for the U.S. Border Patrol, the new unit of southwestern policing. The stories and plotlines of these films of the 1980s are more complex than is evident at first appearance. These B-grade stories are laden with references to other eras of U.S. history; like the Western, they encode many of the traumas of past conflicts and remainders of history. While they appear to raise more issues and conflicts than can be resolved in the time of a feature-length film, they resolve them easily and point to familiar solutions. In each story, the United States suffers from weak borders and a weaker will to police these borders. The solution is to increase the power of the border patrol. Though these films allude to a liberal discourse about immigration, suggesting that immigration is partly an effect of economic and other kinds of exile, this discourse is eclipsed by the larger fear of a U.S. public inundated by immigrants. The southern frontier, the symbol of a modern nation in the postwar Western, became, in the 1980s, a frightening chasm and a porous boundary. In many of these films, the reappearance of the Vietnam veteran on the border is more than just curious; it is a recurring trope that signifies the crises of national identity and the persistent need to resignify failure, Alamo-style, into moral triumph. Many border films depict Vietnam veterans as rogue border denizens whom the films link to failures of national security symbolized by the undefended frontier.

The border that demanded policing in the 1980s became the subject of full-scale war by the late 1980s. By the late 1980s, the war on drugs had reached Hollywood with a vengeance. The border patrol, DEA agents, and Texas Rangers in border drug trafficking films provide cultural redemption from the moral degradation of a globalization that opens borders and lets in agents of an evil Latin American drug empire. These border drug trafficking films contribute to a battle of perceptions between the United States and Latin America, Mexico in particular, and intensify the inter-American drug war. They suggest connections among drugs, border control, and terrorism that would continue to shape cultural agenda into the present.

Border drug trafficking films often feature a "narc" hero whose mission is to bring down drug trafficking kingpins, a simple solution that suggests that hemispheric drug trade is readily "solvable" through the U.S.-sponsored war on drugs. This idea contradicts the work of critics who claim that the war on drugs has been a phenomenal failure and has merely intensified drug trafficking–related violence and increased production across the Americas. Yet, even as the dynamics of the drug trade change, the "war on drugs" in Hollywood border films remains the same.

Critical Latino border films pose a challenge to the prevailing perceptions of the borderlands of Hollywood. Many of these films are based in Los Angeles, a place that many have called the largest border city of the United States. Films like *El Norte, Star Maps*, and *Bread and Roses* associate the national boundary with divisions across the city. These films challenge the polarization of Los Angeles and expose the exclusion and denigration of Latinos, Chicanos, and Latin American immigrants in the largest border city of the Southwest. They expose the disparities and divisions rendered by the fracturing economies of globalization. All of these films, to varying degrees, examine the effects of globalization on those at the very bottom of the labor market. Although all three films are critical of the conditions for Latinos in the city, *Bread and Roses* offers some practical solutions drawn from the history and practices of labor activism, citing actual examples of successful campaigns in Los Angeles. The film guides the viewer through all the steps and possible problems of labor activism, while it also shows the potential outcomes—the workers receive the benefits they were seeking while the protagonist, Maya, is deported for a crime she committed while acting as a "Robin Hood." *Bread and Roses* offers the message that it is possible for undocumented workers to escape the vicious cycle of poverty and invisibility in the largest border city of the United States.

BORDER WESTERN REDUX

It is not surprising that the border Western is the film genre that most readily tackles the issue of the political, racial, gendered, sexual, and ethnic borders of the United States and the relationship of the United States to the rest of the southern hemisphere. Ray Merlock has called the Western one of the major "building blocks" of filmmaking to which films of all genres owe tremendous debt.[2] Since the classical period the Western has undergone many different transformations, including the liberal reconstruction of Western themes and tropes in the 1990s. Tania Modleski finds that nostalgia for classical Westerns coincides with a disdain for the 1990s liberal interventions of the genre that put African-Americans or women at the revisionist narrative helm, such as in *Posse* (1993) or *The Ballad of Little Jo* (1993), thus knocking out the Anglo male center of the moral universe.[3] Many critics do not have the same nostalgic fixation with the revisionist Westerns as they do with the earlier classical and post-classical periods of the genre. Many claim that the 1990s versions of the genre are not Westerns proper because of the changed affect and tone of the tales.

Two contemporary Westerns have changed the mood of the revisionist tale, putting it squarely back into the nostalgic register, albeit with a few significant changes. *Brokeback Mountain* (2005) and *The Three Burials of Melquiades Estrada* (2005) offer new meditations on "American" identity through the country's most hallowed genre.[4] As the most contemporary examples of the Western genre, these films attest to the ways that it is continually being reimagined and redeployed to explore the most salient issues of contemporary culture. These films put both U.S. culture and its major media industry on the line; they force an examination of the myths of the West and the Southwest and their role in national self-definition. Both films deal in some manner with male intimacy, both sexual and emotional, in worlds in which women are secondary and marginal. They explore the fantasies and mythology of the southwesterner: the desert or open plains that signify a freedom of movement and congress and the cowboy-*vaquero* buddies alone on the range without the encumbrance of women and domestic restrictions. As in post–World War II border Westerns and their 1980s and 1990s incarnations, real trouble begins when one member of the couple is murdered; the freedoms they held so dearly are tested and they experience the incursion of culture and society as the pure negation of death.

Jim Kitses describes *Brokeback Mountain*'s relationship to the Western genre as a "confused and contested question" for its "reliance on genre aesthetics and motifs to shape its lament for a broken America."[5] Kitses calls protagonists Ennis and Jack "prototypical cowboys" and "authentic American heroes, self-reliant and brave, honorable and loyal."[6] But this cowboy individualism is at odds with modern liberal culture. Ennis is unable to accept the implications of his love for Jack until it is too late, marking the film's generic turn to melodrama—the film fuses the two genres very much like *Duel in the Sun*.[7] In fact, the painful love story between these two modern-day cowboys eclipsed the generic frame of the story for many viewers. The story appealed more to a gay and predominantly female audience, partly thanks to the way that it was marketed and reviewed as a tragic love story.[8] In fact, Chris Berry notes that director Ang Lee exploited a popular Chinese narrative form in which a gay male romance is framed for a heterosexual female audience. Berry acknowledges that there are small female subcultures of western women who consume gay male stories in popular culture, most notably the "slash" subculture that gains pleasure in turning male buddies into intimate couples.[9]

Annie Proulx wrote the short story on which Ang Lee's film version of *Brokeback Mountain* is based. Her story is an homage to what she calls the "country gay," and the short story was "constructed on the small but tight idea of a couple of home-grown country kids, opinions and self-knowledge shaped by the world around them, finding themselves in emotional waters of increasing depth."[10] "Brokeback Mountain" is about the isolation of Wyoming and also about the destructiveness of rural homophobia. Proulx herself rejects the idea that the story is a cowboy romance, and insists on the dangerous realities for gays in Wyoming, remarking that just one year after the story was published, Matthew Shepard, a student at the University of Wyoming, was beaten to death for being gay. She also reminds us that Wyoming has the highest suicide rate in the country and that the majority of these suicides are elderly single men.

The screenwriters of *Brokeback Mountain*, Diana Ossana and Larry McMurtry, were drawn to the screen adaptation of Annie Proulx's story for the powerful evocativeness of its spare language. Before beginning their work together, they dismissed fears about "being involved in a film that subverts the myth of the American West and its iconic heroes."[11]

The main characters, Jack and Ennis, meet while they are alone tending sheep, a scenario that Proulx takes from the comments of an old sheep farmer who used to send two men out " 'so's if they get lonesome they can poke each other.' "[12] Kitses notes that sheepherders are marginal figures in Westerns, dominated by the cowboy figure of the horse or cattle wrangler. There is nothing heroic in herding sheep, an

5.1 "Prototypical cowboys" Jack (Jake Gyllenhaal) and Ennis (Heath Ledger).

occupation that has often been relegated to immigrants and minorities, as is the case in *The Three Burials of Melquiades Estrada*, in which undocumented *vaquero* Melquiades works with goats.

Jack and Ennis embody the culture and moral values of the Old West in their prosaic speech, rugged survivalism, fierce independence, and stoic masculinity. The isolation of Brokeback Mountain enables them to build an intimacy based on desire, but their reentry into the social world of the sheep ranch immediately destroys their tenuous erotic bond—which culminates in a campfire scene reminiscent of that between River Phoenix and Keanu Reeves in *My Own Private Idaho* (1991). The two men maintain their friendship over the years along with their idealistic recollections of their time together on Brokeback Mountain—clearly a generic citation of the infamous Monument Valley of Ford lore.[13] However, their internalized homophobia leads them to pursue the normative route of heterosexual marriage. They continue to meet periodically at Brokeback Mountain, but are unable to move this intimacy out of the abstraction and isolation of the countryside. Their relationship fades into oblivion when Jack dies unexpectedly.

The death of Jack reminds Ennis that one cannot live in the myth of the isolated and free frontier, because the myth of the Old West and its male utopias is exactly that—a myth. The reality of the modern world is that same-sex sexual and intimate bonds are named, which defines them and gives them political meaning and visibility. Ennis fears the consequences of this reality, which fuels his anxious imagining of Jack's death not as an accident as it is described, but as the result of a brutal gay bashing. But there is yet another source of anxiety for some members of the film's audience, as identified by Ben Sifuentes-Jáuregui:

En la recién estrenada y controvertida película de Ang Lee, Brokeback Mountain (difundida en América Latina con los títulos En terreno vedado y Secreto en la montaña) basada en un cuento de Annie Proulx, hay una escena que me causó mucha ansiedad. No me refiero a las escenas románticas entre los protagonistas, Jack y Ennis, que desataron un debate homofóbico en los círculos de la derecha estadounidense, sino al momento en que Jack decide viajar a la comunidad fronteriza de Cuidad Juárez para encontrar "what he needs" (aquello que necesita).[14]

[In Ang Lee's recent and controversial film, Brokeback Mountain (Prohibited Land and Secret in the Mountain in Latin America) based on the story of Annie Proulx, there is a scene that caused me much anxiety. I'm not referring to the romantic scenes between the protagonists Jack and Ennis, which unleashed a homophobic debate in right-wing circles of the United States, but the moment in which Jack decides to travel to the border community of Ciudad Juárez to find "what he needs."]

Jack goes to the border in search of a Mexican man who will submit to his gay desires. This scene is not only an homage to border Westerns in which everything illicit happens below the border; it also locates the film absolutely and unequivocally in the Hollywood border genre, regardless of its semi-independent lineage and auteur markings. The border remains the place where North Americans can find racialized sexual adventures not permitted on U.S. national terrain. For Sifuentes-Jáuregui, the border encounter is a depressing reminder that Latin/o Americans remain outside the U.S. norm and that Latinos are a fetishized sign of difference to an Anglo and white imaginary, while the borderlands symbolize *ese espacio oscuro de un no yo, o de un yo incompleto*, "this obscure space of a non-I or of an incomplete I."[15] This negation of racial and other outsiders is the legacy of the border genre and its place at the center of questions of 'American' identity. There is no place in U.S. popular culture to examine the complex question of same-sex desire for the anonymous Latino man on the border. The trailer for the twenty-third annual Chicago Latino Film Festival dramatizes this impossibility in a rather phobic manner: two *vaqueros* are leaning against a fence when one leans in to kiss the other, who promptly puts good distance between himself and the offending kisser. A caption surfaces: "This is not Hollywood." The films of the Latino film festival are certainly not funded by Hollywood, and many will not enjoy the promotion or distribution dollars of the Hollywood machine, but the caption raises the question of what differentiates the festival from Hollywood. While implying that the exploration of same-sex desire and intimacy is not the province of the Latino film festival, it misses the more obvious critical target in this citation of *Brokeback Mountain*—that Latino men are not consumable objects of Anglo male heroes—and forges a subtle alliance with the dominant Hollywood filmgoer who is not in favor of seeing two male Western/ranchero heroes in love with each other.

Westerns have always captivated audiences with long panoramic shots of the open desert or plains, a geography cast as the "American" future—the frontier and threshold onto a new way. These films present the promise and the burden of the open range, the leap toward the future and the undertow of the past. The current image of the border has taken danger beyond the limit, beyond the point of no return. Since the border became a militarized zone and thus a place of imperiled passage and risk, the number of deaths from crossing the inhospitable desert has risen drastically. The borderlands, typically associated with risk, are now associated more often with death, from death in passage to the women murdered in the border city of Ciudad Juárez. Even the symbolic resonance of "crossing over" evokes the delimitation of life and death on the border. The threat of death in the harsh borderland desert for undocumented northbound crossers intensifies the symbolic resonance of the partition dividing north from south.

The *Three Burials of Melquiades Estrada* turns the death of one of the protagonists into a negation of a different kind—the death of the U.S.-based mythology of Mexico and the dissolution of the Western fantasy displaced onto Mexico. The film tells of Pete, played by Tommy Lee Jones, and his best friend and hired help, undocumented *vaquero* Melquiades (Julio Cedillo). When Mike, an errant border patrolman, kills Melquiades, Pete kidnaps Mike and drags him and the corpse of Melquiades to his final restitution in Mexico. Tommy Lee Jones, who also directed the film, talks about the film as a collaborative effort with writer Guillermo Arriaga that is equal parts Mexican and U.S. filmmaking. Jones describes the process of developing the guiding themes for the screenplay with screenwriter Arriaga:

First, we began to talk about themes, things that we had concerns about and interests that we had in common. He [Arriaga] wants to make movies about his country and its history, I want to make movies about my country and its history, and you don't have to spend much time [in Mexico] before you see that in a lot of ways the two countries are the same. So we decided early on that we were going to do a study in social contrasts, a consideration of how things are the same on both sides of the river and how things are different.[16]

Eleven drafts later, the screenplay became the final version of this U.S.-Mexican collaboration. The film version, however, is more about the Anglo male couples' journey into the heart of darkness of U.S. myths and cinematic histories of cross-border encounters. In fact the corpse of Melquiades might represent the death of these fantasies about the place of Mexico and Mexicans in the U.S. imaginary.

Tommy Lee Jones claims to have chosen the name Melquiades for the simple reason that it is manifestly difficult for non-Spanish speaking Americans to pronounce. However, he overlooks the reference to a particularly infamous Melquíades, the alchemist gypsy of Gabriel García Márquez's *Cien años de soledad*. It is the nomadic Melquíades who introduces José Arcadio Buendía to the marvels and innovations of the world beyond the small village of Macondo. Though the choice of the name is accidental, the legacy of García Marquez's Melquíades resonates with that of *The Three Burials of Melquiades Estrada*; both characters bring the wonders of elsewhere to a small-town man.

In the final scene, Pete wanders off into the sunset, as do his counterparts in much of Western lore, but he leaves behind Mike, the border patrol agent whom he has taken hostage. The film, as the title indicates, is divided among the three burials, and the final burial is the restitution of Melquiades' body to the fantasy homeland of Jimenez as well as the putting to rest of U.S. fantasies of Mexico. Like that of *El Norte*, the tripartite structure of *The Three Burials of Melquiades Estrada* recalls the cyclical pattern of myths and mythologies, and in both films, the final part unveils the myths and fantasies of the main characters, which coincides with the end of their journeys. The difference in the case of

The Three Burials is that, like some post–civil war Westerns, notably *Vera Cruz*, the border narrative is reversed, with Anglo travelers making a southern Mexico-bound journey. Arriaga, the prolific co-writer of the screenplay, has recently introduced this kind of journey elsewhere in the Hollywood imaginary.

Babel, written by Arriaga and directed by Mexican co-patriot Alejandro González Iñárritu, is comprised of three stories, one of which involves a border crossing into the United States with an entirely different type of migrant. As in *The Three Burials*, the crosser is imagined differently, and this new image serves to critically reconstruct the dominant conception of border crossings. In this story, Amelia, played by Mexican actress Adriana Barraza, is the housekeeper/babysitter of an Anglo couple from San Diego. They leave her in charge of their two young, blonde children while the couple, Richard and Susan Jones, goes on a trip to Morocco. While on vacation, Susan is shot and wounded, and they prolong their stay while she awaits treatment. Amelia must remain with the children longer than expected and faces the possibility of missing her son's wedding in northern Mexico. Rather than miss the wedding, she decides to take the two children with her, crossing the border into Mexico. During this journey, the two blonde children, both under the age of ten, are a continual point of reference as the audience sees everything from their excited and amused vantage, in which all things Mexican register as novelties.

The wedding party comes to an end late into the night and Amelia undertakes the long drive back into the United States with her inebriated nephew, Santiago, played by Mexican actor Gael García Bernal. The checkpoint at the border puts a quick end to any remaining sense of revelry, and panic sets in after routine questioning turns into detainment. The children cry inconsolably in the background as Amelia and Santiago exchange heated words with the patrolling officer. Suddenly, Santiago makes a run for the United States, gunning the car across the border. He drops Amelia and the kids in the desert and continues the high-speed chase with the border patrol to its inevitable conclusion. At this point, the border narrative has shifted ground; the poor, terrified, and weary children elicit our full sympathies as they make their way across the abysmal desert.

The critical innovation in the new border narratives is the reverse focalization on the part of the protagonists, where, for instance, the real process of demythologization begins in *The Three Burials*, with border patrolman Mike, and in *Babel*, with the two Anglo children. The dominant Hollywood audience member identifies with the main Anglo characters in the position of migrants, thereby experiencing their various tribulations in the struggle for survival as they cross the inhospitable desert. *The Three Burials* takes this voyage a bit further. Mike is literally dragged through the desert to face all of his prejudices about Mexicans; for instance, he meets one of the migrants whom he beat up and debased as a border patrol agent and he accepts his fate when she returns the favor. We sense that he is changing at various points in the journey and at the end, when Pete demands that he ask Melquiades for forgiveness, Mike is truly contrite.

In part three of *The Three Burials of Melquiades Estrada*, the narrative moral point of reference shifts entirely from Pete to Mike. When Pete arrives in a town he believes to be close to the town of Jimenez, he asks some people in a local *tienda* for directions, showing them the photo of the alleged wife of Melquiades. The shopkeepers exchange knowing gazes as they inform Pete that there is no such town and that the woman in the picture has another name and husband. This scenario repeats when Pete claims to have found Jimenez as Mike watches him knowingly and with sorrow. We are now aware that Pete finally and irrevocably has crossed the border into insanity in his utter belief of Melquiades' fantasy.

Like *Lone Star*, *The Three Burials of Melquiades Estrada* critiques the myths and everyday experiences of Anglos along the border. But it goes further than *Lone Star* if we consider Rosa Linda Fregoso's critique of the latter as affirmative of a benevolent paternalism. *The Three Burials of Melquiades Estrada* takes the idea of the benevolent Anglo, long a trope of the border film, to its logical extreme. This deconstruction is a unique consequence of the cross-border collaboration between Arriaga and Jones. Arriaga locates the Anglo benevolence as part of an Anglo male fantasy about Mexicans and Mexico. He extends this fantasy to the point where it can no longer sustain itself and crumbles into an abject and ludicrous reality. The film interrupts the mythic history of Mexico created by the Western and its border kin. Melquiades' permanent grimace is a half-mocking smile at the increasingly ridiculous antics of Tommy Lee Jones' character. After *The Three Burials*, we might rethink what it means to "make a run for the border," and what we rethink might be awaiting us when we get there. In the end, as in the final scene of *El Mariachi* (1992), the joke is on the unwitting gringo, who, no matter how culturally reconstructed, or how critical, is still immersed in a North American culture that has defined itself at every turn against Mexico and Mexicans, against Mexican labor and immigration, and against the Mexican culture of the Southwest.

NOTES

PREFACE

1. Michael McCaul, "Investigations Border Report," U.S. House of Representatives Web site.

2. *A Day without a Mexican*, dir. Sergio Arau, official movie Web site.

3. Sergio Arau and Yareli Arizmendi, "Un cambio social de gran magnitude" in *Un día sin inmigrantes: Quince voces, una causa*, ed. Gina Montaner, 23–30.

4. Nicolás Kanellos, *Thirty Million Strong: Reclaiming the Hispanic Image in American Culture*, vii.

INTRODUCTION

1. "Tunnels Show Dangers on Porous U.S.-Mexican Border," *New American*, 7.

2. Ibid.

3. Norma Iglesias, "Reconstructing the Border: Mexican Border Cinema and Its Relationship to Its Audience" in *Mexico's Cinema: A Century of Film and Filmmakers*, ed. Joanne Hirshfield and David R. Maciel, 233.

4. Alex M. Saragoza, "The Border in American and Mexican Cinema," *Aztlán*, 156.

5. María Herrera-Sobek, "Border Aesthetics: The Politics of Mexican Immigration in Film and Art," *Western Humanities Review*, 63.

6. Ibid.

7. Some of the production dates of these films do not correspond to those in the filmography. This could be due to redistribution of the same titles by different companies.

8. María Herrera-Sobek, "The Corrido as Hypertext: Undocumented Mexican Immigration Films and the Mexican/Chicano Ballad" in *Culture Across Borders: Mexican Immigration and Popular Culture*, ed. David R. Maciel and María Herrera-Sobek, 227–258.

9. See Charles Ramírez Berg, "Ethnic Ingenuity and Mainstream Cinema: Robert Rodríguez's *Bedhead* (1990) and *El Mariachi* (1993)" in *Latino Images in Film: Stereotypes, Subversion, Resistance*, 225–227.

10. David R. Maciel and María Rosa García-Acevedo, "The Celluloid Immigrant: The Narrative Films of Mexican Immigration" in Maciel and Herrera-Sobek, *Culture Across Borders*, 149–202.

11. Iglesias, "Reconstructing the Border," 234.

12. Herrera-Sobek, "Border Aesthetics," 60–71.

13. See Allen L. Woll, *The Latin Image in American Film*.

14. Woll, *The Latin Image*, 13–14.

15. Arnoldo De León, *They Called Them Greasers: Anglo Attitudes toward Mexicans in Texas, 1821–1900*.

16. De León, *They Called Them Greasers*, 16.

17. Luis Reyes and Peter Rubie, *Hispanics in Hollywood: A Celebration of 100 Years in Film and Television*, 5.

18. Quoted in Steven W. Bender, *Greasers and Gringos: Latinos, Law, and the American Imagination*, 55. Bender notes that this anti-loitering law created a precedent for contemporary curfew statements and ordinances that use racially neutral language to target racially coded groups and activities.

19. Charles Ramírez Berg, "Stereotyping in Films in General and of the Hispanic in Particular" in *Latin Looks: Images of Latinas and Latinos in the U.S. Media*, ed. Clara E. Rodriguez, 113.

20. Recently, in one of the first depictions of female bandits, the film *Bandidas* (2006) with Spanish actress Penélope Cruz and Mexican Salma Hayek portrays a couple of female social bandits in turn-of-the-century Mexico who rob from the rich to aid the poor.

21. Rosa Linda Fregoso, *MeXicana Encounters: The Making of Social Identities on the Borderlands*, 128.

22. See Ramírez Berg, "Stereotyping in Films," 113.

23. Eric Hobsbawm, *Bandits*. See also María Herrera-Sobek's discussion of the bandit in *Northward Bound: The Mexican Immigrant Experience in Ballad and Song*.

24. The name has been used by a punk rock band of immigrants who reclaimed the title for a bad boy outlaw aesthetic.

25. Joseph Nevins, *Operation Gatekeeper: The Rise of the "Illegal Alien" and the Making of the U.S.-Mexico Boundary*, 79.

26. The plot was rehashed yet again in 1941 in a film of the same name.

27. Walter Prescott Webb, *The Texas Rangers: A Century of Frontier Defense*, 11. The "Indian warrior, Mexican vaquero, and Texas Ranger" were each the respective "representative fighting man" for the "three races that were to struggle for supremacy" in Texas.

28. The term "Native American" eliminates the colonial implications of Christopher Columbus' misnaming of the indigenous peoples of the Americas as "Indians" and it specifies natives of the Americas over those of India. However, in the pre-1960s history and popular culture of the Southwest, the civil rights era term "Native American" seems ahistorical. I use the term "Indian" to describe characters in the terms used within the film or historical texts in which they appear; however, I use the term "Native American" in all other instances. For more on this see Fergus M. Bordevich, *Killing the White Man's Indian: Reinventing Native Americans at the End of the Twentieth Century*.

29. Webb, *The Texas Rangers*, xv.

30. See Gary Clayton Anderson, *The Conquest of Texas: Ethnic Cleansing in the Promised Land, 1820–1875.*

31. Américo Paredes, *"With a Pistol in His Hand": A Border Ballad and Its Hero,* 23–24.

32. Paredes, *"With a Pistol,"* 24.

33. John Weaver, *The Brownsville Raid.* See also Anderson, *The Conquest of Texas;* Julian Samora, Joe Bernal, and Albert Peña, *Gunpowder Justice: A Reassessment of the Texas Rangers.*

34. Herrera-Sobek, *Northward Bound,* 3–5.

35. Ibid., 3.

36. Charles Zurhorst, *The First Cowboys and Those Who Followed,* 12.

37. Ibid., 29–30

38. Ibid., 38.

39. Arnold Rojas, *Lore of the California Vaquero* (Fresno, Calif.: Academy Library Guild, 1958), cited in Maria Herrera-Sobek, *Northward Bound,* 4.

40. See Herrera-Sobek, *Northward Bound,* 4–5.

41. Rick Altman, *Film/Genre,* 13–31.

42. Thomas Schatz, *Hollywood Genres: Formulas, Filmmaking, and the Studio System,* 6.

43. See Thomas Schatz, *Hollywood Genres;* Janet Feuer, *The Hollywood Musical;* John Cawelti, *The Six Gun Mystique.*

44. See Altman, *Film/Genre,* 44–47. Altman cites the example of Darryl Zanuck's attempt to outline Warner's plans for 1933 to produce a larger number of "headliners," or films that have the same impact as the news headlines. The genre of "headliner" did not consolidate, but rather individual films tended to assimilate to other recognizable genre types.

45. See Schatz, *Hollywood Genres,* 16, for this discussion of "static" and "dynamic."

46. Altman, *Film/Genre,* 214.

47. See Janet Staiger, *Perverse Spectators: The Practices of Film Reception.*

48. Schatz, *Hollywood Genres,* 16–17.

49. Gloria Anzaldúa, *Borderlands/La Frontera,* 3.

50. See Héctor Calderón and José David Saldívar, eds., *Criticism in the Borderlands: Studies in Chicano Literature, Culture, and Ideology.*

51. Pablo Vila, *Crossing Borders, Reinforcing Borders: Social Categories, Metaphors, and Narrative Identities on the U.S.-Mexico Frontier,* 1–2. Vila gives the example of the NAFTA-induced border patrol intensification program called Operation Blockade. It surprised many people not of the border region that this program was authored by Mexican-American borderlands native Silvestre Reyes and that it was supported by a majority of Mexican-Americans in El Paso. This scenario, Vila finds, is particular to parts of the borderlands where unreconstructed forms of self-identification are deployed as a means of survival.

52. The history of border cinema often points to this ideological cross fire. This conflict is conveyed in *Lone Star* during a PTA meeting where Anglo parents are angrily contesting the Mexican-American teacher's non-boosterish

depiction of the Alamo. There are two sides to the discussion, not a plethora of voices and perspectives. The immigration issue in this country is also seen more in terms of a debate than a negotiation. It would be reductive to assert two polarizing types of border cinema—Latino and Hollywood—since there is no totalizing image of either; rather, in this study, I explore independent and Hollywood industry films together as part of the same dialogue.

53. Vila, *Crossing Borders, Reinforcing Borders*, 68; María Herrera-Sobek, *The Bracero Experience: Elitelore versus Folklore*, 26–27.

54. See, for example, *Pocho.com: Satire, News y Chat for the Spanglish Generation*; Vila, *Crossing Borders, Reinforcing Borders*, 107.

55. See League of United Latin American Citizens official Web site.

56. Claire F. Fox, *The Fence and the River: Culture and Politics at the U.S.-Mexico Border*, 8–9.

57. Schatz, *Hollywood Genres*, 58.

58. Ibid.

59. A good example of this global anxiety is apparent in the plot of *Gilda* (1946) in which Ballin's designs on world domination are played out in Buenos Aires with the help of "German visitors" and plenty of Pan-American intrigue.

60. See part four of Richard Slotkin, *Gunfighter Nation: The Myth of the Frontier in Twentieth-Century America*, 347–486; Stanley Corkin, *The Cowboy as Cold Warrior: The Western and U.S. History*, 1–18.

61. Slotkin, *Gunfighter Nation*, 349.

62. Chon A. Noriega, ed., introduction to *Chicanos and Film: Representation and Resistance*, xiv–xvii.

63. Charles Ramírez Berg, *Latino Images in Film: Stereotypes, Subversion, and Resistance*, 124–126.

64. Leo Chavez, *Covering Immigration: Popular Images and the Politics of the Nation*.

65. Otto Santa Ana, *Brown Tide Rising: Metaphors of Latinos in Contemporary American Public Discourse*, 69–70.

66. Kent A. Ono and John M. Sloop, *Shifting Borders: Rhetoric, Immigration, and California's Proposition 187*.

67. See Fregoso, *MeXicana Encounters*, 127–128.

68. See Nicholas J. Cull and Davíd Carrasco, eds., *Alambrista and the U.S.-Mexico Border: Film, Music, and Stories of Undocumented Immigrants*.

69. Mike Davis, *City of Quartz*.

70. William V. Flores and Rina Benmayor, eds., "Introduction: Constructing Cultural Citizenship" in *Latino Cultural Citizenship*.

71. Gustavo Leclerc and Michael J. Dear, "Introduction: La vida latina en L.A." in *La Vida Latina en L.A.: Urban Latino Cultures*, ed. Gustavo Leclerc, Raúl Villa, and Michael J. Dear, 3.

72. Leclerc, Villa, and Dear. *La Vida Latina en L.A.*, 1.

73. Flores and Benmayor, *Latino Cultural Citizenship*, 6.

74. Ibid., 10–11.

75. Ibid., 5–6.

76. See Chris Berry, "The Chinese Side of the Mountain," *Film Quarterly*, 33.

CHAPTER ONE

1. James K. Folsom, introduction to *The Western: A Collection of Critical Essays*, 1.

2. Turner's frontier thesis embeds an exceptionalist ideology; he argues that the land was "free" rather than occupied, "settled" rather than conquered, and that progress is defined as the linear onslaught of modernity. In the search for that which is truly "American," the Turner thesis abstracted the United States from a world context.

3. Frederick Jackson Turner, "The Significance of the Frontier in American History," *The Turner Thesis*, ed. George Rogers Taylor, 3.

4. Quoted in Peter Sahlins, *Boundaries: The Making of France and Spain in the Pyrenees*, xv.

5. This short list of films also traces one dimension of the history of Latinos in the Hollywood film industry from marginal and secondary roles in *Rio Grande* (1950), *Vera Cruz* (1954), *Rio Bravo* (1959), *The Comancheros* (1961), and *The Wild Bunch* (1969)—where Cuban-born, Mexican-raised filmmaker Alfonso Arau (*Like Water for Chocolate*, based on the novel written by Arau's wife Laura Esquivel) made his appearance as an actor and protégé of Sam Peckinpah—to the leading role for Mexican actor Jorge Rivero in *Rio Lobo* (1970). By the 1960s, Latinos were more likely to be cast in the lead roles in films, but it was not until the 1990s, with the rise of "Hispanic Hollywood" that these roles had shifted more fully from individuals to the fuller context of family and community.

6. Jack Nachbar, ed., introduction to *Focus on the Western*, 3.

7. See Thomas E. Skidmore and Peter H. Smith, *Modern Latin America*, 370–71.

8. Ibid., 239.

9. Ibid.

10. Albert J. Griffith, "The Scion, the Señorita, and the Texas Ranch Epic: Hispanic Images in Film," *Bilingual Review*, 15–22.

11. Thomas Schatz, "The New Hollywood" in *Film Theory Goes to the Movies*, ed. Jim Collins, Hilary Radner, and Ava Preacher Collins, 11.

12. Reyes and Rubie, *Hispanics in Hollywood*, 110–112.

13. See Reyes and Rubie, *Hispanics in Hollywood*, 111. Reyes and Rubie remark on this unique feature of the story, the centrality of a Spanish surnamed character.

14. Quoted in Reyes and Rubie, *Hispanics in Hollywood*, 112.

15. According to Lewt McCanles, Pearl's father is the "white half"; the name Chavez and the border town location seem to suggest that he is a Creole Mexican of Spanish descent.

16. Jacquelyn Kilpatrick, *Celluloid Indians: Native Americans and Film,* xvii.

17. Laura Mulvey, "Afterthoughts on 'Visual Pleasure and Narrative Cinema'" in *Popular Fiction: Technology, Ideology Production, Reading,* ed. Tony Bennett, 147.

18. See the documentary *Border Bandits: A True Tale of South Texas* (2004).

19. Donald Fixico, *Termination and Relocation: Federal Indian Policy, 1945–1960,* ix.

20. Francis Paul Prucha, ed., *Documents of United States Indian Policy,* 175.

21. The town is immediately recognizable as a Mexican border town for its post-prohibition history of providing vices unavailable in the United States.

22. Linda Williams, "Film Bodies: Gender, Genre, and Excess" in *Film and Theory,* ed. Robert Stam and Toby Miller, 207–221.

23. Mulvey, "Visual Pleasure and Narrative Cinema," 488.

24. Mulvey, "Afterthoughts on 'Visual Pleasure and Narrative Cinema,'" 142–3.

25. Ibid., 142.

26. Ibid., 148.

27. Frantz Fanon, *Black Skin, White Masks,* trans. Charles Lam Markmann, 41–82.

28. Fixico, *Termination and Relocation,* 10–11.

29. Clara Rodríguez, *Heroes, Lovers, and Others: The Story of Latinos in Hollywood,* 2; Reyes and Rubie, *Hispanics in Hollywood,* 548.

30. Reyes and Rubie, *Hispanics in Hollywood,* 548.

31. Robin Wood, "Retrospect" in *Howard Hawks: American Artist,* ed. Jim Hillier and Peter Wollen, 163–174.

32. Laura Mulvey, "Gentlemen Prefer Blondes: Anita Loos/Howard Hawks/Marilyn Monroe" in *Howard Hawks: American Artist,* ed. Hillier and Wollen, 214–229.

33. See Schatz, Hollywood Genres, 70.

34. Edward Buscombe, *'Injuns!': Native Americans in the Movies,* 96–97.

35. Gaylyn Studlar, "Sacred Duties, Poetic Passions: John Ford and the Issue of Femininity in the Western" in *John Ford Made Westerns: Filming the Legend in the Sound Era,* ed. Gaylyn Studlar and Matthew Bernstein, 44; Jane Tompkins, *West of Everything: The Inner Life of Westerns.*

36. Studlar, "Sacred Duties," 45. See also, for instance, Andrew Sarris, *The John Ford Movie Mystery.*

37. Studlar, "Sacred Duties," 64.

38. Slotkin, *Gunfighter Nation,* 358.

39. Charles Ramírez Berg, "The Margin as Center: The Multicultural Dynamics of John Ford's Westerns" in *John Ford Made Westerns,* ed. Studlar and Bernstein, 81–82.

40. Slotkin, *Gunfighter Nation,* 357.

41. Kilpatrick, *Celluloid Indians*, xvii.

42. Ramírez Berg, "The Margin as Center," 90.

43. David E. Lorey, *The U.S.-Mexican Border in the Twentieth Century: A History of Economic and Social Transformation*; Oscar J. Martínez, "Border Indians" in *Troublesome Border*, 48–75.

44. Martínez, "Border Indians," 55.

45. The protection of the border region by neutralizing Native tribes in the United States was part of the terms of the 1848 Treaty of Guadalupe Hidalgo—a small concession for the privilege of annexing half of Mexico's territory.

46. Martínez, "Border Indians," 56.

47. Studlar, "Sacred Duties, Poetic Passions," 64–66.

48. Like Howard Hawks with *Rio Lobo*, *The Comancheros* was Michael Curtis' last film before his death.

49. See Anderson, *The Conquest of Texas*, 6–7.

50. Samora, Bernal, and Peña, *Gunpowder Justice*.

51. See Anderson, *The Conquest of Texas*.

52. Ibid.

53. Richard R. Flores, *Remembering the Alamo: Memory, Modernity, and the Master Symbol*, xvii.

54. Ibid.

55. Flores, *Remembering the Alamo*, 11.

56. Peter Bogdanovich, "Interview with Howard Hawks" in Hillier and Wollen, *Howard Hawks: American Artist*, 65.

57. Judith M. Riggin, *John Wayne: A Bio-Bibliography*, 60–61.

58. See John Mason Hart, *Empire and Revolution: The Americans in Mexico since the Civil War*, 2, for Hart's account of this expansion and the role of the United States in Mexico.

59. See Hart, *Empire and Revolution*, 2–3.

60. Hart, *Empire and Revolution*, 1–5.

61. Lesley Gill, *The School of the Americas: Military Training and Political Violence in the Americas*.

62. Skidmore and Smith, *Modern Latin America*, 238.

63. Paul Seydor, *Peckinpah: The Western Films—A Reconstruction*, 77–84.

64. Schatz, *Hollywood Genres*, 60.

65. See Cull and Carrasco, *Alambrista and the U.S.-Mexico Border*, 16.

66. Garner Simmons, *Peckinpah: A Portrait in Montage*, 86.

67. Robin Wood, "Shall We Gather at the River?: The Late Films of John Ford" in Studlar and Bernstein, *John Ford Made Westerns*, 33.

68. Wood, "Shall We Gather at the River?," 33.

69. Demetrius John Kitses, *Horizons West: Anthony Mann, Bud Boetticher, Sam Peckinpah; Studies of Authorship within the Western*, 161.

70. Quoted in Bender, *Greasers and Gringos*, 156.

71. Skidmore and Smith, *Modern Latin America*, 230.

72. Ibid.

CHAPTER TWO

1. See Robin Wood, "Papering the Cracks: Fantasy and Ideology in the Reagan Era" in *Hollywood from Vietnam to Reagan . . . and Beyond*, 162–188 for his analysis of the "Lucas-Spielberg syndrome."

2. Leo Chavez, *Covering Immigration: Popular Images and the Politics of the Nation*, 100.

3. Lorey, *The U.S.-Mexican Border*, 106.

4. Ibid., 108.

5. However, it should be noted that much of U.S.-based manufacturing was still located in Los Angeles in the 1980s. Charlie's migration parallels the movement of jobs to the border.

6. This has been changing; see the documentary *Maquilopolis* (2006).

7. Guillermo Gómez-Peña, *The New World Border*; Jacques Derrida, *Specters of Marx: The State of the Debt, the Work of Mourning, and the New International*, trans. Peggy Kamuf.

8. James O'Conner, "On Populism and the Antiglobalization Movement" in *Confronting Capitalism*, ed. Eddie Yuen, Daniel Burton-Rose, and George Katsiaficas, 184–5.

9. David E. Simcox, ed., "Overview—A Time of Reform and Reappraisal" in *U.S. Immigration in the 1980s*, 3.

10. Cindy Patton, *Sex and Germs: The Politics of AIDS*, 11.

11. Simcox, "Overview," 2–3.

12. Gil Troy, *Morning in America: How Ronald Reagan Invented the 1980s*, 15.

13. Susan Jeffords, *Hard Bodies: Hollywood Masculinity in the Reagan Era*, 13.

14. See Jeffords, *Hard Bodies*; Troy, *Morning in America*; and Garry Wills, *Reagan's America: Innocents at Home*.

15. See Jeffords, *Hard Bodies*.

16. Ibid.

17. See Nachbar, *Focus on the Western*, 2–3. Similarly, in 1972 Henry Kissinger likened his role in negotiating the Vietnam settlement to that of the Western hero who faces the enemy alone.

18. Quoted in Tom Morganthau, et al., "Closing The Door?," *Newsweek*, 25 June 1984.

19. David Maciel, *El Norte: the U.S.-Mexican Border in Contemporary Cinema*, 55–56.

20. Maciel, *El Norte*, 57.

21. Eithne Luibhéid, *Entry Denied: Controlling Sexuality at the Border*, 3.

22. Ed Guerrero, *Framing Blackness: The African American Image in Film*; Cynthia Fuchs, "The Buddy Politic" in *Screening the Male: Exploring Masculinities in Hollywood Cinema*, ed. Steven Cohan and Ina Rae Hark, 194–210.

23. Jeffords, *Hard Bodies*, 19.

24. Ibid.

25. Lawrence Grossberg, *It's a Sin: Essays on Postmodernism, Politics, and Culture*, 49–62.

26. Gil Troy, *Morning in America*, 16.

CHAPTER THREE

1. Elliott Abrams, "Drug Wars: The New Alliances against Traffickers and Terrorists," *U.S. Department of State Bulletin*, April 1986, 1.

2. Ibid.

3. Abrams, "Drug Wars," 2.

4. Ibid., 4.

5. Ibid., 1.

6. In fact, 1986 is the same year that mandatory minimum sentencing laws were enacted. Strict sentences could be reduced simply by acting as a "narc" and snitching on any ancillary players associated with the defendant's arrest.

7. See Curtis Marez, *Drug Wars: The Political Economy of Narcotics* for an analysis of how the war on drugs has sustained the policing of peoples of color in everyday life from popular to political discourses.

8. Paul B. Stares, *Global Habit: The Drug Problem in a Borderless World*, 24–5. Drug use in the United States reached epidemic proportions in the 1960s due to a number of factors related to the consolidation of late capital and consumer culture and U.S. hegemony. The U.S. economy achieved a leading position in the world, creating conditions of affluence that worked along with the new market economy and consumer desires for greater stimulation and instant gratification. Consumers had more discretionary income than ever before and the population abounded in this baby boom period with youth (ages 15–24) comprising the majority. This era witnessed the rise of a youth-based counterculture that rejected the norms and institutions of the 1950s in a cultural revolution that turned to mind-altering psychotropic drugs as the road to spiritual renewal—echoed in drug guru Timothy Leary's exhortation in 1967 to "turn on, tune in, and drop out." The Vietnam War (1959–1975) intensified the social disaffection of the youth and deepened the divide between generations—later codified as the split between government and the people in 1980s Hollywood.

9. Steven B. Duke and Albert C. Gross, *America's Longest War: Rethinking Our Tragic Crusade Against Drugs*, xvi.

10. Stares, *Global Habit*, 26–7.

11. Coletta A. Youngers and Eileen Rosin, "The U.S. 'War on Drugs': Its Impact in Latin America and the Caribbean" in *Drugs and Democracy in Latin America: The Impact of U.S. Policy*, 4.

12. See Tony Payan, "The Drug War and the U.S.-Mexico Border: The State of Affairs," *The South Atlantic Quarterly*, 863–880; Stares, *Global Habit*, 27.

13. Marez, *Drug Wars*, 3.

14. Stares, *Global Habit*, 33.

15. Skidmore and Smith, *Modern Latin America*, 129.

16. In this role she is alternately docile and a "spitfire" in a reprisal of the

roles taken by Mexican actress Lupe Velez in *Hot Pepper* (1933), *Strictly Dynamite* (1934), and *Mexican Spitfire* (1940).

17. Slotkin, *Gunfighter Nation*, 593.

18. See David F. Musto and Pamela Korsmeyer, *The Quest for Drug Control: Politics and Federal Policy in a Period of Increasing Substance Abuse, 1963–1981*, 50. Incidentally, during the Vietnam War, there were many media reports of servicemen selling, buying, and using drugs due to the availability of cheap and pure heroin from the "Golden Triangle" as well as the wide availability of cannabis. There was testimony in the Senate before the Subcommittee on Juvenile Delinquency in 1970 that addressed the possibility that those involved in the My Lai massacre had been on drugs.

19. See Skidmore and Smith, *Modern Latin America*, 379. The Vietnam War became a beacon in social movements across Latin America; in fact, for Che Guevara it was a model of militancy against U.S. imperialism: "What a luminous, near future would be visible to us if two, three, or many Viet Nams flourished throughout the world with their share of deal and their immense tragedies, their everyday heroism and their repeated blows against imperialism obliging it to disperse its forces under the attack and the increasing hatred of all the peoples of the earth!"

20. See Mark Walker, *Vietnam Veteran Films*.

21. Tom Barry, *Crossing the Line: Immigrants, Economic Integration, and Drug Enforcement on the U.S.-Mexico Border*, with Harry Browne and Beth Sims, 67.

22. Quoted in David W. Houck and Amos Kiewe, eds., *Actor, Ideologue, Politician: The Public Speeches of Ronald Reagan*, 177.

23. The local police force is represented by the "Reverend," who is more clearly connected to the community he polices—this privileging of the local police allows us to hold out hope for the redemption of the policing agencies.

24. Alexander Cockburn and Jeffrey St. Clair, *Whiteout: The CIA, Drugs and the Press*, 289.

25. Samuel I. del Villar, "Rethinking Hemispheric Antinarcotics Strategy and Security" in *The Latin American Narcotics Trade and U.S. National Security*, ed. Donald J. Mabry, 109.

26. Cockburn and St. Clair, *Whiteout*, 7–8.

27. Barry R. McCaffrey, "Perspective on Illegal Drugs: Mass Manipulation of Young Minds," *Los Angeles Times*, 2 Jan. 1997.

28. McCaffrey, "Perspective on Illegal Drugs," 7.

29. Editorial desk, "Television's Risky Relationship," *New York Times*, 18 Jan. 2000; Don Van Natta, Jr., "Drug Office Will End Its Scrutiny of TV Scripts," *New York Times*, 20 Jan. 2000.

30. Eric Schmitt, "Hollywood Is Asked to Join a Campaign Against Drugs," *New York Times*, 20 Jan. 2000.

31. Arthur Allen, "Portrait of a Drug Czar," *Salon*, 30 Aug. 2000.

32. Tim Golden, "Elite Mexican Drug Officers Said to Be Tied to Traffickers," *New York Times*, 16 Sept. 1998.

33. Barry, *Crossing the Line*, 64–66.

34. Richard Porton, review of *Traffic*, directed by Steven Soderbergh, *Cinéaste*, 42.

35. Cited in Porton, *Traffic*, 42.

36. Ted Galen Carpenter, *Bad Neighbor Policy: Washington's Futile War on Drugs in Latin America*, 13.

37. Ibid.

38. Ibid.

39. Skidmore and Smith, *Modern Latin America*, 249; María Celia Toro, *Mexico's "War" on Drugs: Causes and Consequences*.

40. Barry, *Crossing the Line*, 69.

41. Maia Szalavitz, "Breaking out of the 12-Step Lockstep" in *Busted: Stone Cowboys, Narco-Lords and Washington's War on Drugs*, ed. Mike Gray, 81.

42. Youngers and Rosin, "The U.S. 'War on Drugs,'" xi.

43. Ibid., 5.

44. Ibid., 5.

45. Duke and Gross, *America's Longest War*; Citizens' Commission on U.S. Drug Policy, *The War on Drugs: Addicted to Failure*.

CHAPTER FOUR

1. Davis, *Magical Urbanism*; Raúl Homero Villa, *Barrio-Logos: Space and Place in Urban Chicano Literature and Culture*; Fox, *The Fence and the River*; Gómez-Peña, *The New World Border*.

2. Maciel and Herrera-Sobek, eds., introduction to *Culture Across Borders*, 4.

3. Chon A. Noriega and Ana López, eds., introduction to *The Ethnic Eye: Latino Media Arts*, xvi.

4. Davis, *City of Quartz*; Manuel Castells, "Information Technology, the Restructuring of Capital—Labor Relationships, and the Rise of the Dual City (1989)" in *The Castells Reader on Cities and Social Change*, ed. Ida Susser, 285–313.

5. R. D. Laing, *The Divided Self*, 12.

6. Ibid., 17.

7. Ibid.

8. David Harvey, *The Condition of Postmodernity*, 42–3.

9. Davis, *City of Quartz*.

10. Carola Suárez-Orozco and Marcelo M. Suárez-Orozco, *Children of Immigration*.

11. Deepak Narang Sawhney, ed., "Journey Beyond the Stars: Los Angeles and Third Worlds" in *Unmasking L.A.: Third Worlds and the City*, 1–20.

12. José Luis Gámez, "Representing the City: The Imagination and Critical Practice in East Los Angeles," *Aztlán*, 95–120.

13. Chon A. Noriega, *Shot in America: Television, the State, and the Rise of Chicano Cinema*.

14. Ibid., 34

15. Zuzana M. Pick, *The New Latin American Cinema: A Continental Project*.

16. Noriega and López, *The Ethnic Eye*, 16.

17. Christine List, "El Norte: Ideology and Immigration," *Jump Cut*, 27–31.

18. Joel Oseas Pérez, "El Norte: Imágenes peyorativas de México y los chicanos," *Chiricú*, 13–21.

19. List, "El Norte," 30.

20. Kathleen Newman, "Reterritorialization in Recent Chicano Cinema: Edward James Olmos's *American Me* (1992)" in Noriega and López, *The Ethnic Eye*, 95–106.

21. Stanley Cavell, *The World Viewed: Reflections on the Ontology of Film*.

22. Mario Barrera, "Story Structure in Latino Feature Films" in *Chicanos and Film: Representation and Resistance*, ed. Chon A. Noriega, 260.

23. Lucila Vargas, "El Norte," *The Americas Review*, 89.

24. Zygmunt Bauman, *Globalization: The Human Consequences*, 2.

25. Simcox, "Overview," 5.

26. Nicolás Kanellos, *Thirty Million Strong: Reclaiming the Hispanic Image in American Culture*.

27. Rosa Linda Fregoso, "Nepantla in Gendered Subjectivity" in *The Bronze Screen: Chicana and Chicano Film Culture*, 106–10.

28. Charles Ramírez Berg, "Colonialism and Movies in Southern California, 1910–1934." *Aztlán*, 76.

29. Ibid., 77.

30. Incidentally, the actor who plays Carlos, Douglas Spain, will later appear in the campy lesbian love story *But I'm a Cheerleader* as Andre, an unrepentant and un-reformable gay character.

31. Miriam Hansen, "Pleasure, Ambivalence, Identification" in *Film Theory and Criticism*, ed. Leo Braudy and Marshall Cohen, 584–601.

32. Laura Mulvey, "Visual Pleasure and Narrative Cinema" in Stam and Miller, *Film and Theory*, 483–494.

33. Laing, *The Divided Self*.

34. Peter Matthews, review of *Bread and Roses*, directed by Ken Loach, *Sight and Sound*, 36.

35. Leonard Quart and William Kornblum, "Documenting Workers: Looking at Labor on Film," review of *Bread and Roses*, directed by Ken Loach, *Dissent*, 117.

36. Herrera-Sobek, "Border Aesthetics," 63.

37. George Lipsitz, "Learning from Los Angeles: Another One Rides the Bus," *American Quarterly*, 512.

38. Ibid.

39. Janet Abu-Lughod, *New York, Chicago, Los Angeles: America's Global Cities*.

40. George M. Smerk, *Urban Mass Transportation: A Dozen Years of Federal Policy*, 184–185.

41. Dear and Flusty, "The Resistible Rise," 12.

42. Roger Keil. "From Los Angeles to Seattle: World City Politics and the New Global Resistance" in *From ACT UP to the WTO: Urban Protest and Community Building in the Era of Globalization*, ed. Benjamin Shepard and Ronald Hayduk, 328.

43. Ibid., 326–333.

44. Ibid., 329.

45. Davis, *Magical Urbanism*, 146–147.

46. See David Moberg, "Labor Debates its Future," *Nation*.

47. Lance Compa, "Responses," *Dissent*, 66–68.

48. Ibid., 66.

49. Helen Hayes, *U.S. Immigration Policy and the Undocumented: Ambivalent Laws, Furtive Lives*, 25–26.

50. Ronald Hayduk and Benjamin Shepard, "Urban Protest and Community Building in the Era of Globalization" in *From ACT UP to the WTO*, 7.

51. Saskia Sassen, "Analytic Borderlands: Race, Gender, and Representation in the New City" in *Race, Identity, and Citizenship*, ed. Rodolfo D. Torres, Louis F. Mirón, and Jonathan Xavier Inda, 362.

52. Ibid., 363.

53. Ibid.

54. Sassen, "Analytic Borderlands," 356.

55. Ibid., 366.

56. David Shipler, *The Working Poor: Invisible in America*, 12.

57. Ibid.

58. Matthews, *Bread and Roses*, 36.

CONCLUSION

1. Jacques Lacan, *The Four Fundamental Concepts of Psycho-Analysis*, trans. Alan Sheridan.

2. Ray Merlock, "Preface" in *Hollywood's West: The American Frontier in Film, Television, and History*, ed. Peter C. Rollins and John E. O'Conner, ix.

3. Tania Modleski, "A Woman's Gotta Do . . . What a Man's Gotta Do?: Cross-dressing in the Western," *Signs: Journal of Women in Culture and Society*, 519–544.

4. Other films in this nostalgic return to the genre are *All the Pretty Horses* (2000) and *Open Range* (2003).

5. Jim Kitses, "All that Brokeback Allows," *Film Quarterly*, 23.

6. Kitses, "All that Brokeback Allows," 24.

7. Linda Williams, "Film Bodies: Gender, Genre, and Excess" in *Film and Theory*, ed. Robert Stam and Toby Miller, 218. According to Williams, melodrama is marked by its belatedness, when protagonists realize "too late" that they could have impeded the tragic consequences of their decisions.

8. Kitses, "All that Brokeback Allows," 27. Jim Kitses cites J. Hoberman's comments in the *Village Voice* calling the film a "sagebrush Tristan and Isolde"

("Blazing Saddles," 29 Nov. 2005) and Roger Ebert's proclamation in the *Chicago Sun-Times* that "their tragedy is universal" ("Brokeback Mountain," 16 Dec. 2005).

9. See Berry, "The Chinese Side of the Mountain," 34. Berry notes that the idea of the gay love story for female pleasure may not be the basis for the original short story, but that assertion seems to suggest either the universal appeal of the literary tale or the absolute erasure of the author's gaze.

10. Annie Proulx, "Getting Movied" in *Brokeback Mountain: Story to Screenplay,* by Annie Proulx, Larry McMurtry, and Diana Ossana, 130.

11. Diana Ossana, "Climbing Brokeback Mountain" in Proulx, McMurtry, and Ossana, *Brokeback Mountain,* 145.

12. Proulx, "Getting Movied," 132.

13. "Brokeback's majesty and radiance can . . . be said to have a national dimension" that echoes "the language John Ford had helped to shape with the buttes and mesas of Monument Valley." Kitses, "All that Brokeback Allows," 25. See also Proulx, McMurtry, and Ossana, *Brokeback Mountain,* 141 for Larry McMurtry's discussion of the adaptation of the story to the screen in which he likens Ang Lee's use of the landscape to Ford's expressive use of Monument Valley

14. Ben Sifuentes-Jáuregui, "Epílogo: Apuntes sobre la identidad y lo latino," *Nueva Sociedad: Democracia y política en América Latina,* 145–146.

15. Sifuentes-Juáregui, "Epílogo," 146.

16. Jason Guerrasio, "The Walking Dead," *Filmmaker: The Magazine of Independent Film,* 34.

FILMOGRAPHY

Across the Border (1914)

Across the Mexican Line (1911)

Against All Odds (1984)

Alambrista! (1977)

Alamo, The (1960)

Along the Border (1916)

Alvarez Kelly (1966)

American Me (1992)

Americano, The (1955)

And Now Miguel (1966)

. . . and the Earth Did Not Swallow
Him (1995)

Appaloosa, The (1966)

Arizona Escapade, An (1912)

Arizona Wooing, An (1915)

Arms and the Gringo (1914)

Babel (2006)

Bad Man, The (1923)

Bad Man, The (1930)

Ballad of Gregorio Cortez, The (1982)

Ballad of Little Jo, The (1993)

Bamba, La (1987)

Bandido (1956)

Bandit's Spur, The (1912)

Bandit's Waterloo, The (1908)

Bandolero! (1968)

Barbarosa (1982)

Beast of Hollow Mountain, The (1956)

Beauty and the Bandit (1946)

Beneath Western Skies (1912)

Betty's Bandit (1912)

Big Country, The (1958)

Big Steal, The (1949)

Billy the Kid (1930)

Black Sheep, The (1912)

Border, The (1982)

Border Bandits (1946)

Border Cafe (1937)

Border G-Man (1938)

Border Incident (1949)

Border Intrigue (1925)

Border Legion, The (1930)

Borderline (1950)

Borderline (1980)

Border River (1954)

Border Romance (1929)

Bordertown (1935)

Born in East L.A. (1987)

Branded (1950)

Bravados, The (1958)

Bread and Roses (2000)

Break of Dawn (1988)

Breakout (1975)

Bring Me the Head of Alfredo Garcia
(1974)

Brokeback Mountain (2005)

Broncho Billy and the Greaser (1914)

Broncho Billy's Mexican Wife (1912)

Broncho Billy's Redemption (1910)

Burning Hills, The (1956)

California Conquest (1952)

California Frontier (1938)

California Mail (1936)

Californian, The (1937)

Captain Thunder (1930)

Captured by the Mexicans (1914)

Charro! (1969)

Chiquita the Dancer (1912)

Chisum (1970)

Cisco Kid, The (1931)

Cisco Kid and the Lady (1939)

Cisco Kid Returns (1945)

Clear and Present Danger (1994)

Comancheros, The (1961)

Cowboy (1958)

Cowboys, The (1972)

Curse of the Great Southwest (1913)

Daring Caballero, The (1949)

Day without a Mexican, A (2004)

Deadly Trackers, The (1973)

Death of a Gunfighter (1969)

Deep Cover (1992)

Dime with a Halo (1963)

Dirty Dozen, The (1967)

Don Mike (1927)

Dorado, El (1966)

Down on the Rio Grande (1913)

Duck You Sucker (1971)

Duel in the Sun (1946)

Durango Valley Raiders (1938)

Extreme Prejudice (1987)

Falcon in Mexico, The (1944)

Fighter, The aka The First Time
    (1952)

Firebrand, The (1962)

First Texan, The (1956)

Fistful of Dollars, A (1964)

Flashpoint (1984)

Fools Rush In (1997)

For a Few Dollars More (1965)

Fort Apache (1948)

Four Guns to the Border (1954)

Fugitive, The (1947)

Furies, The (1950)

Garden of Evil (1954)

Gatekeeper, The (2002)

Gay Caballero, The (1932)

Gay Caballero, The (1940)

Gay Cavalier, The (1946)

Gay Defender, The (1927)

Gay Desperado, The (1936)

Giant (1956)

Girl and the Greaser, The (1913)

Girl from Mexico, The (1939)

Girl from San Lorenzo, The (1950)

Girl of the Rio (1932)

Goin' South (1978)

Good, The Bad, and the Ugly,
    The (1966)

Greaser, The (1915)

Greaser's Gauntlet, The (1908)

Greaser's Revenge, The (1914)

Guns and Greasers (1918)

Guns for San Sebastian (1968)

Hands across the Border (1926)

Heart of the Sunset (1918)

High Noon (1952)

Hi-Lo Country, The (1998)

His Mexican Bride (1909)

His Mexican Sweetheart (1912)

Hold Back the Dawn (1941)

Hombre (1967)

Honor of the Flag, The (1911)

Hot Pepper (1933)

Hour of the Gun (1967)

Human Cargo (1936)

In Caliente (1935)

Incendiary Blonde (1945)

In Old Arizona (1928)

In Old Caliente (1939)

In Old Mexico (1938)

Joe Kidd (1972)

Juarez (1939)

Juggling with Fate (1913)

Kickback, The (1922)

Kid from Spain, The (1932)

King of the Bandits (1947)

Kiss of Fire (1955)

Land Baron of San Tee (1912)

Lasca of the Rio Grande (1931)

Lash, The (1930)

Last Command, The (1955)

Last Sunset, The (1961)

Left Handed Gun, The (1958)

Life of General Villa, The (1914)

Life of Villa (1912)

Like Water for Chocolate (1992)

Littlest Outlaw, The (1955)

Lonely Are the Brave (1962)
Lone Star (1996)
Lone Wolf McQuade (1983)
Losin' It (1983)
Lost Mine, The (1907)
Love in Mexico (1910)
Lucky Cisco Kid (1940)
Mackenna's Gold (1969)
Magnificent Seven, The (1960)
Man Apart, A (2003)
Man from Del Rio, The (1956)
Man in the Shadow (1957)
Man's Lust for Gold (1912)
Margarita and the Mission Funds
    (1913)
Mariachi, El (1992)
Mark of Zorro, The (1920)
Mark of Zorro, The (1940)
Master Gunfighter, The (1975)
Mexican, The (1911)
Mexican, The (2001)
Mexican Bill (1909)
Mexican Conspiracy Outgeneraled
    (1913)
Mexican Defeat, The (1913)
Mexican Filibusterers (1911)
Mexican Gambler, The (1913)
Mexican Joan of Arc, The (1911)
Mexican Joyride (1947)
Mexican Rebellion, The (1914)
Mexican Revolutionist, The (1912)
Mexican Romance, A (1910)
Mexican's Chickens, The (1915)
Mexican's Faith, The (1910)
Mexican's Gratitude, The (1911)
Mexican's Jealousy, The (1910)
Mexican Spitfire's Blessed Event,
    The (1943)
Mexican Spitfire's Elephant,
    The (1942)
Mexican Spy in America, A (1914)
Mexican's Revenge, The (1909)
Million to Juan, A (1994)
Mi vida loca (1993)
Mixing in Mexico (1925)

Murieta (1965)
My Darling Clementine (1946)
My Family/Mi Familia (1995)
My Man and I (1952)
Naked Dawn, The (1955)
No Country for Old Men (2007)
Norte, El (1983)
No Turning Back (2001)
Old Gringo (1989)
One-Eyed Jacks (1961)
100 Rifles (1969)
One Way Street (1950)
Only Road, The (1918)
On the Border (1909)
On the Border (1914)
On the Border (1917)
On the Border (1930)
Outlaw, The (1943)
Outrage, The (1964)
Ox-Bow Incident, The (1943)
Pan-Americana (1945)
Pancho Villa (1972)
Papita (1910)
Passion (1954)
Pat Garrett and Billy the Kid (1973)
Pedro's Treachery (1913)
Penitent, The (1988)
Pepe (1960)
Picking Up the Pieces (2000)
Plunderers, The (1960)
Pony Express (1907)
Posse (1993)
Professionals, The (1966)
Quantez (1957)
Raiders, The (1952)
Ranchman's Daughter, The (1911)
Rancho Notorious (1952)
Ranger's Reward, The (1912)
Real Women Have Curves (2002)
Red River (1948)
Red Sky at Morning (1971)
Remade, The (1941)
Renegade Ranger (1938)
Return of the Cisco Kid (1939)
Return of the Gunfighter (1967)

Revenge (1990)
Revengers, The (1972)
Reward, The (1965)
Ride On, Vaquero (1941)
Ride the Pink Horse (1947)
Ride, Vaquero! (1953)
Riding the California Trail (1947)
Ring, The (1952)
Rio Bravo (1959)
Rio Conchos (1964)
Rio Grande (1920)
Rio Grande (1950)
Rio Lobo (1970)
Rio Rita (1929)
River's Edge, The (1957)
Robin Hood of El Dorado, The (1936)
Robin Hood of Monterey (1947)
Romance of the Rio Grande (1929)
Romance of the Rio Grande (1941)
Romance of the Rio Grande, A (1911)
Rose of the Rancho (1936)
Rose of the Rio Grande (1938)
Salt of the Earth (1954)
Searchers, The (1956)
Second Chance (1953)
Selena (1997)
Señor Daredevil (1926)
Señorita's Conquest, The (1911)
Serenade (1956)
Seven Cities of Gold (1955)
Shaved in Mexico (1915)
She Came to the Valley (1979)
Sheepman, The (1958)
Sheriff's Blunder, The (1916)
She Wore a Yellow Ribbon (1949)
Showdown (1973)
Sierra Baron (1958)
Slim Gets the Reward (1913)
Sol Madrid (1968)
Song of the Gringo (1936)
South of the Border (1939)
South of Monterey (1946)
South of the Rio Grande (1932)
Spanglish (2004)
Speedy Gonzales (1955)

Stand and Deliver (1988)
Starlight over Texas (1938)
Star Maps (1997)
Steal Big Steal Little (1995)
Streets of Laredo (1949)
Strictly Dynamite (1934)
Stronghold (1951)
Take the High Ground! (1953)
Ten Days to Tulara (1958)
Terror in a Texas Town (1958)
Texas Across the River (1966)
They Came to Cordura (1959)
Tony, the Greaser (1914)
Touch of Evil (1958)
Three Amigos (1986)
Three Burials of Melquiades Estrada,
    The (2005)
Three Caballeros, The (1944)
Three Godfathers (1948)
Three Outlaws, The (1956)
Tijuana Story, The (1957)
Tony the Greaser (1914)
Tortilla Flat (1942)
Touch of Evil (1958)
Trackdown (1976)
Traffic (2000)
Train Robbers, The (1973)
Treasure of Pancho Villa, The (1955)
Treasure of the Sierra Madre,
    The (1948)
Trial (1955)
Two Gun Justice (1938)
Two Mules for Sister Sara (1970)
Two Sides, The (1911)
Undefeated, The (1969)
Under a Texas Moon (1930)
Under Mexican Skies (1912)
Valdez is Coming (1971)
Vera Cruz (1954)
Villa!! (1958)
Villa Rides! (1968)
Viva Cisco Kid (1940)
Viva Max! (1969)
Viva Villa! (1934)
Viva Zapata! (1952)

Western Child's Heroism, A (1912)
When Hearts are Trumps (1912)
Wild Bunch, The (1969)
Wild Wild West, The (1999)
Wings of the Hawk (1953)
Wonderful Country, The (1959)

Wrath of God, The (1972)
Young Guns (1988)
Young Guns II (1990)
Young Land, The (1959)
Zandy's Bride (1974)
Zoot Suit (1981)

MEXICAN

Acá las tortas (1951)
Adiós mi chaparrita (1943)
Alambrado (1991)
Apuros de un mojado, Los (1999)
Arizona (1984)
Asalto en Tijuana (1984)
Aventurera (1950)
Banda del charro rojo, La (1978)
Braceras, Las (1981)
Bracero del año, El (1964)
Carro de la muerte, El (1984)
Chacales de la frontera (1990)
China Hilaria, La (1939)
Cómo fui a enamorarme de ti (1991)
Contrabando humano (1982)
Contrabando por amor (1980)
Cruel destino (1944)
Deportados (1977)
De sangre chicana (1974)
Discriminación maldita (1990)
Dos amigos, Los (1980)
Espaldas mojadas (1955)
Frontera (1980)
Frontera, La (1991)
Frontera norte (1953)
Frontera sin ley, La (1966)
Fronterizo, El (1952)
Herencia de la Llorona, La (1947)
Hombre sin patria, El (1922)
Illegal, La (1979)
Jardín del Edén, El (1994)
Jaula de oro, La (1987)
Llanto de los pobres, El (1978)
Lola la trailera (1983)
Mafia de la frontera, La (1979)
Maldita miseria (1980)
Mamá solita (1980)

Mariachi, El (1992)
Matanza en Matamoros (1984)
Mauro el mojado (1986)
Memorias de un mojado (1988)
Milusos llegó de mojado, El (n.d.)
Misterios del Hampa, Los (1945)
Mojado (1972)
Mojado de nacimiento (1981)
Mojado . . . pero caliente (1989)
Mojado Power (1979)
Mojados de corazón (1987)
Mujeres insumisas (1995)
Murieron a mitad del rio (1986)
Ni de aquí, ni de allá (1988)
Ni sangre, ni arena (1941)
OK Mr. Pancho (1981)
Operación marihuana (1985)
Orgullo de los mojados, El (1992)
Pasaporte a la muerte (1988)
Pecadora (1947)
Pistoleros de la frontera (1967)
Pito Pérez se va de bracero (1948)
Pobres ilegales, Las (1979)
Pocho, El (1970)
Precio del norte, El (2006)
Primero el dólar (1972)
Primero soy mexicano (1950)
Puente, El (1984)
Raíces de sangre (1979)
Remojado, El (1984)
Rompe el alba (1990)
Sangre en Río Bravo (1966)
Sin dejar huella (2000)
Soy puro mexicano (1942)
Terror de la frontera, El (1963)
Tiempo de lobos (1981)
Tres veces mojado (1989)

Tumba del mojado, La (1985)
Ustedes, los ricos (1948)
Vagón de la muerte, El (1987)

Vera Cruz (1954)
Yo soy Mexicano de acá de este lado
(1952)

DOCUMENTARIES

Al otro lado (Amada, 2005)
Al otro lado (Loza, 2005)
Boda, La (2000)
Borderline Cases (1997)
Border War: The Battle over Illegal
Immigration (2006)
Cochise County USA: Cries from the
Border (2005)
Crossing Arizona (2006)
Dying to Get In: Undocumented
Immigration at the U.S./Mexican
Border (2005)
Dying to Live—A Migrant's Journey
(2005)
Forgotten Americans, The (2000)
Gatekeeper, The (2002)
Made in L.A. (2007)

Maquila: A Tale of Two Mexicos
(2000)
Maquilápolis: City of Factories (2006)
Milagros: Made in Mexico (2006)
Mojados: Through the Night (2004)
Natives: Immigrant Bashing on the
Border (1991)
No One (2006)
Performing the Border (1999)
Preguntas sin respuestas (2005)
Roger and Me (1989)
Romántico (2005)
Señorita extraviada (2001)
Sixth Section, The (2003)
Walking the Line (2005)
Wetback: The Undocumented
Documentary (2005)

BIBLIOGRAPHY

Abrams, Elliott. "Drug Wars: The New Alliances against Traffickers and Terrorists." *U.S. Department of State Bulletin*, Washington, D.C.: United States Department of State, April 1986.

Abu-Lughod, Janet. *New York, Chicago, Los Angeles: America's Global Cities.* Minneapolis: University of Minnesota Press, 1999.

Allen, Arthur. "Portrait of a Drug Czar." *Salon*, 30 August 2000. http://archive .salon.com/health/feature/2000/08/30/czar/index.html.

Altman, Rick. *Film/Genre.* London: British Film Institute, 1999.

Anderson, Gary Clayton. *The Conquest of Texas: Ethnic Cleansing in the Promised Land, 1820–1875.* Norman: University of Oklahoma Press, 2005.

Anzaldúa, Gloria. *Borderlands/La Frontera.* San Francisco: Aunt Lute Books, 1987.

Arau, Sergio and Yareli Arizmendi. "Un cambio social de gran magnitude." In *Un día sin inmigrantes: Quince voces, una causa,* edited by Gina Montaner, 23–30. Mexico City: Grijalbo, 2006.

Barrera, Mario. "Story Structure in Latino Feature Films." In Noriega, *Chicanos and Film,* 245–68.

Barry, Tom. *Crossing the Line: Immigrants, Economic Integration, and Drug Enforcement on the U.S.-Mexico Border.* With Harry Browne and Beth Sims. Albuquerque: Resource Center Press, 1994.

Bauman, Zygmunt. *Globalization: The Human Consequences.* New York: Columbia University Press, 1998.

Bazin, André. "The Western, or The American Film *par excellence.*" *What is Cinema?,* Vol. 2. Berkeley: University of California Press, 1971.

Bender, Steven W. *Greasers and Gringos: Latinos, Law, and the American Imagination.* New York: New York University Press, 2003.

Berry, Chris. "The Chinese Side of the Mountain." *Film Quarterly* 60, no. 3 (2007): 32–37.

Bogdanovich, Peter. "Interview with Howard Hawks." In Hillier and Wollen, *Howard Hawks,* 50–67.

Bordevich, Fergus M. *Killing the White Man's Indian: Reinventing Native Americans at the End of the Twentieth Century.* New York: Anchor Books, 1996.

Buscombe, Edward. *'Injuns!': Native Americans in the Movies.* Bodmin, Cornwall: Reaktion Books, 2006.

Calderón, Héctor and José David Saldívar, eds. *Criticism in the Borderlands:*

Studies in Chicano Literature, Culture, and Ideology. Durham and London: Duke University Press, 1991.

Carpenter, Ted Galen. *Bad Neighbor Policy: Washington's Futile War on Drugs in Latin America.* New York: Palgrave, 2003.

Castells, Manuel. "Information Technology, the Restructuring of Capital—Labor Relationships, and the Rise of the Dual City (1989)." In *The Castells Reader on Cities and Social Theory,* edited by Ida Susser, 285–313. Oxford: Cambridge University Press, 2002.

Cavell, Stanley. *The World Viewed: Reflections on the Ontology of Film.* New York: Viking Press, 1971.

Cawelti, John G. *The Six Gun Mystique.* Bowling Green: Bowling Green University Popular Press, 1975.

Chavez, Leo. *Covering Immigration: Popular Images and the Politics of the Nation.* Berkeley: University of California Press, 2001.

Citizens' Commission on U.S. Drug Policy. *The War on Drugs: Addicted to Failure.* Washington, D.C.: Institute for Policy Studies, 2000.

Cockburn, Alexander and Jeffrey St. Clair. *Whiteout: The CIA, Drugs and the Press.* London and New York: Verso, 1998.

Compa, Lance. "Responses." *Dissent* 52, no. 1 (2005): 66–68.

Corkin, Stanley. *The Cowboy as Cold Warrior: The Western and U.S. History.* Philadelphia: Temple University Press, 2004.

Cull, Nicholas J. and Davíd Carrasco, eds. *Alambrista and the U.S.-Mexico Border: Film, Music, and Stories of Undocumented Immigrants.* Albuquerque: University of New Mexico Press, 2004.

Davis, Mike. *City of Quartz.* New York: Vintage, 1990.

———. *Magical Urbanism.* New York: Verso, 2000.

A Day without a Mexican, directed by Sergio Arau. Official movie Web site. http://www.adaywithoutamexican.com/index1.htm

Dear, Michael J., ed. *From Chicago to L.A.: Making Sense of Urban Theory.* Thousand Oaks: Sage Publications, 2002.

Dear, Michael J. and Steven Flusty. "The Resistible Rise of the L.A. School." In Dear, *From Chicago to L.A.,* 3–16.

De León, Arnoldo. *They Called Them Greasers: Anglo Attitudes toward Mexicans in Texas, 1821–1900.* Austin: University of Texas Press, 1983.

del Villar, Samuel I. "Rethinking Hemispheric Antinarcotics Strategy and Security." In *The Latin American Narcotics Trade and U.S. National Security,* edited by Donald J. Mabry, 105–122. New York: Greenwood Press, 1989.

Derrida, Jacques. *Specters of Marx: The State of the Debt, the Work of Mourning, and the New International.* Translated by Peggy Kamuf. New York: Routledge, 1994.

Duke, Steven B. and Albert C. Gross. *America's Longest War: Rethinking Our Tragic Crusade against Drugs.* New York: Putnam, 1993.

Editorial Desk. "Television's Risky Relationship." *New York Times,* 18 January 2000, sec. A.

Fanon, Frantz. *Black Skin, White Masks*. Translated by Charles Lam Markmann. New York: Grove Weidenfeld, 1967.

Feuer, Janet. *The Hollywood Musical*. Bloomington: Indiana University Press, 1982.

Fixico, Donald L. *Termination and Relocation: Federal Indian Policy, 1945–1960*. Albuquerque: University of New Mexico Press, 1986.

Flores, Richard R. *Remembering the Alamo: Memory, Modernity, and the Master Symbol*. Austin: University of Texas Press, 2002.

Flores, William V. and Rina Benmayor, eds. *Latino Cultural Citizenship: Claiming Identity, Space, and Rights*. Boston: Beacon, 1997.

Folsom, James K. Introduction to *The Western: A Collection of Critical Essays*, 1–14. Englewood Cliffs, N.J.: Prentice Hall, 1979.

Foucault, Michel. *Madness and Civilization*. Translated by Richard Howard. New York: Vintage, 1998.

Fox, Claire F. *The Fence and the River: Culture and Politics at the U.S.-Mexico Border*. Minneapolis: University of Minnesota Press, 1999.

Fregoso, Rosa Linda. *MeXicana Encounters: The Making of Social Identities on the Borderlands*. Berkeley: University of California Press, 2003.

———. "*Nepantla* in Gendered Subjectivity." Chap. 5 in *The Bronze Screen: Chicana and Chicano Film Culture*. Minneapolis: University of Minnesota Press, 1993.

Fuchs, Cynthia. "The Buddy Politic." In *Screening the Male: Exploring Masculinities in Hollywood Cinema*, edited by Steven Cohan and Ina Rae Hark, 194–210. New York: Routledge, 1993.

Gámez, José Luis. "Representing the City: The Imagination and Critical Practice in East Los Angeles." *Aztlán* 27, no. 1 (Spring 2002): 95–120.

Gill, Lesley. *The School of the Americas: Military Training and Political Violence in the Americas*. Durham: Duke University Press, 2004.

Golden, Tim. "Elite Mexican Drug Officers Said to Be Tied to Traffickers." *New York Times*, 16 September 1998.

Gómez-Peña, Guillermo. *The New World Border*. San Francisco: City Lights, 1996.

Griffith, Albert J. "The Scion, the Señorita, and the Texas Ranch Epic: Hispanic Images in Film." *Bilingual Review* 16, no. 1 (1991): 15–22.

Grossberg, Lawrence. *It's a Sin: Essays on Postmodernism, Politics, and Culture*. Sydney: Power Publications, 1988.

Guerrasio, Jason. "The Walking Dead." *Filmmaker: The Magazine of Independent Film* 14, no. 2 (Winter 2006): 32–37.

Guerrero, Ed. *Framing Blackness: The African American Image in Film*. Philadelphia: Temple University Press, 1993.

Hansen, Miriam. "Pleasure, Ambivalence, Identification." In *Film Theory and Criticism*, edited by Leo Braudy and Marshall Cohen, 584–601. New York: Oxford University Press, 1999.

Hart, John Mason. *Empire and Revolution: The Americans in Mexico since the*

Civil War. Berkeley, Los Angeles, and London: University of California Press, 2002.

Harvey, David. *The Condition of Postmodernity*. Oxford: Basil Blackwell, 1990.

Hayduk, Ronald and Benjamin Shepard. "Urban Protest and Community Building in the Era of Globalization." In *From ACT UP to the WTO: Urban Protest and Community Building in the Era of Globalization*, edited by Benjamin Shepard and Ronald Hayduk, 1/-9. London and New York: Verso, 2002.

Hayes, Helene. *U.S. Immigration Policy and the Undocumented: Ambivalent Laws, Furtive Lives*. Westport, Conn.: Praeger, 2001.

Herrera-Sobek, María. "Border Aesthetics: The Politics of Mexican Immigration in Film and Art." *Western Humanities Review* 60, no. 2 (Fall 2006): 60–71.

———. *The Bracero Experience: Elitelore versus Folklore*. Los Angeles: UCLA Latin American Center Publications, 1979.

———. "The Corrido as Hypertext: Undocumented Mexican Immigration Films and the Mexican/Chicano Ballad." In Maciel and Herrera-Sobek, *Culture Across Borders*, 227–258.

———. *Northward Bound: The Mexican Immigrant Experience in Ballad and Song*. Bloomington: Indiana University Press, 1993.

Hillier, Jim and Peter Wollen, eds. *Howard Hawks: American Artist*. London: British Film Institute, 1996.

Hobsbawm, Eric. *Bandits*. New York: New Press, 2000.

Houck, David W. and Amos Kiewe, eds. *Actor, Ideologue, Politician: The Public Speeches of Ronald Reagan*. Westport, Conn.: Greenwood Press, 1993.

Iglesias, Norma. "Reconstructing the Border: Mexican Border Cinema and Its Relationship to Its Audience." In *Mexico's Cinema: A Century of Film and Filmmakers*, edited by Joanne Hirshfield and David R. Maciel, 233–248. Wilmington: Scholarly Resources, 1999.

Jeffords, Susan. *Hard Bodies: Hollywood Masculinity in the Reagan Era*. New Brunswick: Rutgers University Press, 1994.

Kanellos, Nicolás. *Thirty Million Strong: Reclaiming the Hispanic Image in American Culture*. Golden, Colo.: Fulcrum Publishing, 1998.

Keil, Roger. "From Los Angeles to Seattle: World City Politics and the New Global Resistance." In *From ACT UP to the WTO: Urban Protest and Community Building in the Era of Globalization*, edited by Benjamin Shepard and Ronald Hayduk, 326–333. London and New York: Verso, 2002.

Kilpatrick, Jacquelyn. *Celluloid Indians: Native Americans and Film*. Lincoln: University of Nebraska Press, 1999.

Kitses, Demetrius John. *Horizons West: Anthony Mann, Bud Boetticher, Sam Peckinpah; Studies of Authorship within the Western*. Bloomington: Indiana University Press, 1969.

Kitses, Jim. "All that Brokeback Allows." *Film Quarterly* 60, no. 3 (2007): 22–27.

Lacan, Jacques. *The Four Fundamental Concepts of Psycho-Analysis*. Translated by Alan Sheridan. New York: Norton, 1981.

Laing, R. D. *The Divided Self*. Middlesex: Penguin, 1972.

League of United Latin American Citizens official Web site. http://lulac.org.

Leclerc, Gustavo, Raúl Villa, and Michael J. Dear, eds. *La Vida Latina en L.A.: Urban Latino Cultures*. Thousand Oaks, Calif.: SAGE Publications, 1999.

Lipsitz, George. "Learning from Los Angeles: Another One Rides the Bus." *American Quarterly* 56, no. 3 (2004): 511–529.

List, Christine. "*El Norte*: Ideology and Immigration." *Jump Cut* 34 (1989): 27–31.

Lorey, David E. *The U.S.-Mexican Border in the Twentieth Century: A History of Economic and Social Transformation*. Wilmington, Del.: Scholarly Resources, 1999.

Luibhéid, Eithne. *Entry Denied: Controlling Sexuality at the Border*. Minneapolis: University of Minnesota Press, 2002.

Maciel, David. *El Norte: The U.S.-Mexican Border in Contemporary Cinema*. San Diego: Institute for Regional Studies of the Californias, San Diego State University, 1990.

Maciel, David R. and María Herrera-Sobek, eds. *Culture Across Borders: Mexican Immigration and Popular Culture*. Tucson: University of Arizona Press, 1998.

———. Introduction to *Culture Across Borders*, 3–26.

Maciel, David R. and María Rosa García-Acevedo. "The Celluloid Immigrant: The Narrative Films of Mexican Immigration." In Maciel and Herrera-Sobek, *Culture Across Borders*, 149–202.

Marez, Curtis. *Drug Wars: The Political Economy of Narcotics*. Minneapolis: Minnesota Press, 2004.

Martínez, Oscar J. "Border Indians." Chap. 3 in *Troublesome Border*. Tucson: University of Arizona Press, 2006.

Matthews, Peter. Review of *Bread and Roses*, directed by Ken Loach. *Sight and Sound* 11, no. 5 (2001): 36–37, 43–44.

McCaffrey, Barry R. "Perspective on Illegal Drugs: Mass Manipulation of Young Minds." *Los Angeles Times*, 2 January 1997, Metro sec.

McCaul, Michael. "Investigations Border Report." U.S. House of Representatives official Web site. http://www.house.gov/mccaul/pdf/Investigations-Border-Report.pdf

Merlock, Ray. "Preface." In *Hollywood's West: The American Frontier in Film, Television, and History*, edited by Peter C. Rollins and John E. O'Conner, xv–xii. Lexington: Kentucky University Press, 2005.

Moberg, David. "Labor Debates its Future." *Nation* 280, no. 10 (2005): 11–14, 16.

Modleski, Tania. "A Woman's Gotta Do . . . What a Man's Gotta Do?: Cross-dressing in the Western." *Signs: Journal of Women in Culture and Society* 22, no. 3 (Spring 1997): 519–544.

Morganthau, Tom, Gloria Borger, Nikki Finke Greenberg, Elaine Shannon, Renee Michael, and Daniel Pedersen. "Closing The Door?" *Newsweek*, 25 June 1984.

Mulvey, Laura. "Afterthoughts on 'Visual Pleasure and Narrative Cinema.'" In *Popular Fiction: Technology, Ideology, Production, Reading*, edited by Tony Bennett, 139–151. London and New York: Routledge, 1990.

————. "*Gentlemen Prefer Blondes*: Anita Loos/Howard Hawks/Marilyn Monroe." In Hillier and Wollen, *Howard Hawks*, 214–229.

————. "Visual Pleasure and Narrative Cinema." In Stam and Miller, *Film and Theory*, 483–494.

Musto, David F. and Pamela Korsmeyer. *The Quest for Drug Control: Politics and Federal Policy in a Period of Increasing Substance Abuse, 1963–1981.* New Haven and London: Yale University Press, 2002.

Nachbar, Jack, ed. Introduction to *Focus on the Western*, 1–8. Englewood Cliffs, N.J.: Prentice-Hall, 1974.

Nevins, Joseph. *Operation Gatekeeper: The Rise of the "Illegal Alien" and the Making of the U.S.-Mexico Boundary.* New York and London: Routledge, 2002.

Newman, Kathleen. "Reterritorialization in Recent Chicano Cinema: Edward James Olmos's *American Me* (1992)." In Noriega and López, *The Ethnic Eye*, 95–106.

Noriega, Chon A., ed. *Chicanos and Film: Representation and Resistance.* Minneapolis, University of Minnesota Press, 1992.

————. "Imagined Borders: Locating Chicano Cinema in America/América." In Noriega and López, *The Ethnic Eye*, 3–21.

————, ed. Introduction to *Chicanos and Film*, xiv–xvii.

————. *Shot in America: Television, the State, and the Rise of Chicano Cinema.* Minneapolis: University of Minnesota Press, 2000.

Noriega, Chon A. and Ana López, eds. *The Ethnic Eye: Latino Media Arts.* Minneapolis, University of Minnesota Press, 1996.

————. Introduction to *The Ethnic Eye*, ix–xxii.

O'Conner, James. "On Populism and the Antiglobalization Movement." In *Confronting Capitalism: Dispatches from a Global Movement*, edited by Eddie Yuen, Daniel Burton-Rose, and George Katsiaficas, 183–195. Brooklyn: Soft Skull, 2004.

Ono, Kent A. and John M. Sloop. *Shifting Borders: Rhetoric, Immigration, and California's Proposition 187.* Philadelphia: Temple University Press, 2002.

Oseas Pérez, Joel. "El Norte: Imágenes peyorativas de México y los chicanos." *Chiricú* 5, no. 1 (1987): 13–21.

Ossana, Diana. "Climbing Brokeback Mountain." In Proulx, McMurtry, and Ossana, *Brokeback Mountain*, 143–151.

Paredes, Américo. *"With a Pistol in His Hand": A Border Ballad and its Hero.* Austin and London: University of Texas Press, 1971.

Patton, Cindy. *Sex and Germs: The Politics of AIDS.* Boston: South End Press, 1985.

Payan, Tony. "The Drug War and the U.S.-Mexico Border: The State of Affairs." *South Atlantic Quarterly* 105, no. 4 (Fall 2006): 863–880.

Pick, Zuzana M. *The New Latin American Cinema: A Continental Project.* Austin: University of Texas Press, 1993.

Pocho Productions. *Pocho.com: Satire, News y Chat for the Spanglish Generation.* http://pocho.com.

Porton, Richard. Review of *Traffic*, directed by Steven Soderbergh. *Cinéaste* 26, no. 3 (Summer 2001): 41–43.

Proulx, Annie. "Getting Movied." In Proulx, McMurtry, and Ossana, *Brokeback Mountain*, 129–138.

Proulx, Annie, Larry McMurtry, and Diana Ossana. *Brokeback Mountain: Story to Screenplay*. New York, London, Toronto, and Sydney: Scribner, 2005.

Prucha, Francis Paul, ed. *Documents of United States Indian Policy*. Lincoln and London: University of Nebraska Press, 2000.

Quart, Leonard and William Kornblum. "Documenting Workers: Looking at Labor on Film." Review of *Bread and Roses*, directed by Ken Loach. *Dissent* 48, no. 4 (2001): 117–120.

Ramírez Berg, Charles. "Colonialism and Movies in Southern California, 1910–1934." *Aztlán* 28, no. 1 (Spring 2003): 75–96.

———. "Ethnic Ingenuity and Mainstream Cinema: Robert Rodríguez's *Bedhead* (1990) and *El Mariachi* (1993)." Chap. 9 in *Latino Images in Film: Stereotypes, Subversion, and Resistance*, 219–239. Austin: University of Texas Press, 2002.

———. *Latino Images in Film: Stereotypes, Subversion, and Resistance*. Austin: University of Texas Press, 2002.

———. "The Margin as Center: The Multicultural Dynamics of John Ford's Westerns." In Studlar and Bernstein, *John Ford Made Westerns*, 75–101.

———. "Stereotyping in Films in General and of the Hispanic in Particular." In *Latin Looks: Images of Latinas and Latinos in the U.S. Media*, edited by Clara E. Rodriguez, 104–120. Boulder: Westview Press, 1997.

Reyes, Luis and Peter Rubie. *Hispanics in Hollywood: A Celebration of 100 Years in Film and Television*. Hollywood: Lone Eagle Publishing, 2000.

Riggin, Judith M. *John Wayne: A Bio-Bibliography*. New York: Greenwood Press, 1992.

Rodríguez, Clara. *Heroes, Lovers, and Others: The Story of Latinos in Hollywood*. Washington: Smithsonian Books, 2004.

Rodriguez, Luis J. *The Republic of East L.A.* New York: Rayo, 2002.

Sahlins, Peter. *Boundaries: The Making of France and Spain in the Pyrenees*. Berkeley: University of California Press, 1989.

Samora, Julian, Joe Bernal, and Albert Peña. *Gunpowder Justice: A Reassessment of the Texas Rangers*. Notre Dame: University of Notre Dame Press, 1979.

Santa Ana, Otto. *Brown Tide Rising: Metaphors of Latinos in Contemporary American Public Discourse*. Austin: University of Texas Press, 2002.

Saragoza, Alex M. "The Border in American and Mexican Cinema." *Aztlán* 21, no. 1–2 (1992–1996): 155–190.

Sarris, Andrew. *The John Ford Movie Mystery*. London: British Film Institute, 1976.

Sassen, Saskia. "Analytic Borderlands: Race, Gender, and Representation in the New City." In *Race, Identity, and Citizenship*, edited by Rodolfo D. Torres, Louis F. Mirón, and Jonathan Xavier Inda, 355–372. Malden, Mass.: Blackwell, 1999.

Sawhney, Deepak Narang, ed. "Journey Beyond the Stars: Los Angeles and Third Worlds." Chap. 1 in *Unmasking L.A.: Third Worlds and the City*. New York: Palgrave, 2002.

Schatz, Thomas. *Hollywood Genres: Formulas, Filmmaking, and the Studio System*. Philadelphia: Temple University Press, 1981.

———. "The New Hollywood." In *Film Theory Goes to the Movies*, edited by Jim Collins, Hilary Radner, and Ava Preacher Collins, 8–36. New York and London: Routledge, 1993.

Schmitt, Eric. "Hollywood Is Asked to Join a Campaign Against Drugs." *New York Times*, 12 July 2000, sec. A.

Seydor, Paul. *Peckinpah: The Western Films—A Reconstruction*. Urbana, Chicago, and London: University of Illinois Press, 1980.

Shipler, David. *The Working Poor: Invisible in America*. New York: Knopf, 2004.

Sifuentes-Jáuregui, Ben. "Epílogo: Apuntes sobre la identidad y lo latino." *Nueva Sociedad: Democracia y política en América Latina* 201 (Enero/Febrero 2006): 145–154.

Simcox, David E., ed. "Overview—A Time of Reform and Reappraisal." Chap. 1 in *U.S. Immigration in the 1980s: Reappraisal and Reform*, 1–63. Boulder and London: Westview Press, 1988.

Simmons, Garner. *Peckinpah: A Portrait in Montage*. Austin: University of Texas Press, 1976.

Skidmore, Thomas E. and Peter H. Smith. *Modern Latin America*. New York, and Oxford: Oxford University Press, 2001.

Slotkin, Richard. *Gunfighter Nation: The Myth of the Frontier in Twentieth-Century America*. New York: Harper Perennial, 1992.

Smerk, George M. *Urban Mass Transportation: A Dozen Years of Federal Policy*. Bloomington and London: Indiana University Press, 1974.

Staiger, Janet. *Perverse Spectators: The Practices of Film Reception*. New York: New York University Press, 2000.

Stam, Robert and Toby Miller, eds. *Film and Theory: An Anthology*. Malden, Mass. and Oxford, Blackwell, 2000.

Stares, Paul B. *Global Habit: The Drug Problem in a Borderless World*. Washington, D.C.: Brookings Institution, 1996.

Studlar, Gaylyn. "Sacred Duties, Poetic Passions: John Ford and the Issue of Femininity in the Western." In Studlar and Bernstein, *John Ford Made Westerns*, 43–74.

Studlar, Gaylyn and Matthew Bernstein, eds. *John Ford Made Westerns: Filming the Legend in the Sound Era*. Bloomington: Indiana University Press, 2001.

Suárez-Orozco, Carola and Marcelo M. Suárez-Orozco. *Children of Immigration*. The Developing Child. Cambridge, Mass.: Harvard University Press, 2001.

Szalavitz, Maia. "Breaking out of the 12-Step Lockstep." In *Busted: Stone Cowboys, Narco-Lords and Washington's War on Drugs*, edited by Mike Gray, 81–83. New York: Thunder's Mouth Press/Nation Books, 2002.

Tompkins, Jane. *West of Everything: The Inner Life of Westerns*. New York and Oxford: Oxford University Press, 1992.

Toro, María Celia. *Mexico's "War" on Drugs: Causes and Consequences*. Boulder, Colo. and London: Lynne Rienner Publishers, 1995.

Troy, Gil. *Morning in America: How Ronald Reagan Invented the 1980s*. Princeton and Oxford: Princeton University Press, 2005.

"Tunnels Show Dangers on Porous U.S.-Mexican Border." *New American* 22, no. 4 (20 February 2006): 7.

Turner, Frederick Jackson. "The Significance of the Frontier in American History." *The Turner Thesis: Concerning the Role of the Frontier in American History*, edited by George Rogers Taylor, 3–28. Lexington, Mass.: D. C. Heath and Co., 1972.

Van Natta Jr., Don. "Drug Office Will End Its Scrutiny of TV Scripts." *New York Times*, 20 January 2000, sec. A.

Vargas, Lucila. "El Norte." *The Americas Review* 14, no. 1 (Spring 1986): 89–91.

Vila, Pablo. *Crossing Borders, Reinforcing Borders: Social Categories, Metaphors, and Narrative Identities on the U.S.-Mexico Frontier*. Austin: University of Texas Press, 2000.

Villa, Raúl Homero. *Barrio-Logos: Space and Place in Urban Chicano Literature and Culture*. Austin: University of Texas Press, 2000.

Walker, Mark. *Vietnam Veteran Films*. Metuchen and London: Scarecrow Press, 1991.

Weaver, John. *The Brownsville Raid*. New York: Norton, 1973.

Webb, Walter Prescott. *The Texas Rangers: A Century of Frontier Defense*. Austin: University of Texas Press, 1935.

Williams, Linda. "Film Bodies: Gender, Genre, and Excess." In Stam and Miller, *Film and Theory*, 207–221.

Wills, Garry. *Reagan's America: Innocents at Home*. New York: Doubleday, 1987.

Woll, Allen L. *The Latin Image in American Film*. UCLA Latin American Studies 10. Los Angeles: UCLA Latin American Center Publications, 1980.

Wood, Robin. *Hollywood from Vietnam to Reagan . . . and Beyond*. New York: Columbia University Press, 1986.

———. "Retrospect." In Hillier and Wollen, *Howard Hawks*, 163–174.

———. *Rio Bravo*. BFI Film Classics. London: British Film Institute, 2003.

———. "*Shall We Gather at the River?*: The Late Films of John Ford." In Studlar and Bernstein, *John Ford Made Westerns*, 23–41.

Youngers, Coletta A. and Eileen Rosin. "The U.S. 'War on Drugs': Its Impact in Latin America and the Caribbean." In *Drugs and Democracy in Latin America: The Impact of U.S. Policy*, 1–13. Boulder, Colo.: Lynne Rienner Publishers, 2005.

Zurhorst, Charles. *The First Cowboys and Those Who Followed*. New York and London: Abelard-Schuman, 1973.

INDEX

Abrams, Elliot, 109, 110, 135
Abu-Lughod, Janet, 172
African-Americans: characters,
    41–42, 140–143; and war on drugs,
    121–130; and Westerns, 187
Alambrista!, 21
Alamo, 2, 11, 28–29, 59, 81, 116, 120,
    185, 199–200n52; Alamo-esque,
    36; and *Rio Bravo*, 61–68; as sym-
    bol, 63–64
Alamo, The, 63
Almodóvar, Pedro, 165
Al otro lado (Gustavo Loza), viii
Al otro lado (Natalia Amada), viii, 4
Altman, Rick, 12, 199n44
American dream, 5, 152, 180
American exceptionalism, 53, 61, 97,
    201n2
American Federation of Labor and
    Congress of Industrial Organiza-
    tions (AFL-CIO), 175
American Me, 23, 124, 146, 154
Anderson, Gary Clayton, 57
anti-miscegenation laws, 33
Anzaldúa, Gloria, 13
Apocalypse Now, 115
Arau, Alfonso, 201n5
Arau, Sergio, viii
Arbenz Guzmán, Jacobo, 72
Arizmendi, Yareli, viii
Arriaga, Guillermo, 25, 192, 193, 194
Arteta, Miguel, 162
A-Team, The, 116

Babel, 11, 193–194
Bad Man, The, 8, 198n26

Ballad of Gregorio Cortez, The, 21
Ballad of Little Jo, 187
Bamba, La, 23
Banderas, Antonio, as "el nuevo
    Valentino," 164–165
Bandidas, 198n20
bandido, 78. *See also* bandits
banditry, 5; female equivalent, 6; in
    Hollywood, 6, 8
bandits, 5–7, 20, 27, 31, 76; and an-
    tithesis, 8; and "gringo," 78
Barker, Eugene C., 9
Barraza, Adriana, 193
Barrera, Mario, 155
Barry, Tom, 118
Bauman, Zygmunt, 156–157
Bender, Steven W., 198n18
Benmayor, Rina, 23
Bernal, Joe, 10, 57
Berry, Chris, 24, 188, 210n9
Blood Meridian, 7
Border, The, 19, 83, 86, 90, 93–96,
    97, 101–103, 115, 170–171, 185,
    204n5
border, borderlands, 2, 15, 19, 27, 42,
    43, 55, 82, 103, 113, 132, 135, 145,
    199n5; border cities and towns,
    1–2, 21–22, 23–24, 33, 35, 37, 75,
    141, 145, 186, 202n21; communi-
    ties, 9; cultural connotations of,
    1–3, 183; and drug trafficking, 1–
    2, 3, 109–143; and history, 28–30,
    104, 184; and industrialization,
    85–86; militarization of, 91, 113–
    114, 115, 151, 191; and national
    identity, 2, 9, 13, 16, 18, 25, 29,

35–36, 48, 49, 52, 61, 69, 82, 104, 146, 183; and national security, vii, 1, 48–49, 56, 87, 88, 95, 108, 114, 183–184, 185–186; southern versus western frontier, 2, 16, 27–29, 72, 81, 183, 184, 185; as symbol, 2–3, 4, 11–12, 13, 15, 18, 19, 25, 29, 33, 46, 48, 51, 53, 82; tunnels, 1–2, 136; as urban division, 21–22, 145–181; and vigilantism, 7, 14, 20, 61

Border Bandits, 7, 9; punk band, 198n24

border bandits, 7–8

border film genre, 2–5, 11–16, 17, 19–21, 24–25, 43, 61, 81, 83, 96, 100, 107, 121, 147, 184, 190, 199–200n52; Mexican, 3–5, 170. *See also* drug trafficking media; Latino film; Westerns

Border Industrialization Program, 85

Borderline, 19, 83, 91–93, 96, 102–104, 106, 107, 115, 116, 185

border patrol, 1, 3, 13, 29, 98–99, 102, 111, 113, 185, 199n51; border guards, agents, patrolmen, 5, 8, 15, 19, 20, 83–108; as buddy cops, 96–97; as corrupt, 95; as messiahs of national security, 88; and signs of fortified nation, 91

Bordevich, Fergus M., 198n28

Born in East L.A., 146

Bracero Program, 19, 69, 85

Bread and Roses, 21, 22, 146, 147, 152, 168–179, 180, 186

bread and roses landmark protest, 168

Brody, Adrien, 169

Brokeback Mountain, 15, 24–25, 187, 188–191, 209–210nn8–9, 210n13; and homosocial utopia, 51

Broncho Billy and the Greaser, 5

Browne, Harry, 118

Buscombe, Edward, 49

Bush, George H. W., 129; administration of, 159

Bush, George W., 109

Calderón, Hector, 13

calvary, 18, 29, 49, 51, 52–53, 82, 184, 185; role of, in Westerns, 76

Cantinflas, 163, 167

Carpenter, Ted Galen, 135

Carranza, Venustiano, 79

Cavell, Stanley, 154

Cedillo, Julio, 191

Central Intelligence Agency (CIA), 119, 126

Chávez, Hugo, vii, 184

Chavez, Leo, 19, 85

Chicago Latino Film Festival, vii–viii, 191

Chicano cinema, 13, 152–153

Chicanos, 186; identity, 14, 15, 148, 153

Chinese Exclusion Act, 20, 35, 85, 174

Cien años de soledad, 192

Ciudad, La/The City, 169

civil rights era, 16, 43, 47, 48, 83, 97–98, 101, 198n28; and feminism, 102; post–civil rights era, 43

Clear and Present Danger, 115

Collateral, 171

colonialism, 3, 6, 27, 40, 146, 148, 151, 180, 198n28

Comancheros, The, 8, 29, 30, 36, 48, 49, 56–61, 184, 201n5

compassion fatigue, 89–90, 103, 108

Cooper, Anderson, ix

Corkin, Stanley, 17, 34, 72

"corporación, la," 111, 136, 138, 139. *See* Latin/o American drug traffickers

corridos, 4, 9, 11; narcocorridos, 113

cowboys, 15, 18, 19, 24, 25, 81, 84, 98, 112, 117, 133, 135, 139, 175, 184, 185, 187, 188; origin of, 10–11;

vigilante cowboy, 137, 139. *See also* vigilantism
coyotes, 159
crack cocaine, 121, 122, 124; crack babies and public health panic, 128; crack houses, 122; origin of, 127–128
Crash, 171
cultural citizenship, 22–24

Davis, Mike, 7, 150
Day without a Mexican, A, viii, 178
Dear, Michael J., 23, 173
Deep Cover, 20, 108, 111, 119, 121–130, 131, 137, 139, 140, 141, 206n23
Del Toro, Benicio, 132
Derrida, Jacques, 86
Díaz, Porfirio, 55
Dobbs, Lou, ix
Drug Enforcement Agency (DEA), 1, 21, 119, 123, 124, 126, 128, 129, 130, 134, 137, 139, 140, 141, 142; agents of, 5, 8, 19, 82, 111, 113, 115, 119, 126, 134, 136, 137, 138–139, 140, 143, 185; origin of, 112–113
drug trafficking, 2, 16; drug traffickers, 20, 126, 134; and national security, 109, 110, 112, 115, 185–186; and terrorism, 110, 142. *See also* globalization; Latin/o American drug traffickers
drug trafficking media, 4, 8, 15, 16, 20–21, 24, 109–143, 185–186
Duel in the Sun, 24, 29, 31–43, 188, 201n13, 201n15, 202n21
Durazo, Maria Elena, 174

Earp, Wyatt, 97
Esquivel, Laura, 201n5
Estudios Churubusco, 15
Extreme Prejudice, 20, 108, 111, 113–121, 123, 126, 130, 140, 141

Fanon, Frantz, 40
Federal Bureau of Investigation (FBI), 21, 119, 123; agents of, 96, 99, 100, 106, 119, 126
Fernández, Emilio, 76
fetishes: racial, 40, 41, 148, 190; sexual, 40
Fixico, Donald, 43
Flashpoint, 19, 83, 84, 88, 96, 97–101, 104, 105–106, 115, 185
Flores, Juan, 7
Flores, Richard, 63
Flores, William V., 23
Flusty, Steven, 173
Folsom, James, 27
Ford, John, 49, 51, 76, 210n13
Foreman, Carl, 64–65
Foucault, Michel, 149
Fox, Claire F., 15
Fregoso, Rosa Linda, 6, 20, 194
Fuchs, Cynthia, 96
Fuerzas Armadas Revolucionarias de Colombia (FARC), 110

Gámez, José Luis, 151, 154
García-Acevedo, María Rosa, 4
García Bernal, Gael, 193
Gatekeeper, The, 14
Giant, 33
Gilda, 200n59
globalization, 2, 3, 84, 86–88, 94, 107, 129, 146, 148, 156–157, 162, 176, 180, 186; and drug trafficking, 111, 112, 129, 185, 205n8; dynamics of, 22; and labor activism, 168–169, 173–178; leftist critique of, 87; right-wing critique of, 87–88; victims of, 102
Gómez-Cruz, Ernesto, 157
Gómez-Peña, Guillermo, 87
González-González, Pedro, 31, 67
González Iñárritu, Alejandro, 193
Good Housekeeping (Buenhogar), 158

Greaser Act (1855 anti-vagrancy act), 6
greasers, 5; greaser films, 5, 11–12; and history, 6
Greaser's Revenge, The, 5
gringo, 75, 80, 120, 159; gringa, 137; history of the term, 78
Grossberg, Lawrence, 107
Guerrero, Ed, 96
Guns and Greasers, 5

Hansen, Miriam, 166
Hart, John Mason, 69, 203n58
Harvey, David, 150
Hawks, Howard, 45, 64
Hayes, Helene, 174
Haymarket Riot, vii
Hays Production code, 33
Herrera-Sobek, María, 3–4, 5, 198n23; and vaqueros, 10–11, 25
High Noon, 17, 40, 64–65, 72, 84, 114, 121
Hispanic Hollywood, 15, 22, 148, 201n5
Hispanophobia, ix, 14, 159
Hobsbawm, Eric, 6–7; and social bandits, 7
homosexuality, 2, 190–191, 208n30; gay and lesbian rights, 83; gay male desire, 24. See also *Brokeback Mountain*
Hotel Employees and Restaurant Employees (HERE), 174
House Un-American Activities Committee (HUAC), 64–65
Huerta, Victoriano, 79

Iglesias, Norma, 3, 4, 5
immigrants, 2, 8, 19, 48, 94–95, 96, 181; criminalization of, 102–103, 177, 184; female immigrants, 15, 101–102; "imaginary illegal aliens," 88, 99–101; immigrant invasion, 3, 19–20, 31, 35, 85, 86, 88–90, 96, 183, 185; male "illegal" immigrants, 86; male immigrants, 16; media coverage of, viii; undocumented immigrants, vii, 14, 20, 23, 92–93, 99, 102, 103, 105, 106–107, 108, 116, 145, 147, 151, 165, 171, 174, 177, 186, 189, 191. See also labor activism
immigration, vii, 2, 16, 19, 20, 21, 24; debates, 145; in film, 4, 8, 24; and policy, 159, 174, 181; post-1965 immigration, 19; psychological impact of, 150–151; and public health, 88–90. See also *specific legislation*
Immigration Act of 1965, 85
Immigration and Naturalization Service, 146, 155, 159–160, 161
Immigration Reform and Control Act of 1986, 22, 89, 91, 159
Indian Reorganization Act of 1934. See Wheeler-Howard Act
Indians, 8, 11, 16, 27, 198n28; characters, 44, 76. See also Native Americans; *and specific films*
Italian Job, The, 171

Jeffords, Susan, 90, 99
Johnson, Lyndon B., 8
Jones, Tommy Lee, 25, 191–192, 194
Justice for Janitors, 148, 174

Kanellos, Nicolás, 159
Keil, Roger, 173
Kennedy, John F., 98; assassination of, 100, 104
Kilpatrick, Jacquelyn, 34; and Native Americans in John Ford's films, 52
Kingpin, 21, 108, 111, 114, 126, 127, 136–139, 141
Kitses, Jim, 187, 188, 209–210n8, 210n13
Korean War, 18
Kornblum, William, 169
Korsmeyer, Pamela, 206n18

labor activism, and undocumented workers, 22, 147, 148, 168–179, 186
Lacan, Jacques, 183
Laing, R. D., 149–150
Lamar, Mirabeau Buonaparte, 10, 11
Latinas, and Westerns, 15, 40
Latin lover, 47, 165, 166
Latin/o American drug traffickers, 20–21, 111, 185; kingpins (drug lords), 111, 122, 128, 142
Latino Cultural Studies Working Group, 23
Latino film, 13, 16, 22, 23, 136, 145–181, 186; Latino border films, 2, 15, 21, 24, 25, 152, 186
Latinos, vii, 19, 22, 23, 43, 145–181, 186, 190–191; celebrities, 174; and criminality, 5–6, 136, 140; in Hollywood, 44–45, 67, 108, 162–170, 201n5; and identity, 15, 23; and labor, 178; in Westerns, 35. See also bandits; greasers
Law, Lindsay, 162
League of United Latin American Citizens (LULAC), 14
Leclerc, Gustavo, 23
Lee, Ang, 24, 51, 188, 190, 210n13
leftist filmmaking, 154
Lipsitz, George, 171–172
List, Christine, 153
Loach, Ken, 168, 169, 178
lone ranger, 107, 117
Lonestar, 11, 14, 63, 64, 104, 194, 199–200n52
López, Ana, 148
López, Enrique Hank, 151
Lopez, George, 169
Louisiana Purchase, 45, 56, 81, 184
Lower East Side Collective (LESC), 175
Lubhéid, Eithne, 93
Lunares, Pio, 7

Maciel, David, 4, 91, 92–93
Madero, Francisco, 79

magical realism, 161–162
Magnum Force, 117
Malavet, Pedro, 78
Mamá solita, 3
Man Apart, A, 20, 108, 111, 126, 137, 139, 140–143
maquiladoras, 85–86; and women, 86
Maquilápolis, viii
Marez, Curtis, 113, 205n7
Mariachi, El, 4, 120, 195
Matthews, Peter, 169, 179
McAllen Ranch, 36
McCaffrey, Barry R., 111, 113, 131–132
McCarran-Walter Act, 175
McCarthy, Cormac, 7
McMurtry, Larry, 188, 210n13
Merlock, Ray, 186–187
mestizaje, 13. *See also* mestizo; mixed race characters
mestizo, 31, 162; characters, 43. *See also* mixed race characters
Mexican-Americans, 199n51; identity, 13–14, 15; neighborhoods, 146, 155, 160; stereotypes of, 19, 163. *See also* bandits; Chicanos
Mexican-American War, 6, 18, 28
Mexican film industry, 3
Mexicans: cinematic depictions of, 2, 5–6, 14, 16, 28, 30, 31, 43–48, 82, 101; and identity, 14, 18; and the Southwest, 10–11; and *The Three Burials of Melquiades Estrada,* 191–192, 194–195; and *Vera Cruz,* 68–74; and *The Wild Bunch,* 74–81; and women, 6, 15, 16, 20, 93, 114
Mexico, 2, 203n58; cinematic depictions of, 13, 15, 16–17, 18, 25, 28, 30–31, 51, 53, 55, 69, 102, 120–121, 134–135, 137, 138, 158, 185–186; fantasies about, 191–192, 194–195
Miami Vice, 110, 111, 113

milusos llegó de mojado, El, 4
Mi vida loca, 21, 146, 169
mixed blood, 34, 37, 43
mixed race characters, 2, 14, 16–17,
    30; relationships, 16–17, 36. See
    also *Duel in the Sun; The Gate-*
    keeper; A Man Apart; mestizaje;
    mestizo; mixed blood; *Rio Lobo*
Modleski, Tania, 187
Mojado de nacimiento, 3
Mojado Power, 4
Monument Valley, 30, 189, 210n13
Morin, Alberto, 61
Mujeres insumisas, 4
multiculturalism, 13, 16, 67, 172
Mulvey, Laura, 166; on *Duel in the*
    Sun, 34, 38–42; on the "Hawks
    woman," 45
Murieta, Joaquin, 7
Musto, David F., 206n18
My Darling Clementine, 40, 114
My Family/Mi familia, 21, 23, 146,
    170
My Lai massacre, 115, 206n18
My Own Private Idaho, 189

Nachbar, Jack, 204n17
narcotics agents, 110; and the narc
    hero, 111, 112, 125, 126, 130, 132,
    137, 139, 143, 186; as "narcs,"
    111, 115, 123, 128, 130, 135, 139,
    205n6
narcotraficante films. *See* drug traf-
    ficking media
National Drug Control Policy, 139
Native Americans, 2, 7, 10, 11, 16,
    203n45; "civilized" tribes, 37;
    history of term, 198n28; and Hol-
    lywood, 49; nation formation, 16;
    status in U.S., 34, 36–37. *See also*
    Indians; *and specific films*
Nava, Gregory, 147, 161, 162
Nevins, Joseph, 7–8
New Latin American cinema,
    152–153, 169

Newman, Kathleen, 154
Ni de aquí ni de allá, 4
Nixon, Richard, 106, 112
No Country for Old Men, 117
Noriega, Chon, 18, 148, 151
Noriega, Manuel, 124, 126, 128
Norma Rae, 148, 178
Norte, El, 14, 21, 22, 23, 146, 147,
    148, 152–162, 167, 170–171, 180,
    186, 192
Norte, Marisela, 171–172
North American Free Trade Agree-
    ment (NAFTA), 15, 22, 133, 134,
    136, 141, 199n51

Office of National Drug Control
    Strategy, 131
Old Gringo, 15
Ono, Kent, 20
Operation Blockade, 147
Operation Cooperation, 133
Operation Gatekeeper, 8
Operation Intercept, 112, 113, 133,
    135
Operation Intercept II, 137
Oseas Pérez, Joel, 153, 158
Ossana, Diana, 188

Paredes, Américo, 9–10, 11
Patton, Cindy, 89
Payan, Tony, 113
Peckinpah, Sam, 78, 80, 115, 120,
    201n5
Peña, Albert, 10, 57
Pistoleros de la frontera, 3
Pocahontas, and origin story, 61
Pocahontas, 41
pochos, 14. *See also*
    Mexican-Americans
Popul Vuh, 147, 155
Porton, Richard, 134
postmodernism, 149
Preguntas sin respuestas, viii
Proposition 187, viii, 20, 147, 159
Proulx, Annie, 24, 188

public transportation, and urban space, 171–173

Quart, Leonard, 169

Ramírez Berg, Charles, 6, 19, 162; and Ford's Westerns, 52
Ramona, 33
Reagan, Nancy, 117
Reagan, Ronald, 90–91, 119; administration, 99, 158, 159; and border, 116; and national security directive, 109, 114; Reaganite concerns, 103; "Reagan Revolution," 90; regime, 158; and Westerns, 91
Reagan era, 16, 84, 86, 90, 107, 134; and globalization, 86; New Right, 107
Real Women Have Curves, 21, 146, 169, 171
Refugee Act of 1980, 157
remojado, El, 4
Reyes, Luis, 201n13
Richardson, Rupert, 9
Richardson, Tony, 84
Riker, David, 169
Rio Bravo, 16, 29, 47, 61–68, 201n5
Rio Grande, 16, 29, 36, 47, 48–56, 61, 117, 201n5
Rio Lobo, 19, 29, 43–48
Rivero, Jorge, 44–45, 201n5
Rodríguez, Luis J., 146
Rodríguez, Robert, 120
Rojas, Arnold, 11
Rosaldo, Renato, 22
Rosin, Eileen, 112, 141
Rubie, Meter, 201n13

Saenz, Rocio, 169
Saldívar, José David, 13
Samora, Julian, 10, 57
Sandino, Augusto, 179
Santa Ana, Otto, 19
Saragoza, Alex, 3
Sarris, Andrew, 51

Sassen, Saskia, 176
Sawhney, Deepak Narang, 151
Sayles, John, 63
Schatz, Thomas, 12, 17, 31, 49
schizopolis, 148–149, 150, 160, 162, 179
School of the Americas (SOA), 69
Searchers, The, 36, 44
Secure Fence Act, vii
Se habla español, viii
Service Employees International Union (SEIU), 148, 174, 175
Shepard, Matthew, 24, 188
Shipler, David, 176–177
Sifuentes-Jáuregui, Ben, 190
Simcox, David, 88–89
Sims, Beth, 118
Sin dejar huella, 4
Skidmore, Thomas E., 206n19
Sloop, John, 20
Slotkin, Richard, 17; and *Rio Grande*, 51–52, 56; and *The Wild Bunch*, 115
Smith, Peter H., 206n19
social realist film, 169, 173. See also *Bread and Roses*
Soderbergh, Steven, 134
Soja, Edward, 173
South Florida Task Force, 113
Spain, Douglas, 208n30
Speed, 171
Stand and Deliver, 23, 146, 171
stardom, 163–164; and Latinos, 162–168. See also *Star Maps*
Stares, Paul B., 205n8
Star Maps, 21, 22, 146, 147, 148, 152, 162–168, 171, 180, 186
Stone Killer, 117
Studlar, Gaylyn, and *Rio Grande*, 51
Suárez-Orozco, Carola, 150–151
Suárez-Orozco, Marcelo, 151

terror de la frontera, El, 3
terrorists, vii, 1, 2, 20; terrorism, 2, 16, 21, 186

Texas ranch epic. See *Duel in the Sun*

Texas Rangers, 5, 7, 29, 36, 111, 113,
114, 119, 121, 123, 184, 185; and
The Comancheros, 8, 56–61, 184;
history of, 8–10, 57; rinches, 9

Thomas, Anna, 147

*Three Burials of Melquiades Estrada,
The*, 11, 15, 25, 187, 191–193,
194–195

Tompkins, Jane, 51

Tony the Greaser, 5

Touch of Evil, 20, 133

Traffic, 20, 88, 93, 108, 110, 111, 121,
131–135, 136, 137, 138, 139, 140,
141

Treaty of Guadalupe Hidalgo, 18,
203n45

Troy, Gil, 90, 107

Truman, Harry, 30

Turner, Frederick Jackson, 27, 201n2

twelve-step programs, 138

24, 1

21 Jump Street, 111

Undefeated, The, 48, 117

U.S. Civil War, 16, 17, 29, 43, 46, 68,
71, 72, 81; battles, 50; Confederates, 75; and masculinity, 50;
officers, 185; post–Civil War, 17,
28, 29–30, 71, 73, 74, 184, 185 193;
and U.S. interventions, 68, 69

vagón de la muerte, El, 4

Valdez, Juan, 156

Valentino, Rudolph, 164–165, 166.
See also Banderas, Antonio

vaquero, 25, 187, 189, 191, 198n27;
history of, 10–11

Vargas, Lucila, 155

Vásquez, Tiburcio, 7

Velez, Lupe, 205–206n16

Vera Cruz, 29, 30, 68–74, 75, 79, 81,
114, 117, 193, 201n5

Vietnam veterans, 104–107, 116, 117,
120, 185

Vietnam War, 2, 8, 18, 83, 84, 103,
104–107, 115, 116, 120, 142,
204n17, 205n8, 206nn18–19; media and, 115

vigilantism, 7, 20, 61, 91, 97, 119,
128, 137, 139, 175; and Dirty
Harry, 99

Vila, Pablo, and social categories of
the borderlands, 13–14, 199n51

Vilar, Pierre, 28

Villa, Francisco "Pancho," 7, 79, 179

Villar, Samuel I. del, 126

Villaraigosa, Antonio, 23

Warnock, Kirby, 7

war on drugs, 109–143, 186; definition of, 112–113; versus "anti-
drug," 131; and war on terror, 21

Washington Office on Latin America,
141

Watts riots, 172

Wayne, John, 8, 19, 20, 31, 80. See
also *The Comancheros; Rio Bravo;
Rio Grande; Rio Lobo*

Weaver, John, 10

Webb, Walter Prescott, 8, 9, 198n27

Welles, Orson, 20, 35

western frontier, 2, 27–29; versus
southern frontier (*see under*
border)

Western Hemisphere Institute for
Security Cooperation (WHINSEC).
See School of the Americas (SOA)

Westerns, 3, 7–8, 11, 13, 15–17,
18–19, 25, 91, 115, 117, 142,
175, 184, 185, 187, 188, 191, 193;
border Westerns, 11, 24, 25, 27–82,
91, 120, 184, 185, 186, 190; as
foundation of border genre, 11–12,
13, 16, 17, 84, 91; and Mexican
women, 114; and nationalism, 84,
187; and oppositions, 102, 137; and
Reagan, 91; revisionist, 15, 24, 51,
187; Western heroes, 15, 17, 18, 25,
47, 93, 204n17

Wheeler-Howard Act, 36, 43
Wild Bunch, The, 29, 74–81, 115, 120, 184, 201n5
Williams, Linda, and melodrama, 38, 209n7
Wilson, Pete, viii
Wilson, Woodrow, 79
Wood, Robin, 45, 64, 76

Young, Robert M., 21
Youngers, Coletta A., 112, 141

Zapata, Emiliano, 79, 179
Zoot Suit, 23, 178
Zurhorst, Charles, and origin of cowboy, 10–11

Lightning Source UK Ltd.
Milton Keynes UK
UKOW030948270912

199705UK00005B/57/P